BILL CLINTON *at the* CHURCH OF BASEBALL

Highly original and exceptionally well researched, this integration of presidential history and sports history makes for a fascinating exploration of baseball's significance as a civil religion in the 1990s. Superbly written and insightful, this book should be equally pleasing to scholarly specialists and general readers—a must read for anyone interested in the Clinton presidency and/or one of baseball's most memorable decades.
—Iwan Morgan, emeritus professor of US History at University College London, and author of *Reagan: American Icon* and *FDR: Transforming the Presidency and Renewing America*

The surprising embrace of baseball and its demigods by a fallen yet ambitious president has found the storyteller it deserves. In this gripping and perceptive book, Chris Birkett explains how Bill Clinton sought leverage and redemption by aligning himself with the uniquely American, culturally unassailable, secular church of baseball. This is a bittersweet story of attempts to rebuild fractured American civic life by appropriating baseball's core narratives: the winning strategy of multicultural teamwork, the glory of running down the American dream and the virtue of uninterrupted hard work. An entertaining and poignant "coming of age" tale of the intertwined fates of an increasingly commercialized and PED fueled national pastime, and increasingly cutthroat national party politics, this book is highly recommended for anyone interested in baseball and political culture, Clintonian leadership, or wonderfully crafted historical narratives of the deepening of our divisions over time.
—Daniel Kryder, Louis Stulberg Chair in Law and Politics, Brandeis University

Like him or not, agree with his policies or not, Bill Clinton was a smart political operator, and this book shows why. Like the man once said, "Whoever wants to know the heart and mind of America had better learn baseball." In a fun recounting of the sport and political history of the 1990s, Chris Birkett shows that Clinton understood the ideas behind that quote and used them well in his effort to connect with the American people and govern.
—Nicholas Evan Sarantakes, author of *Fan in Chief: Richard Nixon and American Sports, 1969–1���*

SPORTS & RELIGION
A SERIES EDITED
BY JOSEPH L. PRICE

Books in the Series

Rebecca Alpert and Arthur Remillard, ed., *Gods, Games, and Globalization: New Perspectives on Religion and Sports*

Chris Birkett, *Bill Clinton at the Church of Baseball: The Presidency, Civil Religion, and the National Pastime in the 1990s*

Arlynda Lee Boyer, *Buddha on the Backstretch: The Spiritual Wisdom of Driving 200 MPH*

Steven Fink, *Dribbling for Dawah: Sports Among Muslim Americans*

Craig Forney, *The Holy Trinity of American Sports*

Robert J. Higgs and Michael C. Braswell, *An Unholy Alliance: The Sacred and Modern Sports*

Bracy V. Hill II and John B. White, eds. *God, Nimrod, and the World: Exploring Christian Perspectives on Sport Hunting*

Allen E. Hye, *The Great God Baseball: Religion in Modern Baseball Fiction*

Steven J. Overman, *The Protestant Ethic and the Spirit of Sport: How Calvinism and Capitalism Shaped America's Games*

Joseph L. Price, ed., *From Season to Season: Sports as American Religion*

Joseph L. Price, *Rounding the Bases: Baseball and Religion in America*

Eric Bain-Selbo, *Game Day and God: Football, Religion, and Politics in the South*

Tracy J. Trothen, *Winning the Race? Religion, Hope, and Reshaping of the Sport Enhancement Debate*

Forthcoming Volumes

Carmen Nanko-Fernández, *¿El Santo?: Baseball and the Canonization of Roberto Clemente*

BILL CLINTON AT THE CHURCH OF BASEBALL

The Presidency, Civil Religion, and the National Pastime in the 1990s

Chris Birkett

MERCER UNIVERSITY PRESS | MACON, GEORGIA

MUP/ P683

© 2023 by Mercer University Press
Published by Mercer University Press
1501 Mercer University Drive
Macon, Georgia 31207
All rights reserved

27 26 25 24 23   5 4 3 2 1

Books published by Mercer University Press are printed on acid-free paper that meets the requirements of the American National Standard for Information Sciences—Permanence of Paper for Printed Library Materials.

Printed and bound in the United States.

This book is set in Adobe Caslon and American Typewriter.

Cover/jacket design by Burt&Burt.

ISBN   978-0-88146-912-7
Cataloging-in-Publication Data is available from the Library of Congress

For M,
Lynda, Pepa, and Freddy

MERCER UNIVERSITY PRESS

Endowed by

TOM WATSON BROWN
and
THE WATSON-BROWN FOUNDATION, INC.

Contents

List of Illustrations	viii
Abbreviations	ix
Introduction	1
1. "Shared Memories and Common Purposes": Bill Clinton and Ken Burns' *Baseball*	26
2. "He Wants to be Savior of The National Pastime": Bill Clinton and the 1994–95 Baseball Strike	51
3. "Going to Work is as American as Baseball": Bill Clinton, Cal Ripken Jr., and Welfare Reform	80
4. Bill Clinton, Affirmative Action, and the Jackie Robinson Myth	110
5. The Summer of '98: Presidential Scandal and the Home Run Race	151
6. Concealment and Confession in the Church of Baseball	187
Conclusion: Baseball, Civil Religion, and the Exercise of Presidential Power	204
Bibliography	209
A Note on Sources	220
Acknowledgments	226
Index	229

List of Illustrations

Clinton's Opening Day pitch, Baltimore, April 1993

Clinton in the broadcast booth, Opening Day, 1993

The First Lady at the White House baseball picnic, September 10, 1994

Don Baer's notes on *Baseball* invitation

Note of Ken Burns meeting, October 18, 1994

Clinton exerts pressure on Bud Selig, February 7, 1995

White House note about Ripken, September 1995

Clinton with Ripken in the Orioles' locker room, Baltimore, September 6, 1995

Clinton and Gore celebrate Ripken's record, September 6, 1995

Clinton at Camden Yards with Kweisi Mfume and Kurt Schmoke, April 5, 1993

Abbreviations

ABC	American Broadcasting Company
AFDC	Aid to Families with Dependent Children
AOL	America Online
AP	Associated Press
BALCO	Bay Area Laboratory Co-operative
BBC	British Broadcasting Corporation
BBWAA	Baseball Writers Association of America
B & O	Baltimore and Ohio Railroad
CBC	Congressional Black Caucus
CEO	Chief Executive Officer
CRC	Civil Rights Commission
C-SPAN	Cable-Satellite Public Affairs Network
EEOC	Equal Employment Opportunity Commission
ESPN	Entertainment Sports Programming Network
FDA	Food and Drug Administration
FOIA	Freedom of Information Act
GDP	Gross Domestic Product
MLB	Major League Baseball
MLBPA	Major League Baseball Players Association
MVP	Most Valuable Player
NBA	National Basketball Association
NBC	National Broadcasting Company

NCAA	National Collegiate Athletic Association
NEH	National Endowment for the Humanities
NFL	National Football League
OIC	Office of the Independent Counsel
PBS	Public Broadcasting Service
PED	Performance Enhancing Drug
POTUS	President of the United States
PTA	Parent-Teacher Association
SOTU	State of the Union Address
UPI	United Press International

Introduction

January 19, 1999
Sammy Sosa at the State of the Union

Nearly an hour into the 1999 State of the Union Address, a speech of intense political drama delivered under the cloud of his impeachment for high crimes and misdemeanors, Bill Clinton called on his fellow Americans to honor a professional baseball player.[1] As Sammy Sosa's name was read out by the President, the Chicago Cubs outfielder watched on from his seat alongside the First Lady in the gallery of the House of Representatives. The previous summer his rivalry with Mark McGwire of the St. Louis Cardinals in pursuit of one of the most hallowed records in American sports had enthralled millions, propelling baseball to the forefront of the national consciousness once again, flooding the media with images of power, masculinity, fatherhood, and racial harmony. In celebrating the virtues of the national pastime, it had offered a cultural counterpoint to the other, more toxic drama simultaneously playing out in the public arena—the political crisis and national moral spasm induced by the sex scandal involving the President and a White House intern. In contrast to Clinton's soiled reputation, Sosa's excellence, competitiveness, and good humor had molded a heroic profile, which was embellished further by his personal contributions to humanitarian relief efforts in the Dominican Republic, the hurricane-devastated country of his birth. Sosa, now a naturalized American citizen, appeared to embody "heroism and sainthood on a human scale."[2] So, in his speech, Clinton set about honoring a figure who had become a significant cultural figure in both his home and adopted countries.

---

[1] William J. Clinton, "Address Before a Joint Session of the Congress on the State of the Union, January 19, 1999," *American Presidency Project*.
[2] Judy Polumbaum, "News For the Culture: Why Editors Put Strong Men Hitting Baseballs on Page One," *Newspaper Research Journal* 21, no. 2 (2000): 23–39, (33).

On the eve of Clinton's address, White House speechwriters had circulated a draft presenting Sosa as a symbol of baseball's enduring relevance in an increasingly self-confident, multicultural nation—a figure who synthesized "our oldest traditions and the best of the new America."[3] But the words Clinton actually delivered the following evening drew upon another set of threads to illuminate baseball's cultural meaning: teamwork, the mystique of record breaking and the generational transmission of its mythical ideals. Pointing up at Sosa, Clinton said: "You know, sports records are made, and sooner or later they are broken. But making other peoples' lives better and showing our children the true meaning of brotherhood, that lasts forever. So, for far more than baseball, Sammy Sosa you're a hero in two countries tonight." Following the example of the President, those on both sides of the aisle rose to their feet to give Sosa a forty-five-second ovation, offering a rare bipartisan display of unity at an otherwise polarized political moment. The television cameras focused on Sosa as he acknowledged the applause. He looked down to the well of the chamber, placing the index and middle fingers of his right hand on his lips, then his heart, in doing so reprising his post-home run-scoring ritual that had become so familiar in ballparks across the country during his battle with McGwire. Amid the turmoil of Bill Clinton's personal and political crisis, at one of the great formal events of American political life, baseball was the vessel through which the nation's supposed virtues and ideals were reaffirmed.

Bill Clinton at the Church of Baseball explores the interplay between the presidency and professional baseball, and that interplay's influence on the political culture of the 1990s, exemplified by Sosa's presence in Washington on the night of the State of the Union Address. It reveals how two 'sacred' national institutions—the presidency and the national pastime—intersected in multiple settings during the Clinton years, helping to shape debates on some of the most contested issues of the time: the legislative battles over welfare reform; Clinton's defense of affirmative action; the presidential response to Newt Gingrich's 'Republican Revolution'; and the fallout from the sex scandal which precipitated the cultural, political, and constitutional crisis of 1998–99. It explains how these events were connected through Clinton's performances and rhetoric to dramas which

---

[3] Draft SOTU speech with notes, OA/ID 14419, Folder: SOTU [State of the Union] 1999 Speech Drafts 1/18/99 [Binder][1], Michael Waldman, Speechwriting, *Clinton Presidential Records*.

engaged, and sometimes enraged, millions of Americans—the unprecedented presidential intervention in a seven-month long players strike (see Chapter Two); Clinton's appropriation of Cal Ripken Jr.'s quest for baseball immortality in 1995 (see Chapter Three); Clinton's role in the 1997 celebrations which marked the fiftieth anniversary of Jackie Robinson breaking professional baseball's race barrier (see Chapter Four); and a shamed president's search for personal redemption by associating himself with the epic, but ultimately drug-tainted, home run race between Sosa and McGwire which lit up America's summer in 1998 (see Chapter Five). In all these cases Clinton summoned the traditional rituals and mythical ideals of baseball in an effort to validate his leadership at times of political peril and personal jeopardy, while all-around dramatic transformations were reshaping American social and economic life.

That Clinton was able to do so is indicative of the resilience of the baseball myth in the mid-1990s, in defiance of the widely held assumption that the elevated place of the national pastime in America's professional sports firmament was in a steady and irreversible decline—beset by intractable labor problems, commercially overwhelmed by the television behemoth, the National Football League (NFL), and deemed lackluster when measured against the spectacle of the celebrity-driven, youth-oriented entertainment offered by the National Basketball Association (NBA). Even soccer, a game hitherto met with indifference by much of the American sports media, had got into the act, muscling its way into the national consciousness in the summer of 1994 when the United States hosted the men's World Cup tournament for the first time. Yet despite this increasingly fierce battle for the hearts, eyeballs, and dollars of sports fans, the final years of the twentieth century saw professional baseball enjoy a commercial and cultural revival, driven in part by a surge in home run hitting and a slew of headline-grabbing assaults on some of the game's most revered records, all wrapped in misty-eyed nostalgia and epitomized by the construction of extravagant retro-styled ballparks as the ambitious architectural centerpieces for revived inner cities. By the time Clinton left office, the doom-mongers who had penned the obituaries of the national pastime just a few years earlier were in retreat—Major League Baseball (MLB) attracted a record 72.8 million fans to the ballpark during the 2000 regular season, and the average franchise was now worth $286 million to its owners, two-and-a-half times more than when the players walked out on their seven-month long strike in August 1994.[4]

Clinton engaged with this resurgence frequently during the course of his presidency: throwing season-opening pitches in gleaming new stadiums in Baltimore and Cleveland; visiting the San Francisco Giants' spectacular new oceanside home (his opening pitch in 2000 fell victim to the Bay Area's inclement weather); being on hand in person to witness the breaking of one of American sports' fabled records in 1995 and interacting on multiple occasions with the heroes of the home run summer of 1998. But importantly, Clinton also engaged with a cultural event which perhaps did more to reestablish the game's presence in the national imagination than anything happening in the ballparks of the American and National Leagues in the 1990s—a television series made by the documentary maker Ken Burns which set out to present the history of the national pastime as a metaphor for the story of America itself. Across nine evenings in the fall of 1994, Clinton was just one of millions of Americans who tuned in to PBS to see their country's turbulent past being retold through the lens of professional baseball. In Burns' words, the national pastime was a "prism in which we can see refracted all our tendencies as a people"; its history was about "the continuity of human experience in America"—an experience of optimism, power and progress, consumerism and corruption, inequality and racism.[5] Just as his earlier multi-award-winning series, *The Civil War*, had sparked a renewal of public awareness of the significance of that conflict in shaping how Americans saw themselves and their country, so some presidential advisors realized that this new Burns production had the potential to speak to similarly big themes, at a time when the administration was anxious to counter the narrative of those who accused Clinton of riding roughshod over American values and traditions. Thus the series premiere was celebrated with a lavish baseball-themed party at the White House, an event which signaled the beginning of a period when Burnsian themes of continuity and compromise increasingly weaved their way into the mindset of key figures in Clinton's communications team (see Chapter One). In an era of extreme polarization and unsettling social change, they understood the potency of baseball's mythology as an

---

[4] Michael J. Haupert, "The Economic History of Major League Baseball," December 3, 2007, *EH.net Encyclopedia*.

[5] Ken Burns, "A Grain of Sand That Reveals the Universe," *US News & World Report*, August 29, 1994.

instrument in the exercise of presidential power. The idea that millions of people still enjoyed significant mutual interests, a meaningful shared heritage, and the continuity of the American experience, found a home in the Church of Baseball.

The Church of Baseball:
The National Pastime as Civil Religion

Clinton's salute to Sammy Sosa in January 1999 was the first time a professional baseball player had been honored in this way during a State of the Union Address—a moment of theater that the White House judged so successful that it would be reprised the following year when Hank Aaron received a similar State of the Union ovation.[6] But the presidential use of baseball as a performative tool had long been a feature of the American political landscape. Ever since the label 'the national pastime' had first been applied to baseball in the mid-nineteenth century, and with its popularity as commercialized entertainment growing steadily in the decades that followed, those seeking votes understood the value of being associated with a game which appeared to define Americanness. The seventeenth president, Andrew Johnson, is thought to be the first to attend a baseball game as a spectator in 1866; the twenty-first, Chester Arthur, was the first to welcome a major league team to the White House in 1883; Benjamin Harrison (number twenty-three) was the first to see a major league team in action in 1892; in 1907, Theodore Roosevelt was the first to be presented with baseball's "golden pass" bestowing upon the holder free entry to all major league games (a privilege he had no intention of using since he privately detested the sport). And three years later William Howard Taft threw the Opening Day pitch in front of a record twelve thousand-person crowd in Washington, so initiating an annual rite which would continue, albeit with interruptions, into the Clinton years and beyond.[7]

For some presidents, such as Richard Nixon, associations with professional sports were an integral part of their campaigning persona. In July 1969, at a reception at the White House, Nixon accepted a gold trophy from the Commissioner of Baseball inscribed to "Baseball's Number One

---

[6] William J. Clinton, "Address Before a Joint Session of the Congress on the State of the Union, January 27, 2000," *American Presidency Project*.

[7] Smith, *The Presidents and the Pastime*, 5–23.

Fan." "I finally made it," beamed a delighted Nixon.[8] For others, like Lyndon Johnson, engaging with baseball was a calculating means to narrower political ends—in his case courting allies in the Senate.[9] Some chief executives had substantial links to the game well before taking office: the thirty-fourth (Dwight D. Eisenhower) was an accomplished outfielder who kept his semi-professional baseball career a secret to avoid being thrown out of West Point; the fortieth (Ronald Reagan), was a play-by-play radio broadcaster during the Depression, reconstructing Chicago Cubs games for listeners from telegraphed pitch-by-pitch reports while he sat in a studio four hundred miles from the ballpark.

Other presidents embraced baseball's cultural meaning once they assumed power by applying its lessons to broader aspects of American life. According to Herbert Hoover, baseball provided young Americans with a solid work ethic and unmatched moral training.[10] His successor, Franklin D. Roosevelt, always keen to strike an intimate tone with his audience, spoke in the language of the ballpark in explaining the inherent risks of some of his New Deal policies: "I have no expectation of making a hit every time I come out to bat," he said in one of his early fireside chats; what he sought instead was "the highest possible batting average, not for himself but the team."[11]

And later, at times of conflict, baseball marched alongside the Commander-in-Chief, from FDR's post-Pearl Harbor Green Light Letter urging the professional game to continue uninterrupted for the national good, to the goodwill tours by star players for the troops in Vietnam after Commissioner William Eckhart declared that baseball supported the war in Southeast Asia.[12] As the historian George Rable observed in 1989, reaffirming American virtues, identifying with a popular sport, and partaking in politically beneficial rituals of fandom had long contributed to a close but complex relationship between baseball and the presidency. But it

---

[8] Richard Nixon, "Remarks at the Baseball All-Star Reception, July 22, 1969," *American Presidency Project.*

[9] Caro, *Master of the Senate,* 210.

[10] "Hoover on Baseball," *US National Archive Blog.*

[11] Franklin D. Roosevelt, "Second Fireside Chat, May 7, 1933," *American Presidency Project.*

[12] "Green Light Letter," Franklin D. Roosevelt to Kenesaw Mountain Landis, January 15, 1942, *FDR Presidential Library;* Florio and Shapiro, *One Nation Under Baseball,* 122.

was a relationship, Rable argued, of diminishing intimacy as America entered the final decade of the twentieth century, when a post-Vietnam, post-Watergate public, increasingly cynical about the performances of those at the pinnacle of national life, was likely to "hoot down" any president who sought to score political points by engaging with baseball.[13] The performance and engagement of the post-Vietnam, post-Watergate, forty-second president, Bill Clinton, suggests that Rable's declension narrative was misguided. Rather than presiding over the waning of the influence of the national pastime, Clinton understood the continuing capacity of baseball's myths and idealized values to align with the aspirations of millions of middle-class Americans. As a result, he would seek to harness the game as a force for cohesion and acculturation in a society unsettled by multiple revolutions—in technology, in the global economy, in diversity, in sexuality and taste—all of which were weakening America's common cultural bonds.

Clinton's embrace of baseball as an enduring emblem of national identity may have been inherited institutionally from his presidential predecessors, but it was also intellectually buttressed by a platoon of scholars, journalists and commentators eager to link baseball to notions of American exceptionalism and, by implication, the existence of an American civil religion—namely a set of commonly held secular beliefs, rituals, symbols, and practices which had acquired quasi-religious meanings and characteristics, and so contributed to a cohesive national ideology and identity.

The concept of civil religion, which had eighteenth-century-roots in the writings of Jean-Jacques Rousseau, had been fleshed out in an American context by the sociologist Robert Bellah in the 1960s, who advanced it as a methodological tool with which to analyze presidential rhetoric and to explain reverence for the country's political institutions, particularly the presidency. Bellah argued that an institutionalized civil religion of Americanism, shaped by shared beliefs, and commonly expressed in presidential speeches, existed alongside, but separate from, the mainstream beliefs and practices of American religious life. A form of national solidarity was conveyed through the religious characteristics of what were essentially secular, state occasions. Thus, in America's civil religion there were prophets,

---

[13] George C. Rable, "Patriotism, Platitudes and Politics: Baseball and the American Presidency," *Presidential Studies Quarterly* 19, no. 2 (1989): 363–72; 371.

martyrs, sacred events, sacred places, and solemn rituals just as there were in the country's more formally recognized religions. It was not, as Bellah was keen to point out, simply the worship of the American nation, but a "heritage of moral and religious experience," a "living-faith" in need of "continual reformation."[14]

It was a contested thesis, with many, including in later years Bellah himself, questioning the existence of any consensus around a nationally cohesive ideology given the degree of public dissent in a society cleaved by conflicts over war, race, social lifestyles, and the nature of capitalism. But despite its detractors, the notion that a fusion of faith and patriotism could be detected in the popular appeal of a range of uniquely American cultural outputs proved to be resilient, thanks in part to those religious studies scholars and sociologists who argued that sources of civil religion could be found not only in the political and historical story of a nation, but also in "religious communities" of "sentiment, taste and style."[15] In this way cultural scholars identified a broad swathe of outputs encompassing the arts (for example Disney characters), music (jazz and rock-and-roll), consumer products (Coca-Cola and McDonald's), and sports as expressions of a civil religious identity with distinctively American attributes. Among those cultural outputs most often cited for its many religious characteristics is baseball—the acknowledged national pastime, a game shrouded in ritual and myth, with its dubious American creation story etched into the national imagination.

It is hardly surprising that baseball is embroiled in the civil religious discourse. Since the organized game's earliest days, baseball and religion had competed for the nation's emotional attention, sometimes clashing on which activity took precedence on the day of worship, at other times, in the words of the religious scholar Joseph Price, "rounding the bases together in muscular expressions of faith."[16] Two twentieth-century-thinkers responsible for melding this sometimes-fractious relationship into a view that baseball should be seen as a quasi-religious expression of American exceptionalism were the philosopher Morris Cohen and the French

---

[14] Robert N. Bellah, "Civil Religion in America," *Daedalus: Journal of the American Academy of Arts and Sciences* 96, no. 1 (1967): 1–21.

[15] Birgit Meyer, "'Praise the Lord': Popular Cinema and Pentecostalite Style in Ghana's New Public Sphere," *American Ethnologist* 31, no. 1 (2004): 92–110; 106.

[16] Price, *Rounding the Bases*, 45.

sociologist Jacques Barzun. In 1919, Cohen posed the question: when the "scholar comes to speak of America's contribution to religion, will he not mention baseball?" For Cohen, baseball was a "national religion" which offered "redemption from the limitations of our petty individual lives and the mystic unity of the larger life of which we are part."[17] The proposition that baseball said something spiritually profound about American life and supposed national characteristics was expanded in 1954 with the oft-quoted declaration by Barzun: "whoever wants to know the heart and mind of America had better learn baseball, the rules and reality of the game." Barzun identified the game as the source of supposed commonly held American virtues which he broadly summed up as accuracy, speed, adaptability, and the capacity to work well in harness with others. Baseball, he wrote "expresses the powers of the nation's mind and body."[18]

Despite by their nature being unprovable, the assertions of Cohen and Barzun nevertheless appear to have influenced the thinking of countless public intellectuals from an array of disciplines, many of whose own sweeping cultural claims seem to be as much the result of youthful enthusiasm for the game and nostalgic memories of childhood as any real intellectual or philosophical inquiry. Take for example the liberal political theorist and devoted baseball follower John Rawls, who strayed from his areas of academic expertise to insist that baseball's physical layout made it "a game perfectly adjusted to the human skills it is meant to display and to call into graceful exercise."[19] Or the cultural theorist Edward Said, who saw each Mark McGwire appearance at the plate during the 1998 home run race as "a religious occasion—the good man confronting danger with courage and simplicity."[20] Or the novelist Philip Roth, who remembered baseball as the literature of his boyhood—a "secular church" with a "mythic sense of itself" that "bound us together in common concerns, loyalties, rituals, enthusiasms, and antagonisms."[21]

---

[17] Morris Cohen, "Baseball: A Moral Equivalent for War," *Dial*, July 26, 1919.

[18] Barzun, *God's Country and Mine*, 159–61.

[19] Letter, John Rawls to Owen Fiss, April 18, 1981, published in "The Best of All Games," *Boston Review*, March 1, 2008.

[20] Edward Said, "The President and the Baseball Player," *Cultural Critique*, 43 (1999): 133–38; 137.

[21] Philip Roth, "My Baseball Years," *New York Times*, April 2, 1973.

Conservative thinkers have been just as captivated by baseball's supposed bigger meaning. The philosopher Michael Novak, offered it as a product of the Enlightenment: in cherishing "individualism, personal honor and the dignity of man, baseball found a perfect match in American culture." It was "as close to liturgical enactment of the white Anglo-Saxon Protestant myth as the nation has."[22] To the conservative commentator George Will, the game was simply "Heaven's gift to struggling mortals."[23] Such confidence in baseball's near-perfection was common. Frequently it was fused with declarations that it was a metaphor for American democracy itself—a discrete contest of pitcher against batter within the setting of a team sport, playing to concepts of rugged individuality being subject to a broader responsibility to others. Its unique physical and technical challenges rewarded the virtues of courage, patience, hard work, honesty, and playing by the rules. The game had become, in the words of the scholar of sports and religion Arthur Remillard, a civil religious ritual, an athletic performance of the American way of life.[24] Bart Giamatti, whose career as President of Yale and Commissioner of Baseball straddled the academy and the ballpark, went further, describing baseball's divine qualities as "part of America's plot, part of America's mysterious underlying design—the plot in which we all conspire and collude, the plot of the story of our national life."[25]

Armed with these insights, major league ballparks become "cathedrals" in the eyes of scholars such as Price who observes religious formality in the repetitive rhythm of the contest and the ritual participatory actions of fans.[26] The cultural historian Roberta Newman, likens baseball to the Mormon Church, with its shared quest to locate "the heavenly home-

---

[22] Novak, *The Joy of Sports*, 58–59.
[23] Will, *Bunts*, 64.
[24] Remillard, "Sports and Religion in America."
[25] Giamatti, *Take Time for Paradise*, 83.
[26] Price, *Rounding the Bases*, 111–75.

plate" in America.[27] This thread of religious exceptionalism is emphasized by the theologian, Christopher Evans, who suggests baseball emerged as the national pastime because it evokes a "sacred mythology" built around the "creation" story of Abner Doubleday and the First Game in 1839 in Cooperstown, New York.[28]

An important constituent of baseball's powerful civil religious presentation stems from the mythologizing of the game's numerous records. And it was on the biggest occasions of record breaking when Clinton most actively and successfully engaged with the game, capitalizing on its capacity to create a widely understood, nationally unifying moment. With baseball's abundance of data facilitating an impulse for record breaking, those moments, in the words of the cultural historian Allen Guttmann, become occasions of "frenzy, a form of rationalized madness, a symbol of our civilization."[29] Thanks to the public's lust for record breaking in the 1990s, competition took place not only in physical spaces (on the field of play) but across time, connecting sporting figures through generations, so cementing baseball's historic continuity. In 1998, McGwire and Sosa were not just competing with one another for the home run crown, but with the earlier holders of the home run record, Babe Ruth and Roger Maris. In 1995, Ripken's extraordinary endurance was inevitably framed by the memory of Lou Gehrig, whose record for consecutive major league appearances he was chasing. The numbers associated with the records—62 home runs, 2,131 appearances—became gauges of greatness in themselves, instantly recognized by millions of Americans. In the media, records which had been held by athletes from an era when the game was supposedly pure and uncorrupted, were labelled 'sacred,' 'hallowed,' and 'revered.' The current day counterparts who seized their mantles were therefore 'saints' and 'immortal,' as long as fans could be assured that they too were virtuous and their records were uncontaminated. The presidential enthusiasm to exploit such elevated moments is easily understood; they were civil religious events—spectacular rituals of celebration in the national pastime, connecting sporting saints, the President, and the people.

---

[27] Roberta Newman, "The American Church of Baseball and The National Baseball Hall of Fame," *Nine: A Journal of Baseball History and Culture* 10, no. 1 (2001): 46–63.

[28] Evans, "Baseball as Civil Religion," 13–34.

[29] Guttmann, *From Ritual to Record*, 51–52.

This belief in the capacity of baseball to project a set of national characteristics and values, and therefore to offer unparalleled moments of national celebration and unity, was not only held by scholars and public intellectuals—it appeared to be shared by politicians, many in the media, and millions of people across the country. This enduring popular embrace of the baseball myth is crucial to understanding Clinton's instrumentalization of the game for political ends. Thanks to an elevated presence in the collective consciousness, with its widely understood set of ideals, rituals, and symbols, baseball was a tool through which Clinton could attempt to forge a cohesive community and to counter the forces which he feared were pulling society apart.

Clinton's American Community
"We Are All in this Together"

Notions of community and the use of communitarian language in pursuit of greater social cohesion were an important part of the forty-second president's rhetorical armory. Articulating the value of communal bonds and a belief in the collective strength in communities had been a core ingredient of Clinton's political offering during his five terms as governor of Arkansas which stretched from 1979 until 1992, albeit with a two-year interruption in the early eighties. In his final gubernatorial inauguration address in Little Rock in January 1991, Clinton had invoked the theme which in subsequent years would echo through his presidency: "Whether we like it or not, we are a community, a community in which we all go forward together, or not at all."[30] Later that year, in a keynote speech in Cleveland to the Democratic Leadership Council, which would cement his position as a future presidential contender, Clinton spoke about what he called a new choice for voters rooted in old values: offering "opportunity," demanding "responsibility," giving citizens more say, "all because we recognize we are a community."[31] It was the first time he had listed the words with which he would attempt to brand his domestic presidency: "opportunity, responsibility, and community"—a trinity which promoted conservative tools of

---

[30] William J. Clinton, Transcript of Inaugural Address, "State's Future in Our Hands, Says Clinton," *Arkansas Democrat Gazette*, January 16, 1991, *Arkansas State Archive*.

[31] William J. Clinton, "[Video] Democratic Leadership Council Keynote Address, May 6, 1991," *C-SPAN*.

individual responsibility to deliver economic and social goals aimed at moderate voters: welfare and health-care reform, a balanced budget, tougher crime laws, and a raft of smaller, values-oriented social programs. Five months later, back in Little Rock to formally announce his presidential bid, Clinton returned to the communitarian theme: "If we have no sense of community the American Dream will continue to wither. Our destiny is bound up with the destiny of every other American."[32]

These invocations of "community," stemming from the shared values of neighborliness and the mutual obligations between citizens and the state, would feature throughout the Clinton era, his speeches embracing "community" as both an abstract concept and as a physical place. Indeed, the word "community" would appear everywhere during his presidency, used more than eighteen thousand times across all forms of White House communications: in radio addresses, news conferences, policy papers, proclamations, press releases, memoranda, fact sheets and briefing documents.[33] In speeches, Clinton would meticulously construct images of communities as spaces of belonging by invoking their real-world, physical manifestations—the church, the PTA, the town hall, the local ballpark. At other times he would draw on the more abstract 'sense of community': the inherited values which were rooted in the tight-knit, social relationships of his Arkansian youth. "You not only knew your neighbors, you looked out for them and your neighbors looked out for you," Clinton recalled during his 1996 campaign.[34]

In using those words, Clinton knew he was grappling with a challenge common to progressive politicians: how to take the broadly understood values of a local community—neighborliness, tolerance, cooperation, participation, belief in equality—and apply them at a national level. David Kusnet, Clinton's first Chief Speechwriter, recalls: "he was always looking for some way to suggest we are bound together by more than geographic proximity, more than family, more than race and ethnicity" in order to

---

[32] William J. Clinton, "Annoucement Speech: Old State House, Little Rock, Arkansas, October 3, 1991," *4President.org*.

[33] Robert F. Durant, "A 'New Covenant' Kept: Core Values, Presidential Communications and the Paradox of the Clinton Presidency," *Presidential Studies Quarterly* 36, no. 3 (2006): 345–72; 368.

[34] Clinton, *Between Hope and History*, 118–19.

build a national family.[35] Don Baer, who served consecutively as White House Director of Speechwriting and Director of Communications between 1994 and 1997, argues that this ideological commitment to community was Clinton's most substantive contribution to late-twentieth-century American political thinking: "Until Clinton came along, no one in politics, Democrat or Republican, was talking about community in the sense of how we help one another."[36]

It was through this lens of community that Clinton invariably viewed the problems of the middle class. As America headed towards the new millennium, Clinton knew he was witnessing a complex and rapidly changing social and economic landscape which was disrupting the fabric of daily life for tens of millions of people. In particular, he saw a society which he believed still cherished the strong communitarian instincts he had experienced in his youth, but which had become increasingly unsettled by the twin forces of globalization and technological change. Everyday life across America was being pulled in different directions by these forces. By the mid-1990s there were plenty of jobs overall, especially in telecommunications and the new computer-based industries, but not in places where deindustrialization had led to plant closures, or where highly paid manufacturing jobs had been exported to low-wage factories abroad, or where commercial life on main street had been all but extinguished by the shopping mall built on an out-of-town highway intersection. There was increasing wealth in aggregate, but it was disproportionally going to the already wealthy. Those struggling on the lower rungs of the economic ladder were working harder and longer than ever for stagnant real wages—often needing to take on more than one job just to get by. In his 1995 State of the Union Address, Clinton spoke of people "getting the shaft" and of communities being "frayed" by the momentum of change.[37]

The perception of societal disquiet was heightened by the broader cultural conflicts of the decade which Clinton's critics insisted were embodied in the style and conduct of his presidency. Clinton represented a new generation of presidential politician—the first to be born after the end of World War II and the first to take office after the end of the Cold War,

---

[35] David Kusnet, Interview by Author, Washington, DC via Zoom, August 4, 2020.

[36] Don Baer, Interview by Author, New York, April 26, 2018.

[37] William J. Clinton, "Address Before a Joint Session of Congress on the State of the Union, January 24, 1995," American Presidency Project.

a conflict that had defined the president's geopolitical role for the previous four decades. But with the collapse of the Soviet Union and the loss of its Eastern European satellites, the Cold War threat had evaporated, and as a result the ties of civic and national unity that a common enemy provided had loosened. Instead, the events of Clinton's politically formative years in the 1960s—the battles over civil rights, gender rights, and the Vietnam War—became the dominant source of competing cultural ideologies, shaping both his own politics and that of his opponents, whose feverish response was driven by their antipathy towards a moral and cultural code inherited from that era. Thus, the howls of indignation which accompanied the array of supposed scandals which afflicted the administration from its earliest days were not only directed at Clinton personally. Many held them up as evidence of a broader deterioration of norms in society, epitomized by high crime rates, falling standards in public schools, the increasing number of births outside marriage, and the perception that popular culture itself had become remorselessly vulgar.

Facing up to the whirlwind of conservative righteous anger, was an equally determined liberal block anxious to protect what it saw as the social, cultural, and sexual freedoms won over the previous thirty years. In 1991, this conflict—grounded in two discordant moral worldviews—had been labelled "the culture wars" by the sociologist James Davison Hunter, one of the scholars whose views were regularly sought by Clinton ahead of major speeches.[38] Hunter's analysis, and the phrase which emerged from it, was weaponized across the political spectrum. At the 1992 Republican National Convention, Pat Buchanan, the arch-conservative presidential candidate who had unsuccessfully challenged George H. W. Bush in the primaries, spoke of an ongoing religious and "cultural war for the soul of America," against homosexual rights, feminists, the purveyors of pornography and pro-choice liberals.[39] As the first baby boomer occupant of the White House—a draft-dodging, pot-smoking (though apparently not inhaling), sexually promiscuous student of the sixties, and the husband of a strong and vocal feminist—Clinton found himself dragged onto the war's virtual front line, in the crosshairs of enemy fire and in the vanguard of his supporters.

---

[38] Hunter, *Culture Wars: The Struggle to Define America*.
[39] Patrick J. Buchanan, "The Cultural War For The Soul of America," *Patrick J. Buchanan Official Website*, September 14, 1992.

It was the convergence of these unstable economic, political, and cultural forces that led the historian Daniel Rodgers to suggest that American society in the 1990s had "disaggregated into a constellation of private acts," with few adherents to the concept of symbolic national unity.[40] Instead it was a "fractured" society where macroeconomic solutions had given way to a fixation with microeconomic behavior and the rediscovery of the market under Ronald Reagan, which in turn had spawned micro-politics; where widely held assumptions about justice, welfare, and equality were under siege from proponents of incentives and individual rights; where disaggregated solutions to the problems of education and race were gaining the upper hand in intellectual and political arenas; where even the teaching of history was entangled in competing claims of ethnic, regional, gender, and religious groups about whose stories should be told. In short, 1990s America, according to Rodgers, was a society which lacked "the metaphors capable of holding in focus the aggregate aspects of human life."[41]

In an academic article published in January 1995 which caught Clinton's attention, the political scientist Robert Putnam tried to explain what was going on: the structures of communal civic life had collapsed. Americans were becoming more insular, more-inward looking and less likely to participate in the institutions which bound them to each other and to their communities. The evidence, Putnam argued, could be found in the disappearance of local bowling leagues—people instead were "bowling alone."[42] Globalization, big government, political disengagement, the television in the living room, the decline in church going, and generational differences were all factors in undermining communal structures and impulses. As a result, America's "social capital" needed rebuilding. Putnam's thesis, which he expounded to Clinton at a Camp David retreat shortly before the 1995 State of the Union Address, struck such a chord with the President that an advisor judged that the two had almost "mind-melded."[43] Journalists were equally intrigued by Putnam's argument and its apparent influence over presidential thinking. Taking their cue, newsrooms dispatched teams of reporters to the dwindling number of bowling alleys in Main Street

---

[40] Rodgers, *Age of Fracture*, 17.

[41] Rodgers, 6.

[42] Robert D. Putnam, "Bowling Alone: America's Declining Social Capital," *Journal of Democracy* 6, no. 1 (1995): 65–78.

[43] William Galston Interview, April 22–23, 2004, *Bill Clinton Presidential Oral History*.

America in search of the mythical blue-collar man, rolling his sixteen-pound ball down sharply polished but sparsely populated lanes, discontentedly alone and fretting about his job and his family's future. Seemingly armed with the evidence, many commentators praised the Putnam thesis for capturing the essence of America's descent into a socially splintered society. And they all had their own pessimistic take. The CBS anchor, Bill Lagattuta, told viewers of the *Evening News* that the decline in bowling leagues was typical of "so many all-American institutions that have gone down the gutter lately."[44] In a monologue on *PBS NewsHour,* the essayist Roger Rosenblatt lamented the rise of the home computer and the increasing amount of time people now spent in cyberspace, linking up with "those who they will never touch or see."[45] In the *New York Times*, Anthony Lewis warned that free market ideology and individualism would not bring contentment to "An Atomized America."[46] Even the stalwart conservative, George Will, asked: "Has individualism become excessive?" and acknowledged that neighborhood and community organizations were "crucial to the success of democracy."[47]

It was amid this sense of restlessness, with the weakening of many of the institutions, symbols, and metaphors of nationhood which bound people together, that Clinton mobilized baseball as a force for civil religious cohesion. Despite fears that baseball was in decline as a cultural force, Clinton understood that the myths of the national pastime still served a purpose in millions of peoples' lives. In a decade of uncertainty, baseball retained a symbolic function in the hands of a president who believed in the potency of its traditions, rituals, and ideals in forging a common national identity, and in his capacity to harness those forces for his own political ends.

---

[44] Transcript, "CBS Evening News (6:00 PM ET)," *CBS News*, February 26, 1995.

[45] Transcript, "The MacNeil/Lehrer NewsHour," *PBS Television*, September 12, 1995.

[46] Anthony Lewis, "Abroad at Home; An Atomized America," *New York Times*, December 18, 1995.

[47] George F. Will, "Look at the Lonely Bowlers," *Washington Post*, January 5, 1995.

Bill Clinton as First Fan

If there was one character trait that aligned Bill Clinton with millions of ordinary Americans, it was his love of sports. In many ways he was the typical fan found sitting in the nation's sixty million ESPN-subscribing living rooms—middle-class, middle-aged, overweight, male, and White. Like most, he usually got no closer to the action than his armchair. It was an image Clinton liked to cultivate whenever he was interviewed on sports broadcasts: his usual end-of-day routine, Clinton claimed, was a TV-dinner with Hillary and Chelsea in the White House kitchen watching the day's highlights on *SportsCenter*.[48] Some evenings Clinton's sports viewing went late into the night, joined by friends on the well-padded sofas of the third-floor Solarium in the White House Executive Mansion. Those around him say he would shout at the TV-set, second guessing the coaches' decisions, just like any fan. When multiple live events were simultaneously broadcast the President would grab the remote control and channel-hop so as not to miss any action.[49] "If you want to be calm and quiet, you shouldn't watch a game with me," Clinton admitted to *Sports Illustrated* in a March 1994 cover-feature headlined "The First Fan."[50] It was an enthusiasm born out of regular-guy instincts, even if Clinton's advisors feared they drained his presidential aura. "He eats too much, he loves sports too much, he talks too much," complained his strategist James Carville.[51] And while he was an enthusiastic and competent golfer (usually playing twice weekly) and a dedicated daily jogger (partly to control his weight), it was as a television-watching spectator that Clinton truly excelled.

While Clinton's authenticity as a genuine, all-round sports lover is undisputed, evidence of a deep, personal passion for baseball, in particular, is less conclusive. His Arkansian friend, Martha Whetstone, insists Clinton always kept up-to-date on the details about team standings and

---

[48] William J. Clinton, "Interview with Dan Patrick of ESPN Radio, November 4, 1999," *American Presidency Project*.

[49] Branch, *The Clinton Tapes*, 111–12.

[50] Quoted in Alexander Wolff, "The First Fan," *Sports Illustrated*, March 21, 1994.

[51] Quoted in Ann Devroy, "Clinton Foes Voice Their Hostility, Loud and Clear," *Washington Post*, May 22, 1994.

individual batting averages.[52] And even after he left the White House, Clinton claimed to enjoy the friendship of several legends of the game, including Stan Musial and Hank Aaron. But his TV-watching companion and close friend, the historian Taylor Branch, judged Clinton's expertise on baseball as only marginally above the politicians' norm.[53] And after observing the candidate on the 1992 campaign trail attempting to commiserate with Pittsburgh Pirates fans after a game seven loss in the National League Championship Series, his advisor Bruce Reed concluded that Clinton's inability to recall accurately the details of the game the previous night was proof that "he was never much of a baseball fan."[54]

It was an observation that may well have been true, especially when set against Clinton's near obsession with the University of Arkansas Razorbacks basketball team which he had begun watching as a young law professor in Fayetteville. He had followed the team avidly as State Attorney General and then Governor and was thought to be the first sitting president to attend college basketball as a spectator when he watched the Razorbacks play Texas Southern University in Fayetteville in December 1993. A few months later, he cheered them on in person twice in the space of a few days at the 1994 NCAA Basketball Tournament in Charlotte, North Carolina. For the championship final on April 4, Clinton flew directly from Cleveland, where he had thrown baseball's Opening Day pitch that afternoon at the Indians' new ballpark, Jacobs Field. It was a sporting double-header which tied together the formal obligations of his office and his First Fan persona. "We're not just citizens, we're fans," Clinton declared in a CBS interview, comments which alluded to the civil religious connections between citizenship and sports, and which prompted the *New York Times* to describe Clinton's sports-hopping day as presenting images of "unsullied Americana."[55]

Clinton's preference for watching NCAA basketball was evident, but it was also clear that he appreciated the prominent position that baseball occupied in the American imagination. Michael Waldman, the White House

---

[52] Takiff, *A Complicated Man*, 236–37.

[53] Branch, *The Clinton Tapes*, 111.

[54] Bruce Reed Interview, February 19–20, 2004, *Bill Clinton Presidential Oral History*.

[55] Douglas Jehl, "Clinton's Doubleheader: Two Cities, Two Sports," *New York Times*, April 5, 1994.

Director of Speechwriting from 1995 to 1999, recalls a consistent willingness to engage with efforts "to resuscitate the glory" of baseball, with Clinton rarely passing up opportunities to publicly profess his love for the game.[56] Such expressions, of course, flowed easily. For Clinton, like most who had grown up in the 1950s, the national pastime possessed an immense cultural and social presence. It had been weaved in multiple ways into the daily fabric of his early life in Arkansas. Throughout his youth he had listened to the radio transmissions of St. Louis Cardinals ballgames, the distinctive tones of Harry Caray beamed by the giant masts of KMOX across the lower midwest and southern states into the Clinton household in Hot Springs. Clinton later reflected that this act of listening to baseball on the radio in the kitchen while doing his homework gave him a sense of belonging to a much wider American community, beyond the confines of his small southern city. It connected him with thousands of other unseen youngsters, spread across the country sharing the experience of listening to the play-by-play broadcasts.[57] In his memoir, Clinton recalls he and his stepfather making the nine hundred-mile roundtrip journey from Hot Springs to St. Louis to see the Cardinals in person.[58] His sadness was that they only did it once—an admission of regret that hints at the absence, in his own life, of a paternal relationship experienced through baseball.

Therefore, it comes as no surprise that when he became president, Clinton would perform the ritual baseball-related presidential duties with respect for the institution and appreciation of the cultural burden he carried. He threw the Opening Day pitch three times: in 1993 in Baltimore, in 1994 in Cleveland, and again in Baltimore in 1996—matching the Opening Day numbers of Nixon and Reagan. Clinton's preparation was thorough: sometimes he would practice in the White House grounds where the regulation 60ft. 6in. between the mound and home plate had been measured out.[59] On game day itself he would go through a warm-up routine below the stands so anxious was

---

[56] Michael Waldman, Interview by Author, New York, June 18, 2019.

[57] William J. Clinton, "The President's Radio Address: October 21, 1995," *American Presidency Project*.

[58] Clinton, *My Life*, 19.

[59] William J. Clinton, "Video: President Clinton Reminisces About Throwing First Pitch Back in 1996," *Clinton Foundation YouTube Channel*.

he to avoid the fate which befell his immediate predecessor, George H.W. Bush—the indignity and damage to masculine and presidential self-esteem of seeing his ball flop into the dirt.

Beyond Opening Day pitches, there were other opportunities for Clinton's communicators to construct baseball-related images of the President as First Fan, from bat-swinging photographs with veteran ballplayers in the Oval Office, to carefully crafted photo opportunities in ballpark locker rooms. Clinton also observed the tradition of the presidential sports encomia—the receptions which honor the achievements of sports champions. Traditionally platforms for a well-worn ritual of presidential praise for discipline, teamwork, and commitment to excellence—all supposed sources of American greatness—baseball encomia were not without a political edge. The New York Yankees, who won four World Series in the Clinton years, had to wait until 1998 for their photo opportunity with the President after a threatened boycott by some Yankee players scuppered a White House appearance for the victorious 1996 team.[60] The Atlanta Braves, the era's most consistent team, with fourteen consecutive divisional titles, five National League titles, and one World Series victory, received their White House reception in February 1996, an occasion at which the political signaling was possibly more to Clinton's liking—the Braves manager, Bobby Cox, told the President, "we're pulling for you" for reelection in November.[61] And the White House appearance of the 1997 World Series winners, the Florida Marlins, an ethnically diverse team with a largely Hispanic fan base, allowed Clinton to deploy them as the sporting embodiment of his broader multicultural outlook: when Americans work together, they win.[62]

A further area of presidential engagement with baseball in которой Clinton excelled was as an occasional broadcast announcer or analyst, a role that linked him to the sports talk radio audience and thus carried

---

[60] Helen Thomas, "Backstairs at the White House," *UPI Archive*, December 18, 1996,

[61] Quoted in "Clinton Honors Atlanta Braves," *UPI Archive*, February 26, 1996,

[62] William J. Clinton, "Remarks to the 1997 World Series Champion Florida Marlins, February 17, 1998," *American Presidency Project*.

political as well as symbolic weight. Over his two terms, Clinton gave several interviews to the sports network ESPN, sometimes calling in from the Oval Office or joining a broadcast live for unscripted conversation while attending a sports event. These broadcasts followed a general pattern: good-natured repartee about the latest newsworthy sports topic, a question about how Clinton managed to find time to follow sports, all rounded off with an opportunity for Clinton to impress the audience by demonstrating his detailed sports knowledge by riffing with the announcer over the course of a few plays. Clinton's performances in the radio and television broadcast booths on the night Cal Ripken Jr. broke the record for consecutive major league appearances were an expert execution of the craft—personal and anecdotal, cementing his presence at a historic moment and allowing him to be identified as an ordinary sports fan in thrall of the national pastime, while simultaneously being the leading celebrant of its historic meaning. It was no one-off. Even on less memorable occasions, Clinton could plunge effortlessly into sports chat, demonstrating a grasp of detail which *Sports Illustrated* described as "dazzling, perhaps even a little eye-glazing."[63] Take, for example, this off-the-cuff analysis of the field dimensions at the new Atlanta Braves ballpark which Clinton performed during a game day interview with Jon Miller on WBAL:

> Miller: Now, you were telling us between innings that you had a chance to go down to Atlanta and see the layout there.
>
> Clinton:...the unique thing about it is...home plate's going to be even tucked in tighter than here, so that the average distance from base line to the stands will be about forty-five feet. And the major league ballparks average something like seventy feet. So even though the Braves have this magnificent pitching staff, they're going to be tested because they won't get as many easy foul-outs.[64]

Even with Clinton's huge capacity to absorb and recycle information, this was an impressive display. Clearly his engagements with baseball were

---

[63] Wolff, "The First Fan."
[64] William J. Clinton, "Interview With Jon Miller and Fred Manfra of WBAL Radio in Baltimore, Maryland, April 2, 1996," *American Presidency Project*.

skillful, sophisticated, and multifaceted—and not entirely rooted in expediency. However much it was performative, Clinton took a considerable degree of personal enjoyment from his First Fandom. Even so, the political dynamic was never far from the surface; being First Fan directly connected him with the electorally important sports fan voters, who would surely have been impressed by his aptitude for talking their language.

Clinton's performances, both as the institutional guardian of the baseball mythos and as the First Fan celebrant of its multiple meanings to American citizens, point to the dual nature of the civil religion of baseball in the closing years of the twentieth century. At one level, notions of baseball as civil religion were deployed symbolically at the pinnacle of public life as a vehicle for presidential rhetoric and ritual, often at moments of high celebration and political drama. At another level, the civil religion of baseball was a revealed faith for the masses—accepted by a broad swathe of the population in that it reflected some of the most traditional, most precious values held by society as a whole. It is this duality of baseball's sacred place in national culture, its part in the creation of an imagined national identity, which Clinton mobilized on multiple occasions.

While I argue throughout this book that the romanticized myths and the revitalized heroes of baseball had a meaningful impact on the politics of the Clinton years, it is equally important to acknowledge that the influence was to a degree innate, assumed and often indirect. At times its use by the President was opportunistic; it was rarely formalized or structured. This book does not suggest the existence in the White House of an organized or rigidly enforced communications policy centered around baseball. There was no individual who came into work every day specifically tasked with inserting baseball references into presidential speeches. Drawing on the virtues of the national pastime did not have the potency, in itself, to reverse the surge of political tides. While David Kusnet recalls transcripts of Ken Burns' output circulating among West Wing staff, even the benefit of hindsight does not make him think that the secret to resisting the Republican landslide of 1994 would have been for Clinton to have talked more about baseball.[65] But it did, as I outline in this book, have a role in framing and delivering policy outcomes and political messages: when Clinton needed to counter accusations of being un-American and morally corrupt, his enlistment of baseball, particularly after the 1994 midterm

---

[65] Kusnet, interview by author.

rout of his party, played a part in propelling the values-driven emphasis of his political fighting back from 1995 onwards.

The impulses at play in this presidential deployment of baseball were in themselves unremarkable, yet they were deeply ingrained and culturally powerful. Like most of those who inhabited the male-dominated, largely middle-aged West Wing, whether in the administration or the media, Clinton had been raised with a deep understanding of the game's traditions and myths; when his communicators reached out for what the historian Gordon Wood labelled in 1997, the "tangible symbols of identity and purpose" required by any cohesive nation, baseball was, unsurprisingly, one of the cultural outputs upon which they alighted—they had experienced it in childhood and talked about it almost every day in adulthood, from spring to fall.[66] To them, it just came naturally. As Michael Waldman points out, Clinton was part of a generation raised in the 1950s in thrall to an American idyll with baseball as part of the national mythos: "It was the American sport. All the stuff that Ken Burns mythologized about—that it's a rural sport, that it doesn't have a clock—had a lot of currency at that time."[67] Indeed, baseball's cultural presence in Clinton's White House was everywhere—in the personal enthusiasms and passions of the staff, in the administration's outward-facing rhetoric, and in the language of internal communication, in watercooler conversation, emails, and memos. Even so, its significance is often underestimated, the relationship between the presidency and baseball taken for granted, accepted as part of the familiar architecture of American public life. The result has been that historians have deemed the presidential-baseball nexus barely worthy of deep and considered interrogation—an act of intellectual neglect which *Bill Clinton at the Church of Baseball* seeks to rectify.

But for all its embrace of some of the most momentous events in baseball in the 1990s, this book is not intended to be a comprehensive account of the professional game during the Clinton years. It is not meant to offer a sporting analysis of the peaks and troughs of the major league teams and their players—how could it possibly do so since the reader will quickly spot that there are only fleeting mentions of the multiple World Series titles claimed by the New York Yankees between 1996 and 2000, or the consistent excellence of the National League's most relentless winners,

---

[66] Wood, "History and Heritage," 193.
[67] Waldman, interview by author.

the Atlanta Braves. Some of the greatest ballplayers of the era, including Ken Griffey Jr., Mike Piazza, Albert Belle, and Jeff Bagwell are noticeable by their absence from the following pages, as are outstanding pitchers such as Randy Johnson, Roger Clemens, and Greg Maddux—all instantly recognizable names to any sports fan. Neither does this book aspire to be a conventional political history of the Clinton administration—I will leave it to others to judge whether his economic record at home and his peace efforts abroad amount to a consequential presidency or merely one of unfulfilled promise, mired in and forever tainted by headline-grabbing scandal. Rather *Bill Clinton at the Church of Baseball* is an examination of the occasions when two cherished, yet fallible, national institutions—the presidency and Major League Baseball—became intimately entwined under Clinton's watch, how that complex relationship was mediated in a rapidly changing landscape, and how it was experienced by the American people, with the result that it both influenced and reflected the tempestuous political culture of the era.

Chapter One

"Shared Memories and Common Purposes": Bill Clinton and Ken Burns' *Baseball*

Scenes at a White House Baseball Picnic

"Nostalgia reigned," observed a *Washington Times* reporter on witnessing the scene on the South Lawn of the White House as the President and the First Lady mingled with hundreds of guests invited to a picnic celebrating the premiere of a television series on the history of baseball.[1] It was September 10, 1994, a balmy late-summer afternoon, and the White House grounds had been temporarily transformed into a shrine to the national pastime; veteran major league ballplayers posed for photographs while celebrities and politicians stood in line at a photo booth, waiting to have their images printed on mocked up baseball trading cards. From time to time the familiar strains of baseball's Tin Pan Alley anthem, *Take Me Out to the Ball Game*, filled the air, struck up on the antique saxhorns of a brass band whose members were dressed in nineteenth-century military uniform. Elsewhere, in a specially erected batting cage, balls were fired at all comers, including cabinet members, legislators, and minor league players kitted out in their throwback knickerbocker uniforms. In a sign acknowledging that those excluded by gender and race from baseball's sentimentalized history nevertheless deserved a place in the afternoon's celebrations, the First Lady took her turn at bat, offering the photo opportunity of the day by swinging at a series of gentle pitches. Close by, a handful of aging stars from the long-defunct Negro Leagues—Buck O'Neil, Riley Stewart, 'Slick' Surratt, and Connie Johnson—chatted with the President. Even the nourishment carried the aroma of the ballpark: hot dogs, popcorn, peanuts, and Cracker Jack—the sickly, caramel-coated, molasses-flavored snack associated with the ritual community singing of the seventh inning stretch. It was an

---

[1] Ann Geracimos, "News Gives Way to Nostalgia at Picnic," *Washington Times*, September 12, 1994.

occasion which played heavily on the myriad of cultural connections which accompanied baseball's elevated place in the American imagination. Unsurprisingly, throughout the event, the President engaged in his favorite pastime, assiduously working the crowd. As his advisors had told him, it was an opportunity to invoke "shared memories and common purposes."[2] Even bad news about the breakdown of the talks to end the strike which had brought the Major League Baseball season to an abrupt halt a month earlier, failed to dampen the mood. Perhaps the national pastime had lost some of its cultural capital, but were fractious relations between workers and owners not just another refrain in the game's mythic narrative and part of America's wider story?

The Clintons had already been instructed that day on baseball's indissoluble connections to national culture and the game's supposed capacity to reaffirm what it meant to be American. Immediately before the picnic they had travelled a few blocks east to the National Theatre, where they had attended a preview screening of the PBS TV series, *Baseball*, hosted by its producer, Ken Burns. The President and the First Lady spent a little over an hour watching as Burns introduced clips from the series and talked about the wider meaning for national character of the myths and memories embedded in the game.[3] What Burns said carried weight; his previous PBS project, a nine-part history of the Civil War, which aired four years earlier, had been a critical and popular triumph—the most-watched series in the history of American public television. It won him Emmys and Grammys and the unofficial title of the country's most influential popular historian. Invitations to dine at the White House had followed.

This latest venture was equally ambitious in scope: over nine episodes (predictably labelled "Innings"), amounting to almost twenty hours of prime-time television, it aimed to present the story of the national pastime as a metaphor for the social and cultural history of twentieth-century America in all its facets. Baseball's history, according to Burns, was a story of immigration and assimilation, race and inequality, capital and labor, class and consumerism, virtue and villainy.[4] It is "the story of us as a

---

[2] Memorandum, Don Baer to Bill Clinton, "September Speeches," August 25, 1994, OA/ID 10993, Folder: Memos, Carolyn Curiel, Speechwriting, *Clinton Presidential Records*.

[3] Baer, interview by author.

[4] Burns and Ward, *Baseball*, xviii.

nation," Burns told reporters at the White House picnic, "a way to see our tendencies, our character, our life, in a subtler, perhaps easier to comprehend form."[5] If the breadth of these claims was not enough, the sense that this was a cultural event of national scope was enhanced by the Clintons' presence. "The film is something the President should definitely take credit for," counselled Martha Chowning of the National Endowment for the Humanities (NEH), the federal agency which had contributed two million dollars to the project.[6]

But the screening and the White House picnic offered more than a mutually beneficial photo opportunity for two fabled emblems of national life. It also presented a public celebration of the connection between the presidency and the national pastime at a time when the cultural power of both national institutions appeared to be on the wane, when trust in many symbols of national identity and social cohesion seemed to be diminishing, and when there was an urgent need, in Clinton's own words that September, "to rebuild the frayed bonds of our American communities."[7] This "fracturing" of public life, as the historian Daniel Rodgers would later label it, was evident in the hyper-partisan political arena where Clinton was being savaged by his Republican opponents as "the enemy of normal Americans" for lacking moral integrity and for promoting policies, such as health-care reform and gay rights, which were "culturally alien to the nation."[8] It could be seen, Clinton's favorite political scientist Robert Putnam argued, in the collapse of communal civic life in towns and cities.[9] It was noted by journalists such as Haynes Johnson, who observed that Americans were now so divided by gender, class, race, and ethnicity that they

---

[5] Quoted in Donnie Radcliffe, "The White House Pitches In," *Washington Post*, September 12, 1994.

[6] Memorandum, Martha Chowning to Ann Stock, White House Social Secretary, September 1, 1994, OAS/ID 10131, Folder: Baseball-Ken Burns, Don Baer, Communications, *Clinton Presidential Records*.

[7] William J. Clinton, "Remarks at a Reception for Senatorial Candidate Ann Wynia in Minneapolis, Minnesota, September 24, 1994," *American Presidency Project*.

[8] Rodgers, *Age of Fracture*; Ken Walsh, "A Polarizing President," *US News & World Report*, November 7, 1994; Mary McGrory, "Gingrich's Buzzword Pudding," *Washington Post*, December 16, 1993.

[9] Putnam, "Bowling Alone".

had "relatively little contact with other large segments of their society."[10] And the fracturing was obvious in baseball as well, where the media and the public turned against the millionaire athletes and billionaire owners whose mutual greed had resulted in the strike which now threatened the very existence of the professional game. "A pox on both your houses," was Labor Secretary Robert Reich's Shakespearian description of the sour mood expressed by millions of fans towards those who played and ran Major League Baseball.[11]

But now, by exploring America's past through his TV series on baseball, Burns believed he had a different story to tell, one which, going forwards, could provide a more optimistic narrative of "the comfort of continuity" and "the generational connection of belonging to a vast and complicated American family."[12] And with this timely revival of the game's relevance in the discourse over national values, Burns also offered something useful to the White House at a moment of political fragility—a rhetorical framework of myths, ideals, and values which Clinton could harness to revitalize his struggling administration.

Baseball: "A Precise Mirror of Who We Are"

Everything about the extensive publicity, extravagant marketing and impeccable provenance of Burns' *Baseball* ensured that the series would be acclaimed as a major cultural event during its primetime run on PBS from September 18 to 28. With *The Civil War* and earlier work, Burns had been credited with reinventing the genre of the historical television documentary. His films were ritualistic, stylized, and self-consciously moralizing: constructed in thematic sections with slow pans across vintage stills, sequences of archive footage set to old-time music, solemn narration, and analysis and anecdote from an opulent cast list of actors, experts, and witnesses. Their sweeping narratives invoked subjects embedded in America's collective memory. "It is more than a game. It is the game of our lives," intoned the television advertisement released to promote the video box set of the series.[13] Likening his own story-telling talents to those of Homer,

---

[10] Johnson, *The Best of Times*, 556.

[11] Quoted in Mark Maske, "The Baseball Race Isn't for a Pennant," *Washington Post*, September 6, 1994.

[12] Burns and Ward, *Baseball*, xviii.

[13] "Ken Burns's Baseball VHS Release Ad (1995)," *YouTube*.

Burns barnstormed the country to generate excitement with a flurry of similarly grandiose declarations: "Baseball is a constant reminder of a vast past and a precise mirror of who we are," he told the *New York Times*.[14] Writing in *US News & World Report*, Burns described baseball as, "a Blakean grain of sand that reveals the universe."[15] To the *Chicago Tribune* he promised to reveal part of America through baseball's disputed and complex history: "If you can reveal the difference between fact and myth you can tell volumes about the myth."[16]

In the preface for the book accompanying the series, Burns and his co-author Geoffrey Ward proposed a set of "mythical contradictions" which, they argued, secured baseball's unique place in the nation's cultural landscape: the pastoral game which thrived in America's cities; the democratic game which possessed a shameful record of exclusion; the archly conservative game with a modern outlook. It was, wrote Burns and Ward, the "American odyssey that links sons and daughters to fathers and grandfathers," while reflecting "a host of age-old American tensions: between workers and owners, scandal and reform, the individual and the collective."[17]

These tensions certainly captured more of the complexities of American history than the questionable claims of some of the game's boosters in the media and the academy who had long romanticized baseball as a game of innate perfection which somehow symbolized the inevitable victory of American democratic values. But the intellectual landing point for Burns was not dissimilar—that the national pastime was fundamental to America's sense of cultural exceptionalism and the creation of a common national character. And he had lined up heavyweight firepower in support. A few minutes into the first episode, the cultural critic Gerald Early suggests that in two thousand years' time the United States of America will be remembered for just three things: its constitution, jazz, and baseball.[18]

While the series undoubtedly reignited interest in baseball's symbolic meaning, the Burns thesis did not go entirely unchallenged. For more than

---

[14] Richard Sandomir, "Hits, Runs and Memories," *New York Times*, September 18, 1994.

[15] Ken Burns, "A Grain of Sand That Reveals the Universe."

[16] Quoted in Steve Nidetz, "Burns' 9-Inning Mini-Series Hits Airwaves Sept. 18," *Chicago Tribune*, August 1, 1994.

[17] Burns and Ward, *Baseball*, ixx.

[18] Ken Burns, *Baseball: First Inning, Our Game*, PBS, September 1994.

a century the media had been the main vehicle for recycling the familiar baseball creed of cultural conditioning, legitimizing its fabricated all-American creation story and celebrating the supposed purity of its values. However, commentators were now divided, with many questioning the game's self-appointed entitlement to moral superiority and its monopoly as the American sport whose cultural meaning was synonymous with national identity. Baseball's persistent labor problems and its diminishing share of the sports entertainment market contributed to a sense that the game was unworthy of the elevated cultural position it enjoyed. With the richly rewarded players on strike since mid-August, and the World Series cancelled for the first time in ninety years, the wave of cynicism which swept over professional baseball inevitably engulfed Burns' pious representation: "Baseball is likened to a religious rite. I didn't know I was at the ballpark to pray," moaned the *Chicago Tribune*'s Jerome Holtzman after watching the series: "I thought I was witnessing a boys' game played by men."[19] Frank McConnell, writing in the Roman Catholic magazine *Commonweal*, complained: "[So] overweening is [the] moral urgency…to make baseball a template for the social history of the American Century that Burns' documentary becomes…spiritually muscle-bound."[20] The nonbelievers were even more withering. The *Washington Post* columnist Tony Kornheiser wrote: "No matter how many quotes from Walt Whitman you dredge up…I won't think its poetry and I won't think its religion and I won't think it explains the history of America."[21] Meanwhile, the *New York Times* columnist Francis X. Clines derided the "nostalgic piffle" of a literary cottage industry of "male bonders and liberal arts graduates on the commercial make for Life's meaning."[22] Harry Waters of *Newsweek* said Burns was "the best reason yet for barring intellectuals from ballparks."[23]

Of course, this admonishment did not discourage scholars from having their say, even if their praise for Burns was guarded. Baseball historians

---

[19] Jerome Hotzman, "Alas Burns' 'Baseball' Provides Rest for The Weary," *Chicago Tribune*, September 25, 1994.

[20] Frank McConnell, "No Fall Classic: Burns's 'Baseball,'" *Commonweal*, November 18, 1994.

[21] Tony Kornheiser, "National Pastime, Past My Bedtime," *Washington Post*, September 22, 1994.

[22] Francis X. Clines, "The Blowhards Have a Shot This Year," *New York Times*, September 11, 1994.

[23] Harry Waters, "Baseball Is Forever," *Newsweek*, September 11, 1994.

were appreciative of the series' mass appeal but irritated by what they considered factual inaccuracies, limited thematic selections and a reliance of the 'great man' theory of history in which the narrative of the professional game's development was driven by the exploits of a few exceptionally talented athletes. "Who attended and who played professional baseball?," asked the historian Steven Riess, an early consultant for Burns who nevertheless criticized the overly sentimental tone of the final product: "One gets the image…that they were either miners or millhands."[24] The baseball scholar Larry Gerlach also complained of the depiction of fans as "hopelessly sentimental cultists." The prevailing view from the academy appeared to be that Burns had overdone the nostalgia and failed to acknowledge recent scholarship on baseball history which painted a more complex picture of its origins, expansion, and economic and social impact. But even from the scholars there was a grudging admission that their reservations about *Baseball* as serious history were not shared by the broader public who "loved it, were excited by it, and informed by it."[25]

Equally, the insistence by some media commentators that the ill will towards professional baseball generated by the strike would somehow undermine the positive glow around the series appeared to be exaggerated. In fact, for many it offered welcome relief, reestablishing the game's nostalgic confidence, and reasserting its place in the canon of American cultural history. Clinton led the chorus of appreciation; he said he had watched the series avidly and described it as "magnificent."[26] Recycling a familiar masculine trope, the *New York Times* television critic Walter Goodman said Burns had stirred emotions about "the generational ties forged by a game that for more than a hundred years American boys have been learning from their fathers and then, as grown-up boys, teaching to their sons."[27] In *Variety*, Jeff Silverman praised Burns for reminding

---

[24] Steven A. Reiss, Jules Tygiel, Larry Gerlach, and S. W. Pope, "Roundtable: Ken Burns's Baseball," *Journal of Sport History* 23, no. 1 (1996): 61–77; 63–76.

[25] Riess et al., 72–77.

[26] William J. Clinton, "Remarks at a Dinner for Governor Mario Cuomo in New York, October 19, 1994," *American Presidency Project*.

[27] Walter Goodman, "9 Revered Innings of American History," *New York Times*, September 15, 1994.

Americans why baseball "continues to mean so much to us, and who we are as a nation."[28]

In the end, the cumulative audience of forty-five million was the second highest ever for a PBS series, its average Nielsen rating of 5.5 more than double the PBS prime-time average.[29] The associated spin-offs—a video box set, a lavishly illustrated sixty dollar coffee-table book, and dozens of souvenir items including trading cards, bats, balls, and calendars—added commercial muscle to the Burns message. And ensuring that a younger generation was not left untouched, General Motors sponsored a learning-aid based on the series, *Lessons of the Game*, which was dispatched to forty thousand schools, reaching more than three million children and their families.[30] These impressive all-round figures suggest that Burns had partly succeeded in reestablishing the game's presence in the national consciousness, restoring some of its sentimental allure and thereby reestablishing its cultural credentials.

Ken Burns and the President's Voice

Among those in the audience with Clinton at the National Theatre on the afternoon of September 10 was the White House Director of Speechwriting, Don Baer, who had been recruited six months earlier to, in his own words, "elevate what the President had been saying and how he had been saying it."[31] Baer was more than just a talented wordsmith; a former lawyer who had risen through the upper echelons of journalism management at the magazine *US News & World Report*, he was instinctively a "big-picture man," an observer of the Clinton inner sanctum noted, "who believed it was important for the President to rise above the day-to-day strife and

---

[28] Jeff Silverman, "Baseball," *Daily Variety*, September 12, 1994.

[29] Edgerton, *Ken Burns's America*, 126.

[30] General Motors Brochure, "Baseball: A Film by Ken Burns," September 1994, OA/ID 10131, Folder: Baseball – Ken Burns, Don Baer, Communications, *Clinton Presidential Records*.

[31] Baer, interview by author.

embrace the kind of values that would resonate with the middle-class."[32] In his boss, Baer soon realized he faced the twin problem of quality and scale. Even by presidential standards, Clinton was unusually loquacious: he spoke in public, on average, 550 times a year. Yet in the early years of the administration much of it had been instantly forgettable—a humdrum assortment of policy and political remarks that might make a quick line for the news agencies but would barely register on the public consciousness. There was little to inspire the country, little, in the opinion of Baer, to "raise their eyes."[33] Now, watching Burns as he introduced four fifteen-minute segments of his series, Baer sensed an opportunity to lead the President to higher ground. With Burns deftly linking each clip with a few words about the emotions and ideals that baseball summoned, it seemed to Baer that a game so familiar to generations of Americans still had the capacity to convey themes of national identity and common values and that those themes had the potential to contribute to a revived presidential rhetoric.

As he took in the images and voices on the screen, and listened to Burns' explanatory remarks, Baer scribbled on the envelope which contained his invitation more than a dozen phrases which he felt were transferable into Clinton's voice.[34] Baer's notes from that day include single words and phrases which, in the mythmaking surrounding the national pastime, connect baseball to the story of America's founding: *journey; memory; glimpse; perfect; this is the end of a long, long journey*. They include half-written expressions of national aspiration: *our dem[ocratic] republic; Am[erica]'s imperishable hope; collective blessing*. Baer's jottings reflect on baseball's supposed virtues, notably the generational transmission of American ideals through the national pastime: *generational connection; those who have gone before; life lessons; now our turn*. And they spell out broad statements of principle against which, Burns suggests, Americans could continue to measure themselves, ideals that made America one community: *the values that shape us as a nation; national character; we need heroes*

---

[32] Kurtz, *Spin Cycle*, 94.

[33] Baer, interview by author.

[34] Notes by Don Baer on "Baseball" Invitation, September 10, 1994, OA/ID 10131, Folder: Baseball: Ken Burns, Don Baer, Communications, *Clinton Presidential Records*.

like these now more than ever. Reexamining his jottings more than twenty years later, Baer comments: "Look at these themes, [they are] enduring, eternal values, things that speak to who we are as a nation and our national character."[35] On the back cover of a publicity brochure for the series, which displayed a vintage photograph of a baseball team in repose, Baer scribbled: "service is never a simple act, it's about you and me and all of us together, who we are as individuals and what we are as a nation."[36] Two days later, these were the exact words Clinton used when swearing in volunteers at the launch of AmeriCorps, the youth community service program which was one of his signature nation-building initiatives.[37] In the search for words that would "raise the eyes" of the country, Burns' imagined America appeared to offer a rhetorical framework of common experiences and community values which drew upon baseball as an expression of a widely shared American civil religion.

Baer had never met the filmmaker before that afternoon in September 1994, but Clinton and Burns already had an established relationship of mutual admiration. They had first met in late-1992 when the President-elect was invited to the home of the publisher of the *Washington Post*, Katherine Graham. Burns recalled plunging into conversation about *The Civil War*, with Clinton displaying "more understanding and insight than any critic or reviewer ever had."[38] When Burns was asked to contribute anecdotes about his relationship with Clinton for a presidential speech, one of the filmmaker's assistants wrote back on his behalf: "Ken feels that President Clinton is, like himself, a great student of history—that he understands the forces that have brought us to this moment, and is sensitive to how complicated history is, how much undertow there is."[39]

On the day of the screening, Baer was so impressed with what he had seen and heard that he introduced himself to Burns and invited him to

---

[35] Baer, interview by author.

[36] Notes by Don Baer on brochure *Baseball: A Film by Ken Burns*, OA/ID 10131, Folder: Baseball: Ken Burns, Don Baer, Communications, *Clinton Presidential Records*.

[37] William J. Clinton, "Remarks in a Swearing-In Ceremony for AmeriCorps Volunteers, September 12, 1994," *American Presidency Project*.

[38] Letter, Paul Beaucorn, to Lowell Weiss, "Anecdotes re: President Clinton and Ken Burns," November 7, 1997, OA/ID 17192, Folder: "Lewis and Clark" 11/9/97, Lowell Weiss, Speechwriting, *Clinton Presidential Records*.

[39] Letter, Beaucorn to Weiss.

meet the rest of his White House writing team.[40] A few weeks later, on the afternoon of October 18, Baer convened a workshop with Burns and the speechwriters in the Old Executive Office Building just west of the White House. A contemporaneous note made by one of the writers, Gabrielle Bushman, gives a flavor of Burns' advice that day.[41] She records that the filmmaker encouraged the writers to revitalize presidential rhetoric by aiming to seize the high ground and capitalize on a unique historical moment: "With the end of the Cold War we have an opportunity to define what we are for." They should write for posterity, Burns advised: "Try to fashion rhetoric as if it was being read 10 years from now." Urging them to have the confidence to deploy religious themes, Burns observed that "POTUS is m[ost] effective when he is the holy ghost," an insight that amounted to the sacralization of the President. When the discussion turned to baseball, one of the speechwriters suggested that the sense of community generated by the national pastime was similar to the appeal of Oprah Winfrey's television broadcasts: it had meaning to those people whose lives were "missing conversation"—an insight which directly addressed the Putnam thesis of America's weakening communal experiences.

The so-called national motto, e *pluribus unum*—"one out of many"— also featured at the meeting. Something of an obsession of Burns, he frequently used the phrase when talking about his ambitions for the series during his nationwide publicity tour. Originally placed on the Great Seal of the United States by the founding fathers, the concept of *e pluribus unum* had come under renewed scrutiny in the 1990s with media commentators fond of debating its relevance for a country with an increasingly diverse and politically polarized population. This renewed prominence in the public arena was thanks partly to the historian, Arthur Schlesinger Jr., whose best-selling 1991 lament, *The Disuniting of America*, had warned of a threat to national cohesion posed by so-called "strident multiculturalism" and proffered *e pluribus unum* as the "brilliant solution for the inherent fragility, the combustibility of a multi-ethnic society."[42] Clearly influenced by Schlesinger, Burns enthusiastically embraced the phrase, frequently

---

[40] Baer, interview by author.

[41] Note by Gabrielle Bushman on Ken Burns Meeting, October 18, 1994. OA/ID 7462, Folder: [Notebook 4], Gabrielle Bushman, Office of Speechwriting, *Clinton Presidential Records*.

[42] Schlesinger, *The Disuniting of America*, 17.

directly quoting JFK's former advisor. "There's too much *pluribus* and not enough *unum*," he told a reporter on the day *Baseball* premiered on PBS: "That's all I'm interested in. I'm interested in more *unum*."[43] A quarter of a century after he first invited Burns to talk to the White House communications team, Baer's still recalls the rhetorical artistry and the power of the filmmaker's argument. Its significance, according to Baer, was that it helped to shape the thinking of the writers, giving them a framework which served as a reference point amid the blizzard of daily speechwriting demands. It was not that writers specifically sought out baseball metaphors to weave into presidential rhetoric but that Burns' language brought context to what they were already trying to do. Put simply, according to Baer, it was "about thinking in the right way."[44]

It is easy to see why Burns' perspective on history and his aspirations for social cohesion would be so appealing to Clinton and those around him. Like the President, Burns embraced a typical liberal-pluralist conceptualization of American culture, which he expressed in the style, content, and underlying themes of his films. Gary Edgerton, an expert on the Burns catalog, notes how the filmmaker always ensured "social and cultural differences between Americans were kept in a comparatively stable and negotiated consensus within the body politic." Like Clinton, Burns believed that the world for many Americans was "unravelling" and that national unity was even more dependent on the "alchemy" of a "few pieces of paper and a few sacred words."[45] Indeed, in December 1995, a White House memo suggested asking Burns to contribute ideas for the forthcoming State of the Union Address precisely because his films "remind us of why we should be together."[46] Although not a follower of an organized religion himself, Burns often presented this yearning for national cohesion in the language of civil religion: "My mission—and I'm happy to say there is a huge evangelical dimension to what I'm doing—is preaching the

---

[43] Quoted in Susan King, "Taking Us Back to the Ballgame: PBS' 'Baseball' Holds a Mirror Up to America," *Los Angeles Times*, September 18, 1994.

[44] Baer, interview by author.

[45] Gary Edgerton, "Mystic Chords of Memory,'" 16.

[46] Memorandum, Michael Lessin, "SOTU Outreach Biographies; December 14, 1995," OA/ID 10986, Folder: SOTU [State of the Union] [1], Terry Edmonds, Speechwriting, *Clinton Presidential Records*.

gospel of Americanism," he explained in a 2008 interview. "At the heart, every religious teaching is about reconciliation. It's about making one of the many. It is *e pluribus unum*. All my films are about that in some way."[47]

The problem for some critics was a perception that this culture of shared beliefs common to Burns and Clinton had a decidedly liberal tinge. Clearly irritated by the tone Burns adopted in the television series in retelling the story of Jackie Robinson and the integration of professional baseball, the religious commentator George Weigel accused him of being, "a child of the 1960s intent on driving home a certain interpretation of the American national experience of race (and to a lesser extent class)." Weigel's watching of *Baseball* prompted him to complain of being exhausted by the "claims of continuing victimhood" coming from liberals who supported racial quotas in affirmative action, the "ever-expanding welfare state" and the "lunacies" of Afrocentric school curricula.[48]

However, that Clinton-Burns consensus so loathed by Weigel was not as he described it. While Burns and Clinton admittedly shared a liberal approach to some social issues, such as civil rights, they combined it with a reverence for other, more traditional expressions of American values and national institutions. This synthesis was one of the continuing threads of Clinton's New Democratic philosophy on which he had built his 1992 election victory. "New choice, old values," "old-fashioned American values for a new time," and a "common community" had all been phrases from Clinton's presidential nomination acceptance speech in 1992.[49] Michael Waldman, who would succeed Baer as Director of Speechwriting in 1995, argues that it was a post-New Deal, socially liberated vision of politics which was sensitive to the conservative strain of working and middle-class voters buffeted by economic and social change. It was this blend which made Clinton such an unusual politician. His rapid acceleration from a modest Arkansas upbringing, through Ivy League and Oxford, into the highest rungs of meritocratic, socially liberal, global society gave Clinton, "a willingness to embrace the traditional 1950s values of small-town

---

[47] Quoted in Timothy Larsen, "An Interview With Ken Burns," *Christian Century*, July 15, 2008.

[48] George Weigel, "Politically-Correct Baseball," *Commentary*, November 1, 1994.

[49] William J. Clinton, "Address Accepting the Presidential Nomination at the Democratic National Convention in New York July 16, 1992," *American Presidency Project*.

America in a way that all the other Rhodes scholars, all the other Yale Law graduates, all the other McGovern campaign officials [Clinton had helped run George McGovern's presidential campaign in Texas in 1972] would have looked down their noses at."[50] So when Burns and Ward loftily suggested that baseball "encoded and stored," "the genetic material of our civilization—passing down to the next generation the best of us," Clinton would have understood better than most what they were talking about— namely how baseball expressed the continuity of the American experience.[51] And no doubt he would have appreciated the political resonance of such sentiments. To Clinton, these Burnsian notions were embedded in the social and economic consensus of his Arkansas youth which celebrated many of the traditional aspects and underlying principles of American culture. Those notes Don Baer scribbled on the back of an envelope on the afternoon of September 10, 1994—*the values that shape us as a nation, America's imperishable hope, those who have gone before, now our turn*—embodied a Clintonian liberal-pluralist concept of "One America." A liturgy for America's civil religion was being expressed through the history of baseball.

In all, Clinton would host White House receptions for screenings of three Burns historical documentary projects, *Baseball* (1994), *Thomas Jefferson* (1997), and *Lewis & Clark* (1997), all sweeping stories which reverberated with the American myth. On the last occasion Clinton introduced the filmmaker as "the incomparable Ken Burns" and spoke of his work as a "journey of learning" and a "precious gift to future generations." Clinton said he hoped Burns' example would inspire others to "honor our past and imagine our future" as the new millennium approached.[52] This was the essence of American civil religion under Clinton—the linking of the nation's destiny and mission to its history and commonly held values—and Burns was the preeminent preacher.

"It's Not About Baseball, It's About America"

In the fall of 1994—the season when tens of millions of Americans watched the Burns *Baseball* series on television but were unable to tune in

---

[50] Waldman, interview by author.
[51] Burns and Ward, *Baseball*, xviii.
[52] William J. Clinton, "Remarks at a Screening of Ken Burns' 'Lewis and Clark', November 10, 1997," *American Presidency Project*.

to the cancelled World Series—the challenging political outlook was a source of concern and frustration at the White House. The first year and a half of the administration had been bumpy, full of misplays and errors. There had been early controversy over plans to lift the ban on gay people serving in the military; taxes had increased on high-income earners, but also on fuel, which hit the less well off. The campaign promise of a middle-class tax cut had not materialized. Neither had Clinton's much-heralded pledge to "end welfare as we know it." GDP growth was steady but unspectacular; real wages were stagnant.[53] Significant achievements on international trade, gun control, crime, unemployment, and the federal budget were offset by the collapse of Clinton's ambitious health reform plans and by the expanding investigation into the First Family's real estate investments on the Whitewater River in Arkansas. A sense of sleaze surrounding the administration was fueled by a string of scandals of varying substance, usually adorned with the 'gate' suffix. Some were indeed serious, or had serious consequences, albeit in the longer term, including the suicide of the Deputy White House Counsel, Vince Foster, in July 1993, and the sexual harassment suit brought against Clinton by Paula Jones in May 1994, which contained the seeds of the impeachment crisis of 1998–99.[54] These events, and others of less consequence, were endlessly amplified in the hyperventilating and expanding universe of conservative talk radio.

The media narrative that the former Arkansas governor was out of his depth in Washington was further stoked by the publication in June 1994 of *The Agenda* by Bob Woodward.[55] The celebrated Watergate reporter had written a 350-page, fly-on-the-wall account of the tensions and rivalries in the White House over the economic plan which formed the centerpiece of the administration's first year agenda—and it was not

---

[53] Statista business database, "Gross Domestic Product of the United States 1990–2022," and "Median Inflation Adjusted Weekly Earnings of Full-Time Wage and Salary Workers in the United States from 1979–2020," *statista.com*.

[54] In addition to Whitewater, the 'scandals' of 1993–94 included: 'Nannygate', which concerned the failed nomination of Zoe Baird as Attorney General; 'Travelgate' which involved allegations of corruption, embezzlement, and nepotism within the White House Travel Office (and which is thought to have contributed to Foster's suicide); and 'Troopergate' in which it was alleged that Arkansas state troopers had procured women for Clinton during his time as Governor. One of the women was Paula Jones.

[55] Woodward, *The Agenda*.

flattering to Clinton. "Those running the country functioned in near total disorder," reported *Newsday*, under the headline "Absolute Chaos," the day after CBS *60 Minutes* gave national TV exposure to the claims in Woodward's book.[56] It all contributed to a depressing political outlook as the midterm elections approached; never before had a president experienced such consistently poor approval ratings across the first two years in office, stuck for most of the time at around forty percent.

Clinton addressed this bleak reality by expressing irritation that his successes were not recognized by the public. He aimed a special venom at press commentators who he believed unfairly portrayed him as "a wild eyed liberal who wanted to tax them into the poorhouse and take their doctors and guns away."[57] His exasperation was evident both in public ("I have to find ways to communicate better with the American people," he admitted in a radio interview in late August) and in private: Taylor Branch noted in his meetings with his old friend, "a plaintive tone of uncertainty mixed with political gloom."[58]

Republicans in Congress, urged on by the House minority whip Newt Gingrich, sensed Clinton's vulnerability and were determined to make the midterm elections a referendum on the President. Gingrich identified the need to redirect the Republican campaign away from its typically local orientation, and instead present a unified national message which articulated positive policies alongside the inevitable avalanche of negative attacks on the President. Gingrich's chosen vehicle was a big-picture legislative agenda, the *Contract with America*, which he persuaded 367 Republican congressional candidates to sign in a ceremony on the steps of the Capitol six weeks before election day. The *Contract* promised a Republican victory would deliver a ten-point, hundred-day action plan of institutional reform, congressional term limits, tax cuts, budget cuts, and welfare reform to bring about what Gingrich called the "renewal of American civilization."[59]

---

[56] Andrew Smith, "'Absolute Chaos': Book Cites Rage, Indecision in Clinton White House," *Newsday*, June 4, 1994.

[57] Clinton, *My Life*, 619.

[58] William J. Clinton, "Interview with Gene Burns of WOR Radio, New York City, Wednesday, August 24, 1994," *American Presidency Project*; Branch, *The Clinton Tapes*, 209.

[59] Republican House Representatives, "Republican Contract with America," *billofrightsinstitute.org*; Newt Gingrich, "Speech to Christian Coalition of America, September 10, 1993," *C-SPAN*.

The Democratic offering, embodied in a languishing president who had not even been able to deliver his signature health-care plan despite his party controlling both the House and the Senate, looked limp in comparison.

At a meeting with his senior communications advisors a few days after the White House baseball picnic, Clinton revealed the depth of his concerns about his political prospects. A transcript of that meeting reveals Clinton moaning about an unwarranted assault from the media and complaining that no matter how many times he said things were getting better people refused to believe him. He feared the lack of a coherent presidential message was dragging him into the trenches of the culture wars: "They think we sin publicly and privately....And they believe I go to dinner every night with a homosexual abortion doctor." Clinton fretted over his political positioning ("I'm over here too far to the left on cultural issues without a magnet to generate any enthusiasm") and demanded a change of direction in his communication strategy. "All I'm just telling you is if every speech is a new set of pretty words, it's a failure," he said. "There has got to be a story line. It's got to be something people hear. Something people repeat."

Responding to the President's analysis, his aides at the meeting advocated a more emotional response in the presidential rhetoric—Americans wanted to be inspired both "as a nation and as individuals." Clinton's rhetoric, they argued, should concentrate on selling his drive and vision; he should "raise the level of the rhetoric" by "calling for sacrifice, and challenging and recognizing human emotions."[60] One of the aides then referred Clinton to a document containing ideas expressed by Ken Burns. The specific document is not identified in the transcript, but we do know that a press cutting of an article authored by Burns from the August 29 edition of *US News & World Report*, on which several sections had been hand-highlighted, was circulating at the time among staff in the West Wing. The underlined sections included:

---

[60] Transcript, speechwriting meeting, the White House, September 1994, OA/ID 10131, Folder: Presidential Interviews, Don Baer, Communications, *Clinton Presidential Records*. The exact date of the meeting is not clear from the document, although references to the 'Cairo Conference' place it at around September 12–13. The President is the only contributor named: others are unidentified, although Don (Baer) is referred to as is Phil (Lader, Deputy Chief of Staff).

> There is something in baseball…that teaches continually the tiny margin between success and failure and that does so within a sense of community in which in order to win you sacrifice.[61]

A few paragraphs later, the notion of what Burns called a "tribal Americanness" was highlighted, along with the observation that the shared memory of baseball represented the "continuity of human experience" in America.

> So few of us are aware of the union from which so many of our blessings flow, and we need to struggle to find those institutions that provide the continuity and time and memory, and that seem to feed a kind of larger, tribal Americanness.

And on the following page, in a highlighted paragraph reflecting on the intransigence of the opposing parties in the baseball strike, Burns had written of the virtues of compromise as a way of moving forward: "In baseball you always win by giving up something. Quite often…we forget the genius of America is compromise."

Some of these themes—community, sacrifice, continuity, and compromise—had formed the rhetorical spine of a notable series of speeches Clinton had delivered in France three months earlier to mark the fiftieth anniversary of the D-Day landings. Baer had overseen those speeches; "the generational connection was a key part," he recalls, "'we are the children of your sacrifice' was meant to be a statement from one generation to another about their commitment, their devotion, their sacrifice not being in vain."[62] Now, at this September 1994 communications strategy meeting, Clinton's aides proposed that Baer's Normandy conceptualization of generational connection and Burns' notion that baseball was an emblem of continuity in the American experience, could be blended to offer a rhetoric of generational transmission, sacrifice, and compromise that could reinvigorate the Clinton message.

> UNIDENTIFIED: Normandy did speak to this country at a level it wants to be spoken to. Because it said—and that's why I gave you this Ken Burns excerpt here —it's not about baseball, it's about America. It said when we work together, we win. When we find common ground

---

[61] Press cutting of Burns article with markings, *US News & World Report*, August 29, 1994, Staff Member: Don Baer, OAS/ID 10131, Folder: Presidential Remarks, Don Baer, Communications, *Clinton Presidential Records*.

[62] Baer, interview by author.

and we pull together in this and we're willing to make some sacrifices at the edges from each of us, we win. We each are better than we could be—

PRESIDENT: —If you're trying to do anything, you have to find a way to make compromise honorable again.

UNIDENTIFIED:...And for you to be the carrier of the message, that when we work together, we win —if we can find a way to fit that into the story line of these accomplishments, then I think we take it to a higher ground, we inspire Americans to do something bigger....That's the story line.[63]

This notion of 'working together to win' had long been part of Clinton's rhetorical armory and an integral element of his New Democratic, communitarian appeal. In this context, the entreaty to work together was invoking Clinton's abstract sense of community—a renewal of the commonly held attitudes and values that stirred Americans to greater feats. According to Waldman, it was grounded in Clinton's youth and a nostalgic desire to recreate the national community of World War II and the Cold War, when middle-class was not just an economic label but also a construction of values about people working hard, being responsible, and sharing a measure of equality. It was a sense of community that had shrunk by the 1990s, disrupted by the relentless march of commercialism and weakened by social and economic forces beyond the control of individuals.[64] Clinton knew that despite strong headline numbers, the economic experience of middle-class Americans in the mid-nineties was mixed; inequality continued to rise rapidly until the end of the decade, with wage earners working longer hours for less money. And although unemployment rates were historically low, long-term job security was declining with the onset of globalization and rapid technological change. For many, simply eking a living in late-twentieth-century America, Clinton claimed, was "like walking across a running river on slippery rocks" where you could "lose your footing at any time."[65] It pointed to a widespread belief that

---

[63] Transcript, speechwriting meeting.
[64] Waldman, interview by author.
[65] William J. Clinton, "Exchange With Reporters Aboard Air Force One, September 22, 1995," *American Presidency Project*.

community life had been stronger in previous generations—more evidence, it seemed, of an American civic malaise.[66]

The spiritual damage caused by this sense of a fragmented and anxiety-ridden national life was highlighted in a memo sent to Clinton by the Yale law professor Stephen Carter, who had been solicited for ideas for the upcoming State of the Union Address. Carter argued that Americans were losing their faith in government: they viewed one another as "adversaries competing for the same limited resources, and even as enemies out to do harm to the values that really matter." Carter continued: "Americans need to be brought back to the theme of community so that we can learn to see each other as friends and neighbors."[67] It reinforced the analysis of other scholars in the Clinton orbit, such as Putnam. America was suffering from a decline in its social capital—the networks, contacts, and reciprocal social relations provided by social structures, including parents' associations, churches, and sports teams. Americans, Putnam said, needed to reconnect with one another.[68]

Again, this was familiar territory for Clinton. He had spoken in the past about the value of the civic structures in promoting community engagement, frequently citing institutions of education, local democracy, religion, and sports. In his 1992 nomination speech, Clinton had mourned the plight of overworked parents who had "gotten the shaft," leaving them with little time for their children or the PTA, the Little League, or Scouts.[69] In Normandy, Clinton had declared that the young American soldiers who had liberated Europe had been "driven by the voice of free will and responsibility, nurtured in Sunday schools, town halls, and sandlot ballgames."[70] And Clinton would use similar imagery at the memorial

---

[66] Putnam, *Bowling Alone*, 25.

[67] Memorandum, Stephen L. Carter to the President, January 10, 1995, OA/ID 1031, Folder: State of the Union Memos, Don Baer, Communications, *Clinton Presidential Records*.

[68] Putnam, *Bowling Alone*, 28.

[69] Clinton, "Address Before a Joint Session of Congress on the State of the Union, January 24, 1995."

[70] William J. Clinton, "Remarks on the 50th Anniversary of D-Day at the United States Cemetary in Colleville-Sur-Mer, France, June 6, 1994," *American Presidency Project*.

service after the bombing of the Alfred P. Murrah Federal Building in Oklahoma City in April 1995, in his most vivid expression of the aggregated American community, when he spoke of those who had died as being friends and neighbors, from churches, the PTA, civic clubs, and the ballpark. "You have lost too much, but you have not lost everything. And you have certainly not lost America, for we will stand with you for as many tomorrows as it takes."[71] In the face of tragedy, Clinton had summoned Burnsian notions of the universality of the American experience and applied the sacred elements that bound that imagined American community together—parenting, civic duty, and the national pastime.

The healing power of these institutions surfaced again a few months later when Clinton spoke of baseball helping "to hold us together; it helps us come together." In a weekly radio address on the theme of "American renewal" he painted an idealized picture of American communal life, where "communities large and small grow up around baseball: kids play a pick-up game until it's too dark to see, folks getting together for softball after work, families walking together to see a home game at their local ballpark."[72] Mike McCurry, Clinton's Press Secretary from 1994 to 1998, identifies in this rhetoric a religious dimension; there was an analogy between the bleachers at sports venues and the pews in churches—they were both spaces of social and democratic equality where people could put aside their political divisions and just watch the game: "Clinton understood the role sports play in creating a common thread that brings people together at the end of the day and weaves people together in a national ideal." Of course, McCurry acknowledges, Clinton knew there were limits to what sporting events could do to heal the country in divisive times, "but on the other hand, there weren't that many opportunities for him to find things that would break down barriers between people....There were very few

---

[71] William J. Clinton, "Remarks at a Memorial Service for the Bombing Victims in Oklahoma City, Oklahoma, April 23, 1995," *American Presidency Project*.

[72] Clinton, "The President's Radio Address: October 21, 1995."

places where that happens."[73] Like the church, the ballpark was one of those sacred spaces.

Reconnecting the Clinton Presidency

By the time Don Baer again wrote to Ken Burns, two months after the speechwriters workshop, the political landscape in Washington had dramatically shifted. Like Carter, Burns was among several public intellectuals asked to contribute thoughts for the State of the Union Address, the first presidential set piece of 1995—a year in which the White House hoped to restore Clinton's authority in the wake of a disastrous midterm defeat in November which had delivered Republican majorities in both the chambers for the first time since 1952. The scale of the punishment meted out to the Democrats—a fifty-four-seat gain for the Republicans in the House, and an eight-seat gain in the Senate—had exceeded the expectations of almost all experts and shocked Clinton, who admitted to being "profoundly distressed" by the results.[74] The discouraging prospect now facing him was two years of an energized Republican majority pressing ahead with the conservative program laid out in the *Contract with America*, sidelining Clinton in the domestic legislative arena, while continuing to harry him as "the enemy of normal Americans" for his lack of moral leadership and support for gay rights. "It was a very bad time," recalls Clinton's Commerce Secretary, Mickey Kantor: "He saw what it did to his presidency and how difficult it was going to be—he related it to his own reelection two years hence."[75] Carolyn Curiel, one of the senior writers on Baer's team, explains the impact of the midterms defeat: "It forced all of us to reach deeper down into the gut and figure out what we stood for and how to express it."[76] Baer acknowledged as much in his letter to Burns: "The political circumstances have indeed changed considerably since last year," but "what has not changed is that the President has an opportunity in this

---

[73] Mike McCurry, Interview by Author, Washington, DC, November 6, 2019.

[74] Clinton, *My Life*, 630

[75] Michael (Mickey) Kantor Interview, June 28, 2002, *Bill Clinton Presidential Oral History*.

[76] Carolyn Curiel, Interview by Author, Chicago via Skype, July 23, 2020.

address to identify the challenges facing the country in ways only a President can."[77]

Seeking input on the way forward, Clinton hosted a dinner at Camp David on January 14, 1995, for a group of sympathetic scholars and public intellectuals. Their combined analyses mirrored the divisions within the wider Democratic party: half thought the President had not been full-throated enough with progressive policies in the first two years of his administration; the rest believed he had drifted too far from the moderate, New Democrat agenda on which he had campaigned successfully in 1992. But it was a contributor with a foot in both camps, Robert Putnam, who in the words of one of those present "stole a piece of the show." Putnam presented to the group his "bowling alone" decline of community thesis which had been published in article form that month. Of everything Clinton heard that evening, this was what resonated most with his own views about the need to protect community values from encroaching social and economic disruption.[78] And this is what had been missing from Clinton's rhetoric in 1993 and 1994, according to Waldman: Clinton's synthesis as the communitarian New Democrat who wanted to preserve traditional values in a disrupted world and to "aspire to build and rebuild a national community." The "opportunity, responsibility, community" language had fallen out of his speeches in the previous two years, says Waldman, "part of what he now wanted to do was reconnect with that vision."[79]

Addressing Congress on January 24, Clinton deployed his New Covenant and the "opportunity, responsibly, community" mantra in a major speech for the first time since the 1992 campaign. He reflected on the disquieting state of civic life—people worked together less, he noted, and shouted at each other more: "The common bonds of community which have been the greatest strength of our country from its very beginning are badly frayed." And he again offered the PTA, the town hall, and the ballpark as institutions which strengthened "the bonds of trust and cooperation."[80] They were examples of tangible civic structures that helped to define Clinton's vision of a presidency focused on an idealized American

---

[77] Letter, Don Baer to Ken Burns, January 4, 1995, OA/ID 10138, Folder: SOTU Scholars, Don Baer, Communications, *Clinton Presidential Records*.

[78] Galston interview.

[79] Waldman, interview by author.

[80] Clinton, "Address Before a Joint Session of Congress on the State of the Union, January 24, 1995."

community. Dick Morris, the strategist to whom Clinton was increasingly turning for polling-driven policy advice, was also urging that the President should project "compromise, reconciliation, values and healing."[81] The Secretary of Housing, Henry Cisneros, pressed a similar point in a lengthy memo to the President: "When everything else is changing confusedly, people look to the leader for…the affirmation of enduring values," adding that it was important to "evoke a remembrance of history."[82] These were the themes Baer had identified in Burns' films and that had been championed by the filmmaker himself in the whirlwind of publicity surrounding the premiere of *Baseball*.

In the weeks immediately after the State of the Union, Clinton would summon the symbolism of baseball on multiple occasions, often invoking its cultural meaning in his efforts to end the baseball players strike which now threatened to disrupt spring training and the upcoming regular season. In doing so he repeatedly advocated compromise and reconciliation, which he hoped would bring healing to the game, and by implication, the nation. Clinton's embrace of baseball as a symbol of national cohesion can therefore be understood as one response to the incoming Republican-controlled Congress of 1995. Clinton had been portrayed by the Republicans as the "enemy of ordinary Americans" and "culturally alien" to American values. So, revisiting his successful 1992 formula of faith, family, and flag and reconnecting his presidency with the people through the values expressed by a sacred institution such as baseball made sense. Burns' rendering of the national pastime had presented the game once more as a meaningful emblem for a unified national creed. By engaging with the problems facing baseball, Clinton had the opportunity to fashion himself as the protector of wider American values against the increasingly strident and hyper-partisan Republicans, whose zeal for cutting government spending would prove politically costly in the federal budget standoff at the end of 1995. It was a neat reversal of the respective party positions the previous year—Clinton could once again present himself as the moderate against an overreaching Republican Party. "The whole project of 1995 was to try to restore a sense of the President's connection to the whole country," Baer recalls. "To the extent that [the country] had been deprived of him by the

---

[81] Morris, *Behind The Oval Office*, 40.
[82] Memorandum, Henry Cisneros to Bill Clinton, August 14, 1995, OA/ID 10131, Folder: Cisneros, Don Baer, Communications, *Clinton Presidential Records*.

Republican leadership, to make it clear that he was very much of the country and leader of the whole country."[83] And what could make him appear leader of the country more than saving the national pastime from self-destruction?

However, the arena in which Clinton initially engaged with baseball in the early months of 1995 was messy. The bitterness surrounding the strike, which started in August 1994 and would not end until the following April, engulfed players, owners, and fans. Despite its rating success and its rediscovered cultural resonance, Burns' televisual homage to the game sat uneasily with those fans whose most recent major league experience was of a closed ballpark, an abandoned World Series, and a sport disfigured by what looked like reckless greed. If anything, the increasing sentimentalization of baseball's past propagated by Burns had sharpened views about the professional game on all sides, particularly among those who had already given up following it in the belief that it had lost its way. Certainly, millions of Americans and many influential journalists were losing the faith. Professional baseball needed a savior. But few people outside the Oval Office were convinced that the right person to perform that role was the President.

---

[83] Baer, interview by author.

Chapter Two

"He Wants to be Savior of the National Pastime": Bill Clinton and the 1994–95 Baseball Strike

"The Owners Suck, the Players Suck, Baseball Sucks"

On February 6, 1995, Pamela Owens, a mother from Texas who was campaigning for better educational opportunities for her autistic son, felt compelled to write to Bill Clinton about his misplaced priorities. She had heard on the radio that the President wanted to get directly involved in negotiations between players and owners in an effort to end the strike in Major League Baseball which had dragged out over the past six months. "I would think there are a lot of more important matters to be handled by the President of the United States than the issue of baseball," Owens wrote. "Truly these grown wealthy men should be able to come to some understanding on their own while they still have a few fans left." Perhaps, Owens mused, she had overvalued the position of the presidency.[1]

Pamela Owens was not alone in thinking that Clinton was misguided in his willingness over the winter months of 1994–95 to step into an ill-tempered labor dispute, one that had led to the abrupt end to the previous baseball season, the cancellation of the World Series for the first time in ninety years, and had left millions of fans furious, both with the billionaires who ran and the elite professional athletes who played the national pastime. "The owners suck. The players suck. Baseball sucks," fumed Steve Wulf in *Sports Illustrated*, reflecting the disgust of many of its readers. "They take our money, but they take us for suckers and they take us for granted."[2] It seemed, moreover, that Wulf was not only speaking for the

---

[1] Letter, Pamela Owens to Bill Clinton, February 6, 1995, OA/ID 9947, Folder: [Unrelated General Mail and Form Letters] [Loose] [10], Roger Goldblatt, Health Care Task Force, *Clinton Presidential Records*.

[2] Steve Wulf, "Fans, Strike Back!" *Sports Illustrated*, September 26, 1994.

exasperated, die-hard fan. When readers of the *Chicago Sun-Times* voted on whether the President should be involved in solving the strike almost three-quarters said no.[3] A more scientific *Washington Post-ABC News* poll painted a similarly emphatic picture of public opinion.[4] Some in Clinton's cabinet also harbored doubts about the wisdom of presidential intervention; Vice President Al Gore feared his boss was risking his prestige "in a scorpion fight."[5] Labor Secretary Robert Reich, who had been tasked by Clinton to bring the warring parties together, recalled theories championed by the political scientist Richard Neustadt, about the contingency of the persuasive powers of the presidency and the danger of presidential authority being "frittered away on lost causes."[6] Commentators were similarly unconvinced of the merits of intervention, suggesting that Clinton, in trying to bang together two stubborn sets of heads, was simply wasting his time. In the *New York Times,* Claire Smith wondered whether the President was "the last American willing to invest emotional energy in baseball."[7]

Yet, despite public suspicion, the caution of colleagues, and the skepticism of much of the media, Clinton persisted in his belief that he had a role in saving professional baseball from self-destruction: he could not afford to let the national pastime die on his watch. And one of the driving forces behind his thinking was the myth that had been propagated by journalists, scholars, and politicians since the early-twentieth century and had just been reinforced by Ken Burns—that the health of the national pastime was somehow a measure of the health and vitality of American society itself. It was an association which had been typically presented in positive

---

[3] Facsimile, Baker & Hostetler to Bruce Lindsey, February 8, 1995, OA/ID 24792, Folder: Baseball Strike – Letters/Comments/Polls [3], Bruce Lindsey, Counsel Office, *Clinton Presidential Records.*

[4] Washington Post-ABC News Poll, "Americans Go To Bat For Owners; Poll: Clinton, Congress Should Stay Out of Baseball Dispute," *Washington Post,* February 1, 1995.

[5] Branch, *The Clinton Tapes,* 241.

[6] Reich, *Locked in the Cabinet,* 239–40; Neustadt, *Presidential Power and the Modern Presidents.*

[7] Claire Smith, "Fans Should Turn Their Backs, Too," *New York Times,* February 10, 1995.

terms, but as 1994 drew to a close, with baseball engulfed in its own existential crisis and the country's political institutions awash with partisan antagonism, the mythical connection had more dispiriting implications. It was Burns himself who made the point most succinctly: "Beset by the pernicious effects of self-interest and narcissism, and an inability to find common ground...I could be describing the country as a whole as I describe the problems that beset baseball."[8] By this logic, it followed that the mess in which baseball now found itself reflected badly on the state of the country and, by association, Clinton's administration. And Clinton appeared to agree: "If our national pastime was being cancelled things could not be going in the right direction."[9] Channeling this belief, Clinton became the first sitting president publicly to get involved in trying to settle a labor dispute in professional sports—a decision he presented as one of institutional obligation, if not sacred duty. Mike McCurry, briefing reporters two days after Pamela Owens had written her letter, insisted that the President in practice had little choice: Clinton's intervention was, in effect, an assertion of his civil religious role. "He is the President, and we're talking about baseball and baseball is the national pastime and plays a unique role in our history and our culture."[10] In a single sentence McCurry had framed Clinton's actions as a matter of patriotic, indeed civil religious duty, rather than the meddling of an overzealous and ill-advised chief executive.

Of course, McCurry was right: the relationship between baseball and the presidency was ingrained in the cultural architecture of the office of President. From the early-century Opening Day ritual to late-century baseball-jacketed appearances on the pitcher's mound; from White House receptions for championship teams to the deployment of the language of the ballpark in speeches and broadcasts, presidents had engaged with the national pastime to validate their claims to national leadership. Clinton had already seized his first two formal opportunities: pitching on Opening Day in Baltimore in 1993 and Cleveland in 1994. But Clinton's engagement with the strike was not solely motivated by a desire to fulfill his

---

[8] Burns, "A Grain of Sand That Reveals the Universe."
[9] Clinton, *My Life*, 620.
[10] William J. Clinton, "Press Briefing by Mike McCurry, February 8, 1995," *American Presidency Project*.

ceremonial obligations—the political landscape of 1994–95 played a part too. The President's approval ratings remained in the doldrums. Under fire as "the enemy of normal Americans" for his lack of moral leadership and for pushing health-care reforms which were "culturally alien" to the nation, the new Republican-led Congress of January 1995 now promised an active legislative program to, in Gingrich's phrase, "restore American civilization."[11] Clinton's hopes of delivering his own domestic agenda ahead of the 1996 presidential election looked set to be frustrated. He appeared to be an executive lame duck, destined for a one-term presidency. Even Clinton's own Labor Secretary observed that Speaker Gingrich and Senate Majority Leader Bob Dole appeared "to have taken charge of the United States Government."[12] In short, Clinton's presidency was being dismissed as "irrelevant."[13]

The baseball strike offered Clinton a chance to chip away at the narrative of irrelevance, the opportunity for him to be an activist, albeit in a narrowly defined setting, and to demonstrate that he could still pull on the levers of persuasion his office provided, especially where there were potential swing-state votes at stake. By cherishing a national institution and bringing an end to conflict in the national pastime, Clinton thought he could prove that the Republicans were wrong; that he did share the values of "normal Americans." By advocating compromise and reconciliation in baseball, he could heal a broken game, and, by implication, a fractured nation.

August 12, 1994: The Strike Begins

The immediate cause of the strike in which Clinton would eventually get entangled was the breakdown in talks over a new collective bargaining agreement between MLB owners and the Major League Baseball Players Association (MLBPA). But the dispute was situated on a much longer arc—one whose trajectory was defined in 1922 when baseball was granted

---

[11] Ken Walsh, "A Polarizing President," *US News & World Report*, November 7, 1994; Mary McGrory, "Gingrich's Buzzword Pudding, " *Washington Post*, December 16, 1993.

[12] Reich, *Locked in the Cabinet*, 115.

[13] William J. Clinton, "The President's News Conference, April 18, 1995," *American Presidency Project*.

exemption from the nation's antitrust laws by the US Supreme Court.[14] That ruling allowed clubs to maintain a monopoly of the professional game in a given regional market and to benefit from the monopsonistic labor practice of the reserve clause, which tied players to their teams in perpetuity—a dynamic which would be the source of much of professional baseball's labor turmoil as the century progressed.[15] Twice the Supreme Court revisited the antitrust exemption, in 1953 and 1972, and twice left it largely intact. In the words of Justice Harry Blackmun's 1972 majority opinion, it was an "established aberration."[16] By the mid-nineties baseball's unique legal and commercial arrangements had become a source of instability rather than security, with industrial disruption endemic. The game had experienced labor-related disputes in 1972, 1973, 1976, 1980, 1981, 1985, and 1990. Strikes, or the threat of them, had become commonplace because they were the union's only viable weapon, given that franchises had little to fear from an antitrust suit.

There was relative cultural decline as well: no longer did baseball occupy an unrivaled position in the American sporting imagination as it had in the halcyon postwar years. That mantle had long been surrendered to the explosively televisual, brilliantly marketed NFL, and, increasingly in the 1990s, to the Michael Jordan-fueled NBA. Enjoying the revenue-sharing freedom allowed by the Sports Broadcasting Act of 1961, the NFL had built a nationally visible league with teams competing on a broadly equal footing. More condensed in its narrative and action and more in tune with Cold War sensibilities, professional football was, as the journalist Ted Anthony describes, "battlefield poetry, the civilian made military, an American aesthetic if ever there was one."[17] By 1972, according to most

---

[14] US Supreme Court, "259 US 200 (1922) Federal Baseball Club of Baltimore v. National League," *Justia.com*.

[15] "Monopsony" is a specific economic term in which a single buyer (e.g., MLB) controls the market as the sole purchaser of services (e.g., the players). It is a different concept from a monopoly, which refers to sellers of goods and services rather than buyers.

[16] US Supreme Court, "407 US 258 (1972) Flood v. Kuhn, No. 71–32," *Justia.com*.

[17] Ted Anthony, "What Is America's Game? 3 Sports, 3 American Eras," *Associated Press*, October 25, 2019.

measures, it had overtaken baseball as America's most popular sport.[18] In contrast, baseball, according to *Sporting News*, had lost its sense of purpose, caught between trying to satisfy fans who wanted things to "stay as they were in grandfather's day and a new breed of sports followers who want more action."[19] While the NFL concentrated on securing national television deals which ensured its games were seen each week across the entire country, a Darwinian economic model persisted in baseball, where local broadcast deals magnified the inequalities—teams in small markets struggled to compete with the revenue-rich, big-market franchises for the recruitment and retention of the top talents. How income should be shared among the clubs, and divided between the owners and players, was never resolved. Wage inflation associated with the rise of free agency added to commercial and labor-related uncertainty. In 1976 major league ballplayers made eight times the earnings of the average US worker; by 1991 they were earning forty-seven times the average wage.[20] Despite revenue remaining healthy, these soaring costs were biting into the owners' profits and making the leagues even more financially unequal. In June 1994, with the collective bargaining agreement lapsing six months earlier, MLB owners proposed a new deal: revenue sharing and a salary cap across the industry. The players asserted that as free agents they should be able to sell their services to the highest bidder. The union rejected the deal and set a strike date of August 12, fifty-two days before the scheduled end of the regular season. The hopes of millions of baseball fans that the finale of the 1994 season would witness Matt Williams of the San Francisco Giants breaking the single-season home run record, or Tony Gwynn of the San Diego Padres achieving the magical 0.400 batting average had disintegrated thanks to a dispute about how to divide revenues between two enormously wealthy groups—the twenty-eight owners of MLB franchises (collective 1993 operational revenue approximately $1.9 billion) and the 750 members of the MLBPA (combined 1994 payroll approximately $1.1 billion).[21]

As the strike date approached and with negotiations stalled, Clinton was well aware of the frustration of fans. During a campaign trip in late

---

[18] Lydia Saad, "Gallup Vault: Football's Rise as a US Spectator Sport," *Gallup*, February 2, 2017.

[19] *Sporting News*, May 3, 1969.

[20] Burk, *Much More Than a Game*, 274.

[21] Associated Press, "1994 Strike Was Low Point for Baseball," *espn.com*, August 11, 2004; Table 5.1 in Jennings, *Swings and Misses*, 101.

July to Cleveland, home of the division-leading Indians, he experienced those frustrations firsthand: "The first fifteen people I shook hands with said: 'can't you do anything about the baseball strike?'."[22] Two days later Reich took a call from Bruce Lindsey, the Deputy White House Counsel: "You guys doing anything about this baseball thing?" Reich, who believed that presidential abstention from industrial disputes was usually the best course, sensed this time there was an appetite in the White House for Clinton to be seen to be saving the baseball season. "Moreover," Reich noted in his diary, "without baseball, blue-collar America will be even more depressed than it is now and blue-collar blues aren't good for the party in power in a midterm election year."[23] It was an example, Michael Waldman believes, of a kind of Democrat "muscle memory" among those in the White House who assumed that "Democrats get hurt when there's a sports strike," because people "get mad at the unions."[24]

Ten days before the strike was due to begin, reporters raised the issue in the White House press briefing for the first time—was the President personally doing anything or making any calls? Not according to Clinton's press secretary, who said the administration was offering to "be helpful," preferring to leave it to the two sides "to work out their differences across the table."[25] Nevertheless, a few days later Clinton remarked to William Gould IV, who he had recently appointed to chair the National Labor Relations Board (NLRB): "If you guys could resolve this, they would elect me president for life."[26] For now, however, Clinton remained at arm's length, not wishing yet to intervene directly, heeding instead the warnings of his staff that the ill will surrounding the negotiations offered a high risk of failure.

But with the players taking their final at bats on August 11, there were no last-minute initiatives and no fresh talks scheduled. For the union, Don Fehr accused the owners of forcing the shutdown: the owners' chief

---

[22] William J. Clinton, "Remarks at a Reception for Joel Hyatt in Mayfield Heights, Ohio, July 30, 1994," *American Presidency Project*.

[23] Reich, *Locked in the Cabinet*, 186.

[24] Waldman, interview by author.

[25] William J. Clinton, "Press Briefing by Dee Dee Myers, August 2, 1994," *American Presidency Project*.

[26] William B. Gould IV, "The 1994–'95 Baseball Strike and the National Labor Relations Board: To the Precipice and Back Again," *West Virginia Law Review*, no. 110 (2008): 983–97; 990.

negotiator, Richard Ratvich, blamed the players for "a tragedy for millions of fans and tens of thousands of people whose livelihood will be interrupted."[27] From the White House, Clinton spoke in pessimistic terms, warning both sides they were setting out on a perilous path: "They always have to consider in the end their customers and what will happen if they lose their customers. In a great event like the baseball strike, I think there's an assumption that the customers are always there."[28] Clinton clearly implied it was a misplaced assumption; a prolonged strike had the capacity to diminish the fan base and thus threatened baseball's special place in the heart of Americans.

These twin commercial and cultural threats were raised with Clinton by a New York State senator whose district included Yankee Stadium. Pedro Espada Jr. wrote to Clinton urging him to follow "a long tradition of presidential persuasion" and intervene to avert a possible one hundred million dollar hit to New York's economy.[29] The fans also mobilized their own networks to express their fears for the game: grassroots organizations sprung up around the country, including three in New York (*Sports Fans United*, *Strike Back*, and *Strike Three—The Fans Are Out*) and others in Boston (*Ball Four—The Fans are Walking*), Cleveland (*Fans First*), Los Angeles (*Strikebusters '94*), Minnesota (*Ball Park Tour*), and Georgia (*Professional Sports Fans Association*). These groups were loosely affiliated under the umbrella of the National Union of Fans and Families, which made a broad case for political intervention in professional baseball in a submission to Congress laced with civil religious imagery. Invoking the founding fathers, the National Union asserted that baseball's antitrust exemption was an abuse of the free market economy and, even more fancifully, a violation of the Constitution of the United States: the failure to address it severely weakened "the social and economic foundations [of the

---

[27] Quoted in Richard Justice, "With Baseball's Last Out, A Strike," *Washington Post*, August 12, 1994.

[28] William J. Clinton, "Remarks Announcing the Appointment of Abner Mikva as White House Counsel and an Exchange With Reporters, August 11, 1994," *American Presidency Project*.

[29] Letter, Sen. Pedro Espada Jr. to Bill Clinton, August 18, 1994, OA/ID 24792, Folder: Baseball Strike – Letters/Comments/Polls [2], Bruce Lindsey, Counsel Office, *Clinton Presidential Records*.

country]."[30] Separately, representatives of the fan groups sent a letter to the White House calling on Clinton to impose an emergency sixty-day back-to-work order and to explore legislative ways to end the antitrust exemption. "For too long the baseball of money has intruded upon our baseball of National Pastime and National Spirit," declared the signatories, firmly committing their rhetoric to a civil religious framework. "Baseball is the tie that binds across towns, across the country, across generations, across time. Quite simply, Baseball Fans still Believe. You, Mr. President, of all people must appreciate the importance of this rare element in today's society."[31] Clearly in this instance, the narrative of baseball as American civil religion was being shaped not only from above—by the President and the media—but also from below, by the fans. Their entreaties addressed Clinton's known sensitivities and chimed with his ambition to restore the American family and to renew a sense of community among those who were suffering a "tenuous quality of life."[32]

A few days later, the President hosted the nostalgia-laden, baseball-themed picnic at the White House to mark the premiere of Burns' documentary series. Despite the celebratory mood, the strike offered a sobering backdrop. Talks between the union and owners had broken down and there was now only the faintest chance of postseason play. Questioned by reporters on the South Lawn, Clinton urged both parties to "elevate the idea of baseball over the specifics of this disagreement."[33] Baseball, in this typically Clintonian interpretation, was not a business, or even a game, but an "idea," just as in his 1993 inauguration he had spoken of the need to rededicate the country to "the idea of America."[34] Donnie Radcliffe in the *Washington Post* appeared unconvinced about Clinton's abstract,

---

[30] Statement by the National Union of Fans and Families to the House Subcommittee on Economic and Commercial Law, September 22, 1994, OA/ID 24792, Folder: Baseball Strike – Letters/Comments/Polls [1], Bruce Lindsey, Counsel Office, *Clinton Presidential Records*.

[31] Letter, Fans First to Bill Clinton, September 6, 1994, OA/ID 24792, Folder: Baseball Strike – Letters/Comments/Polls [2], Bruce Lindsey, Counsel Office, *Clinton Presidential Records*.

[32] William J. Clinton, "The President's Radio Address, September 3, 1994," *American Presidency Project*.

[33] Quoted in Radcliffe, "The White House Pitches In."

[34] William J. Clinton, "Inaugural Address, January 20, 1993," *American Presidency Project*.

intellectual appeal to the protagonists, speculating that the Burns' series could be the "epitaph to baseball as Americans know it."[35]

On September 14, four days after the White House picnic, Bud Selig, the acting MLB commissioner, announced what most by then had assumed inevitable—the cancellation of the 1994 World Series. For the first time since 1904, there would be no championship decider between the winners of the American and National Leagues. In the eyes of some commentators, it was an act of destructive self-indulgence that detached the sport from its spiritual roots. "A perfidy beyond calculation," thundered George Weigel in *Commentary*, who accused the owners and players of "risking the wrath of Heaven."[36] The verdict of columnist and baseball historian George Vecsey was equally brutal: the game was no longer worthy of the designation national pastime—American history was being "severed" by a group of "nouveau-riche gangsters."[37] The *New York Times* carried an "In Memoriam" notice on the front page, black-bordered and headlined in funereal font: "The National Pastime, which was buried yesterday, died a long time ago," wrote Robert Lipsyte, adding, "somewhere between the myth of the Pastime and the glory of the game was the annual major league season which seems to have collapsed of exhaustion towards the tail end of a century-long search for its soul." Lipsyte may have sounded the death knell of the professional game of baseball, but in the same column he also celebrated the resilience of the national pastime's generational myths and iconic tropes, recalling the family farm, the prairies, the Little League, and "daydreaming of drinking the same beer with your dad as he drank with his dad."[38] Lipsyte was marking out the clear distinction between baseball as a business and the mythical game which remained an abundant source of cultural inheritance. In the absence of the World Series, this alternative story played out, one which continued to project a romanticized version of baseball—a pastoral game, nurtured and grown in the nation's small towns and emerging cities, of American values and social rituals, of integrity and hard work, of ballgames played in streets, on sandlots, and in municipal parks. And it was weaved through the sentimental optimism of Burns' series, with its confident reassertion of the

---

[35] Radcliffe, "The White House Pitches In."

[36] Weigel, "Politically-Correct Baseball."

[37] George Vecsey, "Owners Strike Out in Betrayal of History," *New York Times*, September 12, 1994.

[38] Robert Lipsyte, "In Memoriam," *New York Times*, September 15, 1994.

game's generational ties and its secure place in the canon of American history.

This notion, that baseball as a commercial enterprise operated in a different realm to the game so preciously cultivated by generations of ordinary Americans, was seized upon by public intellectuals, among them the literary scholar, George Grella. Writing in the *Los Angeles Times*, Grella argued that the presumption that the major leagues embodied the soul of baseball was like "some devout worshipper imagining that God only dwells in the great cathedrals of the faith.... No strike can destroy the purity, joy and significance of the essential game as practiced in the church of baseball."[39] One of Clinton's picnic guests, the actor-activist Ossie Davis, also recognized the religious parallel: "I don't look at the game today as a game. It's business. To me baseball was an act of communion,...like I used to feel teaching Baptist Sunday school. We were lifted out of ourselves by just being together. Baseball was a secular equivalent of that."[40] Clinton similarly expressed concern that baseball had become "just another business in America."[41] For him this was the "ultimate hazard" of the strike: "If it becomes so painfully clear that it's no longer a sport and that it's just a business, then the customers may decide to take their business elsewhere." Baseball, Clinton warned, would be played only in Little Leagues and local ballparks, "almost the way soccer is"—a comment alarming to those sporting chauvinists convinced of the innate superiority of the supposedly purer, made-in-America pastime.[42]

It was into this complex cultural and commercial environment—in which the professional version of baseball embodied the sins of commercialization, yet the mythologized national pastime still shouldered a significant cultural burden—that Clinton attempted to throw the weight of his office. Baseball's rituals, ideals, and heroes had been a source of social cohesion for more than a hundred years—a symbol of national identity. Clinton's role now was to ensure that the emotional connection between baseball's two diverging but equally authentic histories—the commercial

---

[39] George Grella, "Perspective on Baseball: A Religion That Goes to Our Roots," *Los Angeles Times*, August 11, 1994.

[40] Quoted in Geracimos, "News Gives Way to Nostalgia at Picnic."

[41] William J. Clinton, "Interview With Wire Service Reporters on Haiti, September 14, 1994," *American Presidency Project*.

[42] William J. Clinton, "Interview With Tony Bruno and Chuck Wilson of ESPN Radio, March 25, 1995," *American Presidency Project*.

and the sacred—was not irreparably severed. His chosen rhetorical device was a synthesis of 'the presidency,' 'baseball,' and 'the people,' through which he expressed a discourse of reconciliation and American cultural exceptionalism.

In one of his first public comments on the strike, Clinton fashioned himself "as a lifelong baseball fan" and spoke of "heart-break for the American people."[43] On the eve of the shutdown, Clinton was equally solemn, adopting a tone reminiscent of a wartime leader: "Today I would like to speak on behalf of the country because this is an unusual situation." He went on to call the strike "a great event" that threatened the happiness of generations of Americans—"kids and not-so-little kids"—placing to the fore his guardianship of baseball's celebrated generational connection. He urged the players to return to work and finish a season that had promised to be one of the most exciting for decades. "I think the people ought to be taken into consideration here and I hope they will be."[44] When the cancellation of the World Series was confirmed, Clinton suggested baseball's antitrust exemption was at risk, "in light of what has happened to the American people."[45] Elsewhere he spoke of "America living without baseball for too long" and "getting baseball back for America"; the strike was "trying the patience and depressing the spirits of millions," again inferring the health of the nation was at stake. Even baseball's mythical values were under threat: "rancor and cynicism" were "shadowing the American ideal of baseball."[46] In an interview with Tom Brokaw on *NBC Nightly News*, Clinton urged the players and owners to "give baseball back to the American people," an implication that they had stolen a national treasure. He spoke of the "significant percentage of American people—you and I among them—who really believe baseball is something special."[47] Embedded in his role as president, Clinton acknowledged a duty to protect the status of the national pastime in the American cultural landscape. The *Washington Post* columnist, Thomas Boswell, agreed: it was only the office

---

[43] William J. Clinton, "The President's News Conference, August 3, 1994," *American Presidency Project*.

[44] Clinton, "Remarks Announcing the Appointment of Abner Mikva."

[45] Clinton, "Interview With Wire Service Reporters on Haiti."

[46] William J. Clinton, "Statement on the Baseball Strike, January 26, 1995," *American Presidency Project*.

[47] William J. Clinton, "Interview with Tom Brokaw of NBC Nightly News, January 26, 1995," *American Presidency Project*.

of the presidency that possessed that fusion of patriotic weight and persuasive power which could realistically change hearts.[48]

While his rhetoric reflected baseball's historic cultural status, the political imperatives driving Clinton were equally powerful, and linked by the seasonal ritual of spring training in Florida and Arizona. Each February and March the major league franchises decamped their playing operations to those two states for training games which cumulatively attracted tens of thousands of sun-seeking baseball tourists eager to escape the northern and mid-western winter, filling the hotels around the athletic complexes where the teams competed. When they were not watching baseball, fans spent their dollars in restaurants and at the multiple attractions close by. Twenty major league teams were due to hold their 1995 training camps in Florida, where Clinton had lost to George H. W. Bush by less than one percent in 1992: in Arizona, which hosted the other eight franchises, the 1992 election result had also been close, with Bush victorious by just under two percent. If the dispute dragged beyond the winter, thousands of spring training jobs were at risk in the hotels, restaurants, and tourist venues in two states which were very much in play in the 1996 presidential election. Florida Governor Lawton Chiles and Senator Bob Graham warned Clinton that the strike could put a billion tourism dollars at risk in the state—an economic impact "not unlike that of a natural disaster." The context was clear: when it came to cleaning up after hurricanes in Florida, the federal government was expected to lend a hand, and this strike was potentially as devastating. "No state can afford these type of revenue losses," Chiles and Graham told Clinton.[49] The voters would have their say if spring training was cancelled. Conversely, for Clinton, there was the opportunity to secure votes in key states if his actions were seen as successful. A handwritten note faxed to Bruce Lindsey, who was the White House liaison on the strike, made the point directly: "Bruce, the re-election is on your shoulders." It was scribbled next to a cartoon from the

---

[48] Thomas Boswell, "Step Up to the Plate, Mr. President," *Washington Post*, September 14, 1994.

[49] Letter, Lawton Chiles and Bob Graham to Bill Clinton, September 7, 1994, OA/ID 24792, Folder: Baseball Strike – Letters/Comments/Polls [3], Bruce Lindsey, Counsel Office, *Clinton Presidential Records*.

Miami Herald depicting Clinton's poll ratings soaring if the strike ended.[50] It seemed the political temptations for Clinton to intervene were aligned with the cultural expectations embedded in his office.

Clinton Intervenes: "This is Baseball, and I am the President"

The President's first direct intervention came when the strike was into its third month with invitations to Selig and the MLBPA Executive Director, Don Fehr, to come to separate meetings at the White House, at which Clinton asked them to accept the appointment of a special mediator, William Usery, who had been Labor Secretary under Gerald Ford. Since leaving government, Usery had gained a degree of celebrity for his stamina in negotiating settlements in violent disputes in the auto and mining industries with his no-nonsense style, including apocryphal tales of locking protagonists in negotiating rooms until they reached agreement.[51] Selig and Fehr were told that Usery would attempt to broker a deal and that Clinton would back his recommendations.[52] Both sides agreed to his appointment, and Usery was introduced to the media by Reich at a late-night West Wing news conference on October 14, a signal that he was there at the behest of Clinton. Reich, making biblical allusions, described Usery as "no ordinary man."[53] Deploying the well-worn baseball metaphor, the *Washington Post* heralded Usery as a "heavy hitter." In his initial remarks, Usery referred to baseball as America's "great game" and "the national pastime," embedding his role in the sport's cultural significance.[54] To begin with the prospects looked positive: four days after the appointment, the owners and players representatives met for the first time in more than a month. That morning, October 19, Clinton left the White House for his daily jog wearing a sports shirt emblazoned with the words "Play Ball." It was a display that implied presidential credit for the resumption of talks and placed

---

[50] Facsimile to Bruce Lindsey, February 3, 1995, OA/ID 24792, Folder: Baseball Strike – Letters/Comments/Polls [3], Bruce Lindsey, Counsel Office, *Clinton Presidential Records*.

[51] James Risen, "Baseball: Former Labor Secretary Has a Reputation for Getting Results in Difficult Situations," *Los Angeles Times*, October 15, 1994.

[52] Selig, *For the Good of the Game*, 165.

[53] C-SPAN, "Baseball Strike Negotiations," *c-span.com*, October 14, 1994.

[54] Frank Swoboda, "Clinton Gets Heavy Hitter to Mediate Baseball Strike," *Washington Post*, October 15, 1994

Clinton's voice at the center of calls for the restoration of the national pastime to its place of cultural preeminence.

However, Clinton's T-shirt entreaty went unanswered. Talks through November and December produced no progress—each potential compromise advanced by Usery rejected. Nor did Congress show any appetite for enforcing a resolution or addressing baseball's historic antitrust exemptions. On New Year's Day, Anthony Lake, Clinton's National Security Advisor, who like many in the administration was a keen baseball fan, was invited onto *Meet the Press* to talk about the world's trouble spots—North Korea, Bosnia, and Chechnya. But he soon found himself quizzed about the baseball strike: "I'm not sure…you can make a distinction between the future of the world and the future of baseball," Lake remarked. "If baseball's in serious trouble, we're all in serious trouble."[55] However light-hearted Lake intended his comments, this was the man responsible for counselling the President about potential threats facing the country framing the debate about a strike in baseball in terms of national security.

At the beginning of 1995 problems were mounting for Clinton in other arenas too. The Office of Independent Counsel, led by Kenneth Starr, was probing ever deeper into the Clintons' tangled financial affairs around their real estate investments on the Whitewater River in Arkansas, while the journalist David Maraniss had put Clinton's pre-presidential personal life in the spotlight during research for an upcoming biography. Maraniss had compiled an authoritative and sympathetic account of Clinton's youth and early career. But there were also sections in the book about tensions within his marriage and allegations about Clinton's sex life, in particular that his long-time assistant, Betsey Wright, had admitted to covering up his use of state troopers to solicit women while he was Arkansas governor.[56] According to Morris, Clinton was deeply upset—he felt that the book was "violating" him. To regain the initiative, Morris suggested to Clinton that he divert public attention by "focusing on hard news events." He advised Clinton to try to settle the baseball strike.[57]

---

[55] Transcript NBC News, "Meet The Press," January 1, 1995, OA/ID 420, Folder: [Anthony] Lake-Transcripts, Robert Boorstin, Speechwriting, *Clinton Presidential Records.*.

[56] Maraniss, *First In His Class*, 440. Wright later claimed Maraniss had "misunderstood" her remarks.

[57] Morris, *Behind The Oval Office*, 113–14.

With a new Congress convening in January and strike negotiations becalmed, there were renewed efforts by the White House to increase the pressure on both parties via Usery, while intimating that should he fail, other solutions to enforce arbitration would be explored.[58] On Capitol Hill, sympathetic legislators introduced a series of baseball-related bills: the Major League Play Ball Act, and the National Commission on Professional Baseball Act both contained measures which specifically aimed at ending the dispute, including making it subject to binding arbitration. The Baseball Fans and Communities Protection Act, the National Pastime Preservation Act, and the Professional Baseball Antitrust Reform Act all targeted the game's antitrust exemption as a way of exerting pressure on the owners. The Justice Department let it be known that, in principle, it supported such limiting legislation, arguing that baseball players should have the same antitrust recourse that was available to other professional athletes.[59] Clinton's speechwriters, meanwhile, drafted a passage for the upcoming State of the Union Address with a warning for the players and owners: "The young people of America are watching. You have a responsibility to worry less about how many millions you can make and more about what kind of role models you make."[60] The passage was intended for inclusion in a broader section themed "responsibility is for everybody," and although it did not make the final cut, it demonstrates the degree to which the strike featured in White House thinking about the emerging themes of accountability and obligation which would become an important part of Clinton's rhetoric from 1995 onwards.

Another problem presented by the strike was the possibility of an asterisk against one of baseball's most hallowed records.[61] At risk was Cal

---

[58] Jennings, *Swings and Misses*, 110–11.

[59] Draft letter, Anne K. Bingaman to Sen. Patrick Leahy, Senate Judiciary Committee, March 31, 1995, OA/ID 24792, Folder: Baseball Strike – Letters/Comments/Polls [3], Bruce Lindsey, Counsel Office, *Clinton Presidential Records*.

[60] Draft speech with notes, State of Union Speech 1995, January 23, 1995 OA/ID 10131, Folder: SOTU - Edits by Admin Officials [1] Draft 2, Don Baer Communications, *Clinton Presidential Records*.

[61] An * [asterisk] is assigned to a record if its achievement is thought to be tainted. In this case, had baseball resumed with non-unionized players, it was suggested that Ripken (who would have refused to play) could have continued his

Ripken Jr.'s unbroken thirteen-year-long sequence of more than two thousand appearances for the Baltimore Orioles, which had put him within sight of the once-thought-impregnable major league record for consecutive games played, held by the legendary 'Iron Horse' of New York, Lou Gehrig. Six decades after he set the record of 2,130 consecutive appearances for the Yankees, Gehrig still embodied a particularly American sporting ideal: a model of steadfastness and hard work whose tragic early death had cemented a mythical place for him and his record in the public imagination. With the owners threatening to deploy non-union players for the approaching season, Ripken, a dependable union member, faced seeing his run end and therefore the country deprived of a historic moment of celebration in the national pastime later that year. Clinton faced losing Ripken's record-breaking feat as a prime example of the American work ethic and a useful rhetorical presence in the presidential case for welfare reform. As Taylor Branch noted after chatting with the President about the pursuit of the Gehrig record, Clinton fully understood "the symbolic stakes for national character" of Ripken's quest.[62]

Less urgent, though perhaps just as culturally significant, was the crisis facing Arthur Shorin, chairman of Topps, the company which made the baseball cards collected and traded by millions of Americans. With production falling to a thirty-year low, Shorin wrote to Clinton, observing that Topps was "only one in a long line of innocents" being adversely affected by the strike. "How can kids celebrate or collect heroes of the diamond when there are no heroes in sight?" Shorin lamented, offering to print a commemorative bubblegum trading card of the President should he broker a deal. Clinton scribbled on the letter: "I need an answer to this."[63]

Days later, Clinton invoked the memory of the greatest baseball legend of them all, George Herman Ruth Jr., to support his strike-ending efforts. The upcoming one hundredth anniversary of the birth of 'The Babe,' had already generated a wave of nostalgic reflection and related commercial activity, signifying Ruth's huge presence in America's

---

consecutive game streak once unionized players returned, albeit with an * against his record.

[62] Branch, *The Clinton Tapes*, 231–32.

[63] Letter, Arthur T. Shorin, to Bill Clinton, January 31,1995, OA/ID 24792, Folder: Baseball Strike – Letters/Comments/Polls [1], Bruce Lindsey, Counsel Office, *Clinton Presidential Records*.

collective memory. Commemorative memorabilia was produced in all shapes and sizes—trading cards, balls, books, calendars, and postage stamps; Nestlé launched a year-long campaign for its 'Baby Ruth' candy bars, featuring three period-style television commercials retelling the story of Ruth's extraordinary hitting.[64] Close to his birthplace in inner-city Baltimore, a statue of Ruth was unveiled. In the *Washington Post*, the nonagenarian columnist, Shirley Povich, who was old enough to have reported on Ruth's exploits in the flesh, expounded with biblical devotion: "Fivescore years ago, the wife of a fat Baltimore saloon keeper brought forth upon this earth the infant-man child born to captivate our nation with each swish of the baseball bat."[65] These centenary celebrations offered an opportunity for Clinton to weave the memory of one of the most significant figures of twentieth-century American popular culture into the narrative of the game's current labor crisis. The 'Great Bambino' had rescued the reputation of baseball once before: in the aftermath of the Black Sox Scandal, Ruth's home run hitting had restored public confidence in a game whose integrity had been rocked by the revelations of Chicago players throwing games in the 1919 World Series on the orders of a betting syndicate. Now the celebration of Ruth's birthday allowed him to be posthumously called-upon to polish-up the national pastime's tarnished image a second time. "It struck me as a good day to settle the baseball strike," Clinton told to a group of mayors visiting the White House. The dispute was imperiling the livelihoods of tens of thousands of workers and "depressing the spirits of millions of fans." It was "time to play ball." Clinton set the owners and players a deadline of 5:00 p.m. on February 6, the day of the Ruth centenary. Either they would reach a deal on that symbolic date, or Clinton would instruct Usery to make recommendations for settlement—a step which exceeded his official mediation role and carried an implicit threat of legislative intervention backed by the President. Clinton chose the date, he said, because he identified with Ruth: "He's a little overweight and he struck out a lot—but he hit a lot of home runs because he went out to bat."[66] Like Ruth, the President was batting for America. A day later Clinton pressed home the point, warning that the negative effects of the

---

[64] "Baby Ruth Candy Bar Television Commercial, 1995," *YouTube*.

[65] Shirley Povich, "Legend, Truth Mix With Ruth: 100th Anniversary of Babe's Birth," *Washington Post*, February 5, 1995.

[66] William J. Clinton, "Remarks to the U.S Conference of Mayors, January 27, 1995," *American Presidency Project*.

strike were "a big deal," and promising his administration was "working hard" on the issue, all the time weaving a rhetoric which emphasized both baseball's economic importance and the emotional and patriotic responsibilities of those entrusted with ensuring the game's health.[67]

Initially, the Ruthian deadline provoked activity, with revised proposals and counteroffers. The White House attempted to keep up the pressure by indulging in Ruth-flavored rhetoric; at a daily briefing McCurry suggested that Clinton was prepared to "take a 40-ounce Louisville Slugger to both parties and tell them to get a settlement," referencing Ruth's favorite heavyweight bat.[68] But both sides remained deaf to the jocular threat from the White House, intransigent in their demands and showing few signs of compromise. The Ruth centenary passed without progress. Clinton set another deadline—3:00 p.m. on February 7. There would be one last White House effort to resolve the tensions between baseball as a commercialized business and the national pastime as a quasi-religious myth. The instability and contradictions of this dynamic would now be laid bare in the symbolic setting of the sacred center of national power.

Clinton threw his final pitch of the strike drama at the White House, on the evening of February 7. Events earlier in the day did not augur well. That afternoon Usery had presented his latest set of proposals at a meeting at the Mayflower Hotel, a fifteen-minute stroll from the White House. Usery's document outlined complex arrangements for revenue sharing, free agency, and arbitration which so enraged one union negotiator that he said it looked like the work of someone who was senile.[69] On Capitol Hill the Republican leadership made it clear they remained opposed to getting involved. Senate Majority Leader Dole warned the President not to count on legislative cooperation from his side of the aisle.[70] Gingrich was even more emphatic: "It's nice the President is trying to be helpful," he commented acidly, but this was "a straight-out labor-management struggle."

---

[67] Clinton, "Statement on the Baseball Strike, January 26, 1995."

[68] William J. Clinton, "Press Briefing by Mike McCurry, February 3, 1995," *American Presidency Project*.

[69] Michael Bevans, "Let's Make a Deal," *Sports Illustrated*, February 20, 1995.

[70] Ross Newhan and Doyle McManus, "Clinton Pitches Baseball Strike to Congress," *Los Angeles Times*, February 8, 1995.

It was "not a matter of national survival."[71] Not all members of the White House press corps appeared to share the apparent indifference of the Republican leadership. At a lunchtime White House briefing, there was talk of a "national emergency" and questions to McCurry about the powers of the President in such circumstances. McCurry explained Clinton's strategy: "When the President looked at the question of getting involved he said, 'listen this is baseball: I am the President; it makes every sense in the world to use whatever authority I can to bring the conflict to an end.'"[72] Again Clinton's role as defender of the national pastime was projected as the main force for dispute resolution. Four hours later, McCurry hosted a second briefing: the President was "exasperated" that his 3:00 p.m. deadline had lapsed. He had therefore decided to summon an extraordinary meeting at the White House that evening.[73]

Despite all the signs to the contrary, there is evidence that Clinton thought there was still an opportunity to force a settlement. Twice in the lunchtime briefing McCurry had mentioned Clinton's belief in the value of "jawboning," a term which recalled Lyndon Johnson's legendary talents at arm-twisting and verbal persuasion.[74] And in the later briefing McCurry had hinted at the existence of an 'or else'—an implied threat of some action initiated by the President if the sides did not settle.[75] In addition, Reich thought Clinton was always "convinced there was a deal lying out there somewhere....He is absolutely certain that every single person he meets—Newt Gingrich, Yasir Arafat, whoever—wants to find common ground. It is simply a matter of discovering where it is," Reich wrote in his diary. "He smells a deal. He'd like to be savior of the national pastime."[76]

At 6:05 p.m. thirteen men, comprising the players and owners representatives, sat down on opposite sides of the large mahogany table in the

---

[71] "Bad Sports," *New York Magazine*, February 20, 1995.

[72] William J. Clinton, "Press Briefing by Mike McCurry, 1:15 p.m. February 7, 1995," *American Presidency Project.*

[73] William J. Clinton, "Press Briefing by Mike McCurry, 5:10 p.m. February 7, 1995," *American Presidency Project.*

[74] Clinton, "Press Briefing by Mike McCurry, 1:15 p.m. February 7, 1995."

[75] Clinton, "Press Briefing by Mike McCurry, 5:10 p.m. February 7, 1995."

[76] Reich, *Locked in the Cabinet,* 238.

Roosevelt Room in the West Wing.[77] Named for the dynastic family that provided two celebrated presidents, the windowless room was decorated with presidential artifacts and imagery: appropriately, given the confrontational circumstances and the aims of the meeting, America's first Nobel Peace Prize, awarded to Theodore Roosevelt for negotiating a treaty between Russia and Japan in 1905, was on display; portraits of Theodore Roosevelt as the 'Roughrider' on horseback and Alfred Jonniaux's depiction of FDR hung on the walls. The setting made a powerful statement about the historic, institutional, and emotional weight of the office of the presidency. "I was humbled being there," admitted the players representative, Scott Sanderson of the Chicago White Sox. Gore, Usery, and Reich opened the meeting by reviewing the proposals which had been rejected over the previous six months. Clinton joined the group at 7:20 p.m. David Cone, the New York Yankees pitcher, recalled Clinton pointing to the Roughrider painting and giving a history lesson on the 'bully pulpit,' the term coined by Theodore Roosevelt to describe the agenda-setting authority of the office of a president.[78] In invoking both the bully pulpit and Johnson's jawboning, Clinton was placing his initiative in a historic framework of presidential activism. He acknowledged the legal limits to his powers but returned to his emotional pitch which focused on presidential duty and the importance of the sport to American life: "I don't want to impose a solution on anyone, and I know that I am getting criticized for getting involved in sports. But there are a lot of Americans who really love baseball and I feel an obligation to them. So, I am urging all of you, let's try to figure out a way to solve this tonight."[79] At that point the meeting adjourned, with the parties caucusing in separate rooms in the West Wing.

---

[77] This account of the 'summit' draws on the recollections of McCurry (interview by author) and the memoirs of Selig and Reich: Bud Selig, *For The Good of The Game*, 166–71; Reich, *Locked in the Cabinet*, 237–40. Also the news conference given by Reich and Usery at 11:00 p.m. on February 7: William J. Clinton, "Press Briefing by Secretary of Labor Bob Reich and Former Secretary of Labor Bill Usery, February 7, 1995," *American Presidency Project*. The official schedule gives details of Clinton's movements that night: Daily Schedule, Office of Scheduling, "President Clinton's Daily Schedule for February 1995," *Clinton Digital Library*.

[78] Bodley, *How Baseball Explains America*, 53–54.

[79] Quoted in Pessah, *The Game*, 125.

In the Chief of Staff's office, Clinton shared a sofa with Selig, an encounter colorfully recalled by Reich as "full intensity Clinton":

> 'Now all you need to do'—B[ill]'s voice becomes even softer and he moves his face closer to Selig's—'is agree to have this thing arbitrated. It's in your interest Bud.' B[ill] pauses and looks deeply into Selig's eyes. 'And it's also in the interest of …… America.'…The performance is spellbinding. Selig's thin body seems to be shaking.

The President believed, according to Reich, that he had "hit a home run" with his arguments.[80] But Selig, with a markedly different memory of the sofa encounter, says he lost his temper with the presidential entourage, swearing at them in uncompromising language when it became clear that they favored arbitration over the proposals made by Usery, their own appointed mediator.[81] With Selig now nursing a deep sense of betrayal, the indirect talks stuttered on with no apparent progress. At one stage Clinton left the West Wing to attend a reception for freshman legislators elsewhere in the White House, but even then he could not escape the dispute, with a representative from Kentucky presenting him with a personalized Louisville Slugger bat.[82] During other breaks, Reich observed the players snacking on pretzels and soda giving the symbolic center of American power the appearance of a ballpark clubhouse.[83] Clinton contributed to this transformation of the White House into a sports venue by socializing with the players, even practicing his golf swing in the corridor with Tom Glavine, the Atlanta Braves pitcher. "He made us feel very welcome that night. We had a lot of one-on-one time with him," recalled Glavine.[84]

After almost five hours of indirect talks, Gore made an appeal to both sides to accept binding arbitration. The players agreed but the owners said they would only arbitrate parts of Usery's proposed settlement. The players rejected it as "cherry picking."[85] Clinton made one final proposal: the 1995

---

[80] Reich, *Locked in the Cabinet*, 239.

[81] Selig describes himself as "barely containing" his fury; he felt Clinton was siding with the players union and had "betrayed a nation of baseball fans." Selig, *For the Good of the Game*, 168–70.

[82] Chris Duncan, "For Louisville Slugger Company, Strike Is a Real Corker," *Associated Press*, February 12, 1995.

[83] Reich, *Locked in the Cabinet*, 239.

[84] Quoted in Bodley, *How Baseball Explains America*, 65.

[85] Jennings, *Swings and Misses*, 115.

season would go ahead with the unionized players while a presidential committee worked on a longer-term framework for negotiations. The MLBPA agreed; the owners did not. Out of options, Clinton called the two negotiating committees back into the Roosevelt Room: "Both of you have a lot at stake, and I'm afraid you're both going to wind up losers."[86] The bully pulpit and jawboning having proved impotent, Clinton's gamble to hold a White House baseball summit had also failed. He would now call on Congress to intervene. Reich noted in his diary: "B lost big tonight."[87]

Shortly before 11:00 p.m., Clinton addressed the members of the White House press corps who had been waiting all evening in the West Wing briefing room for news of the talks. Acknowledging that mediation had failed, Clinton announced he would send legislation to Congress the next day to seek binding arbitration. He conceded that legislators would be reluctant to intervene but said the players and owners had left no alternative: "Clearly they are not capable of settling this strike without an umpire." Clinton again referred to the continuity of baseball and the frustrations of the American people.

> If something goes on for that long without interruption, seeing our nation through wars and dramatic social changes, it becomes more than a game, more than simply a way to pass time. It becomes part of who we are. And we've all got to work to preserve that part.[88]

Amid his lament, there was something "concerned citizens" could actively do, Clinton said: lobby their senators and members of congress to back his plan. It was now up to the people. Neither Clinton's attempts to instrumentalize the myth of baseball, nor the weight of his office, nor the hallowed White House setting had been sufficient to sway the parties in a game caught between its fabled place in the American story and its indissoluble commercial realities.

---

[86] Quoted in Douglas Jehl, "President Will Call on Congress to Impose Baseball Arbitration," *New York Times*, February 8, 1995.

[87] Reich, *Locked in the Cabinet*, 240.

[88] William J. Clinton, "Remarks and Exchange With Reporters on the Major League Baseball Strike, February 7, 1995," *American Presidency Project*.

Media reaction to the failure of the summit combined sympathy at Clinton's apparent humiliation with outrage aimed at the players and owners. "If the president says what you're doing hurts the country, *you're supposed to stop doing it* [his italics]," complained Boswell in the *Washington Post*.[89] "What an embarrassment," declared Smith in the *New York Times*: "Here was baseball, in the shadow of all that power and all that history that Clinton brought to bear....And still Clinton was rebuffed."[90] Nevertheless, true to his word, the following day Clinton sent the Major League Baseball Restoration Act, which proposed binding arbitration, to Capitol Hill. Identical co-sponsored bills were introduced in the Senate and the House. But in the face of Republican opposition to intervention, neither progressed. The same fate befell a separate legislative initiative which aimed to narrow the antitrust exemption.

Clinton's hoped-for wave of public backing also came to nothing—members of Congress reported few calls or letters on the issue.[91] Instead, Gingrich proposed an altogether more spiritual way forward. The best way to break the deadlock, he suggested, was for the owners and players to sit down together and bond over the baseball movie, *Field of Dreams*: "They ought to...ask themselves, 'isn't there some spirit of cooperation here? Isn't there some spirit of caring about our national pastime?'"[92] Although he was refusing in any practical way to play ball with the President, Gingrich appeared to share his belief that baseball's virtues could somehow prevail over the game's hyper-commercial realities. It was not to be so. A day later—a week after the Ruth deadline—political reality kicked in: Lindsey wrote a memo urging Clinton against expending more political capital. Do

---

[89] Thomas Boswell, "Same Pitch, Same Catch," *Washington Post*, February 8, 1995.

[90] Smith, "Fans Should Turn Their Backs, Too."

[91] David Hess, "Fans' Message to Congress: Stay Out of the Baseball Strike," *Philadelphia Inquirer*, February 11, 1995.

[92] Quoted in Associated Press, "Gingrich now Pitching 'Field of dreams' After 'Boys Town,' A Hollywood Solution for the Baseball Strike," *Philadelphia Inquirer*, February 12, 1995.

nothing, "certainly not in public," Lindsey counselled. "You should not expose yourself politically unless success comes closer."[93]

"American Renewal": the World Series Returns

The longest labor stoppage in the history of American sports finally ended after 234 days, on April 2, 1995, not as the result of presidential or congressional intervention but following a ruling by a federal judge. It had been made three days earlier in the Manhattan courtroom of the US District Court, where the future Supreme Court justice, Sonia Sotomayor, granted a request from the NLRB for an injunction against the owners of baseball's twenty-eight major league franchises. In comments that again saw the judiciary acknowledging the game's special status, Sotomayor wrote of the need to protect "the public interest" and to ensure that the "symbolic value" of Opening Day was "not tainted by an unfair labor practice."[94] With the injunction reinstating the terms of the previous collective bargaining agreement, the players offered unconditionally to return to work; the owners unanimously decided not to lock them out. Opening Day of a shortened season would be April 25, a little over three weeks away. Ripken, his streak unbroken, would resume the quest for Gehrig's record, offering the prospect of a dazzling moment of baseball celebration later in the season, one which would be enthusiastically embraced in presidential rhetoric and performance. Clinton issued a brief statement: it was good news for baseball, its fans, and the cities whose economies had suffered.[95] Clinton agonized over whether to resume his ceremonial duty by throwing the Opening Day pitch, telling Branch that "his job was to stand for continuity in hope."[96] But this time, fearful of encountering the lingering ill-will of the fans, caution prevailed, and Major League Baseball returned without a presidential pitch. Instead, Clinton performed his duties on a different stage, throwing the first pitch at the National Amateur All-

---

[93] Memorandum, Bruce Lindsey to Bill Clinton, "Baseball Update," February 13, 1995, OA/ID 24792, Folder: Baseball Strike, Letters, Comments Polls [2], Bruce Lindsey, Counsel's Office, *Clinton Presidential Records*.

[94] US District Court for the Southern District of New York, "Silverman v. Major League Baseball Player Relations Inc., 880F. Supp. 246 (S.D.N.Y), April 3, 1995," *Justia.com*.

[95] William J. Clinton, "Statement on the Major League Baseball Strike Settlement, April 2, 1995," *American Presidency Project*.

[96] Branch, *The Clinton Tapes*, 248.

Star Baseball Tournament in his home state of Arkansas, describing it as "the real heart and soul of baseball in our country," in a barely concealed jibe at the major league game.[97]

Even with the players back on the field, the presidential intervention had been a chastening experience for Clinton—more proof, after the failure of his health-care plan, that the power of his office could be a blunt weapon in the absence of meaningful congressional cooperation or broad public support. And while nine decades of precedent suggested that presidential engagements with baseball usually had mutually beneficial outcomes, it was clear from the strike that this was contingent upon factors beyond presidential control, including the mood of the media and the willingness of athletes and other actors to bend to presidential will.

So why, in the face of reluctant colleagues, an uneasy public and an unsupportive press, did Clinton persist in placing himself and the presidency at the center of a conflict which even the battle-scarred Usery considered extraordinarily hostile? The answer offered by two of those inside the administration is that Clinton sensed a political opportunity and was drawn inexorably towards activism because he miscalculated the weight of the presidential voice. As McCurry recalls: "Clinton had a fair amount of hubris, and thought by force of moral suasion, using the presidency, he could make it work."[98] Reich also saw an unerring self belief as "a supersalesman."[99] Both these observations have merit, and also illustrate the travails that characterized the early years of Clinton's administration: a tendency to overestimate his own, and his office's, muscularity. By this measure the President emerged from the strike with a losing record—the reality of his apparent impotence acknowledged by Clinton himself in the bland, single sentence description of the baseball summit which appears in his memoir: "I even invited representatives of the owners and the players to the White House, but we couldn't settle it."[100]

But taking a broader perspective, it is possible to detect in Clinton's motives and performances a principled seam of presidential obligation combined with political expediency, a fusion of purpose and pragmatism which places his strike intervention firmly in the context of his post-1994

---

[97] William J. Clinton, "Interview with Gary Matthews of ESPN in Pine Buff, June 24, 1995," *American Presidency Project*.
[98] McCurry, interview by author.
[99] Reich, *Locked in the Cabinet*, 238.
[100] Clinton, *My Life*, 620.

presidency. From this viewpoint, rather than offering more evidence of Clinton's early ineptitude in government, the intervention instead marked the stirrings of a values-oriented rhetoric, with an emphasis on the components of national character which would contribute to the revitalization of presidential communications from 1995 onwards. One notable observer within the administration, the Assistant Secretary of State, Richard Holbrooke, felt that by late-1994 Clinton had developed a good grasp of what he called "the symbolic use of the presidency."[101] His growing enthusiasm to deploy symbols of national identity was both genuinely held and politically effective. Clinton saw such symbols as sources of cohesion at a time when, in his own words, communal bonds were "frayed" by the momentum of social, cultural, and economic change.[102] The social anxiety caused by the fracturing of American life appeared to be profound and visible everywhere: in the hyper-partisan political arena where Clinton was being savaged by his opponents for being un-American; in the decline in participation in civic institutions; in the country's racial divisions which surfaced in strident debates over affirmative action and education. And now it was being witnessed in the broken national pastime. Against this background of unease and discord, Clinton's intervention in the strike for the more noble purpose of rescuing and restoring one of the foundations of American culture seemed entirely reasonable—it was an act of leadership. As McCurry pointed out to reporters at the time of the baseball summit: "He is the President, and we're talking about baseball [which] plays a unique role in our history and our culture. The president thinks the American people expected [him]…to do what he could to try to save baseball."[103] And although Selig sensed that Clinton had always been more sympathetic to the union case, the acting commissioner still reflected on the summit in similar terms: "It was a very emotional day and again it proved how really important baseball is to America and society. When you have the President of the United States involved it says everything."[104]

In cherishing the national pastime in the early months of 1995, Clinton advanced language which he would later use to invoke broader notions

---

[101] From Holbrooke's Bosnia Audio Diary, November 8, 1994, quoted in Packer, *Our Man*, 298.

[102] Clinton, "Address Before a Joint Session of Congress on the State of the Union, January 24, 1995."

[103] Clinton, "Press Briefing by Mike McCurry, February 8, 1995."

[104] Quoted in Bodley, *How Baseball Explains America*, 54.

of a "national community" and the "renewal of America," recurring themes as he endeavored to reestablish his relevance in the wake of the November midterm disaster. Distinct from partisan issues like health care, or culturally divisive issues such as gay rights and gun control, the efforts to save baseball had ostensibly been in service of the entire American community, one Clinton imagined comprised of families of active citizens whose values were embodied in their presence at church, at the PTA, at town hall meetings, and at the local ballpark.[105] In advancing a misty-eyed vision of old-time baseball, Clinton adopted an inclusive tone which had fallen out of his speeches. "It's an interesting thing to do in the context of the time," observes Don Baer, "when everyone is focused on government breakdown, to connect yourself so directly, in your rhetoric or your role as leader of a nation, to something that's as fundamental as baseball."[106] From that perspective, at least, his intervention had a constructive side—less damaging to his long-term authority and reputation than it appeared in the immediate, embarrassing aftermath of the White House summit.

These threads converged again in October 1995, on the eve of the World Series, which returned to its traditional place in the fall calendar after the hiatus of the previous year. In his weekly radio broadcast, Clinton revisited the theme of "American renewal" which had formed the rhetorical spine of his First Inaugural Address in 1993. The return of the World Series was the "renewal of our national pastime," of a common heritage, and a shared national memory: "No matter where you go in America, sooner or later, there will be a patch of green, a path of dirt and a home plate," he said. Baseball's familiar icons, artifacts and images were scattered through Clinton's words—legendary players like Stan Musial and Cal Ripken; the "arc of the home run," the Little League, the "snap of the ball in the back of a mitt." So were a set of idealized American values: teamwork, tolerance, dedication, and optimism; "winning with joy and losing with dignity." Baseball, said Clinton, was "more than a Field of Dreams"— it was something the country still badly needed with the challenges of the twenty-first century looming. In World Series week, this was the rhetorical reconnection of the big-league game with its mythical community roots—an association on which Clinton had placed so much emphasis

---

[105] These four examples of community life made frequent appearances in Clinton's speeches: for example, Clinton, "Address Before a Joint Session of Congress on the State of the Union, January 24, 1995."

[106] Baer, interview by author.

during his efforts to end the strike. It was the celebration of national ideals and civic institutions which transcended cultural and partisan divisions. It was the President performing the reconsecration of the national pastime, blotting out the lingering bitterness of his failed intervention and attempting to reestablish the game's sacred place in the American imagination.

By the time the final postseason pitch was thrown, it was clear that the professional incarnation of America's national pastime had, for the moment at least, survived. The game may have been "debilitated," as the economist Andrew Zimbalist observed, but it was "still alive." [107] Even so, attendances in the 1995 season had plunged more than twenty percent, and the fans' continuing resentment towards the strike protagonists meant that those motivated enough to go to the ballpark often did so to vent their anger noisily at everyone involved. And though it had not died on his watch, Clinton could scarcely claim much credit. The tensions between the game's mythic inheritance and its capitalist impulses exposed by the strike had been contained but not resolved. However, there remained one figure, a player, who did have the capacity to align baseball's myths and commercial interests—and to Clinton this presented another opportunity to connect with the game. Over the post-strike summer of 1995, Cal Ripken Jr. emerged as the real savior of the national pastime, a heroic symbol of the American work ethic who in the hands of the President would also become an avatar for one of the most contested domestic policies of the era—the overhaul of the welfare system.

---

[107] Zimbalist, *In the Best Interests of Baseball?* 149.

Chapter Three

"Going to Work Is as American as Baseball": Bill Clinton, Cal Ripken Jr., and Welfare Reform

September 1995: Americans at Work

On the morning of September 8, 1995, Bill Clinton hosted a multifaith prayer breakfast for more than seventy religious leaders in the State Room of the White House. It was the third time in his presidency that Clinton had held this gathering close to the Labor Day break—an occasion he had used in the past to muse on the role of faith in public life and the need to find common ground amid America's religious diversity. This time Clinton expanded his themes, speaking for more than half-an-hour about the shared values that he felt were required "to move into the next century with the American Dream alive." One of the homespun stories he offered his audience was about a bus driver from Virginia who had not missed a day's work for eighteen years. The driver had featured on a local television news bulletin watched by Clinton late the previous night. He recalled it in some detail: The driver "was meeting the people that he picked-up every day and let off every day and talking about how his daddy told him he was supposed to work, that he didn't think it was unusual [to work every day for eighteen years]." His story, said Clinton, was a reaffirmation of "the personal responsibility, the dignity of work, the devotion" of the working American. Clinton continued: "I think it sort of reinforced to me this idea that in spite of all the differences in the country, there really are lots of things that bind us together, that we believe very deeply."[1]

Clinton was not alone in celebrating the work ethic over the Labor Day holiday: across the country, across multiple forms of media, the public were offered heroic images of "ordinary" Americans at work. The *Los Angeles Times* profiled Gloria Acosta, an immigrant from the Philippines,

---

[1] William J. Clinton, "Remarks at a Breakfast With Religious Leaders, September 8, 1995," *American Presidency Project*.

who had not missed a day's work since taking her first job as a nursing assistant thirteen years earlier: "She is simply one of thousands of Angelinos who go quietly and efficiently about their work each day, unsung and unheralded."[2] In Chicago, a bar owner called Max had served customers for ten years, day-in and day-out, "one of countless small businessmen" who "open the store, shop or office every day or they don't make any money," wrote the *Tribune*.[3] The readers of America's most popular celebrity magazine, *People*, were presented with a photo-feature about six "hardworking Americans," all of whom had not missed a day's work for at least thirty-five years, among them Audrey Stubbart, one hundred years old but still proofreading her local newspaper. "The day I call in," she said, "I won't be sick I'll be dead."[4] And the thread weaving together these diverse stories of duty and resilience, the inspiration for editors all over the country to fill columns with tales of ordinary folk just doing their jobs, was the career of a professional baseball player. The Virginia bus driver "would have never been on television," the President told his audience of clergy, "if it hadn't been for Cal Ripken breaking Lou Gehrig's record."[5]

Like the bus driver, the nurse, the bartender and the centenarian, Calvin Edwin Ripken Jr., the thirty-five-year-old shortstop for the Baltimore Orioles, exemplified a story of selfless endurance. Ripken had been showing up for work every day in the ballparks of the American League for more than thirteen years—never rested, never stood down through injury, never benched through loss of form. But his durability had a significance beyond sporting longevity—it established Ripken as an unusual cultural icon for the 1990s, a figure whose nationwide celebrity was built on a clean-cut image and his capacity just to turn up and do his job. Two days before the White House prayer breakfast Ripken had surpassed a hallowed mark in baseball, breaking the record for playing consecutive major league games hitherto held by Lou Gehrig, one of the greatest heroes in the pantheon of American sports. In celebrating Ripken's achievement, a much broader narrative was disseminated, one of the renewal of the national

---

[2] Beverly Beyette, "Cal Ripken Isn't The Only One on a Streak," *Los Angeles Times*, September 6, 1995.

[3] Mike Royko, "Ripken's New Record Deserves an Asterisk," *Chicago Tribune*, September 7, 1995.

[4] "Unmissing Persons," *People*, October 16, 1995.

[5] Clinton, "Remarks at a Breakfast With Religious Leaders, September 8, 1995."

pastime following the trauma of the strike and the reawakening of traditional notions of work, duty, and family at a time when, by the President's own admission, "the common bonds of community were badly frayed."[6] When people cheered Ripken, Clinton explained, it was because in recognizing his character, his strength, his perseverance, his commitment to teamwork, they were sharing something "we desperately need to elevate and preserve as long as this country exists."[7]

The interested parties in the propagation of Ripken's narrative of work, duty, and responsibility were multiple. Importantly it was a story of mutual benefit to two connected industries: the multi-billion-dollar baseball industry, whose owners craved a heroic role model to recapture the strike-alienated fan base and reconnect them to the game's supposedly wholesome past; and the media enterprises whose revenues relied on the popularity of its sports content for readers, viewers, and advertisers. It resonated in the political arena too: public declarations of admiration for the universal qualities embodied by Ripken allowed politicians of all hues to appear above the partisan fray at a time of intense cultural conflict and noisy jeremiads of national decline. Finally, the uplifting Ripken story was of particular advantage to the President: Ripken's potency as a cultural symbol, whose endurance embodied the American work ethic, aligned with Clinton's promotion of a policy at the core of his domestic agenda—the transformation of the welfare system by ending benefit dependency and pushing people toward work. In embracing the story of Cal Ripken Jr.'s steadfastness at work, Clinton was uniting two elements of America's civil religion—baseball's nostalgic representation of the ideals of community and integrity and a belief system that associated the work ethic with self-fulfillment and personal independence.

"Ending Welfare as We Know It"

Clinton's convictions about the virtues of work drew on two sources: his own experiences from his modest southern upbringing and an anti-welfare thread embedded in national ideology. As Clinton often acknowledged in his speeches, American reverence for the work ethic wound back to the

---

[6] Clinton, "Address Before a Joint Session of Congress on the State of the Union, January 24, 1995."

[7] Clinton, "Remarks at a Breakfast With Religious Leaders, September 8, 1995."

nation's Puritan forefathers, when, as the historian Daniel Rodgers points out, the New World was "a land pre-occupied by toil," where a moral life was one of struggle and determination, of sobriety and industry.[8] With prosperity growing off the back of labor during the late-nineteenth-century industrialization, the work ethic as an idealized virtue became uncoupled from its Puritan roots, though it lost none of its centrality to definitions of American values. By the early twentieth century, immigrant workers were powering the factories of capitalist mass production, and the link between work and Americanization was explicit. "Workers, to be good workers, to be the kind of workers that make for mass production, must have the American point of view," declared an editorial in 1918 in *Automotive Industries* magazine. "They must have American ideals and ambitions."[9] In this industrialized setting a belief in work-focused virtues was almost universally held. Idleness was not only an unjust economic burden on those working hard for a living but a moral affliction too: charity for the non-working poor merely encouraged dependency. This ideological legacy survived into the late-twentieth century, to underpin popular and political support for work-based welfare reform.

It was this work-centered impulse in American history which would provide Clinton with the rhetorical spine in his effort to fulfil his 1992 campaign pledge to overhaul the benefits system "and welfare as we know it."[10] In a typical speech in Kansas City in June 1994, Clinton spoke of the need to restore faith in the three founding principles: "the bond of family, the virtue of community, the dignity of work." And he argued that changes in the welfare system had to be rooted in getting people back to work: "Work is the best social program this country ever devised. It gives hope and structure and meaning to our lives."[11]

Clinton would insist that his attachment to such sentiments was personal—incubated in his Arkansas childhood, growing up in a poor family with a working mother: "[Work] kept food on the table, but it gave us a sense of pride, meaning and direction," Clinton recalled. "I know it is sometimes hazardous to extrapolate your own experiences...but on this I

---

[8] Rodgers, *The Work Ethic in Industrial America 1850–1920*, 5.

[9] Quoted in Gartman, *Auto Slavery*, 227.

[10] William J. Clinton, "The New Covenant Speech: Part One. October 23, 1991," *Scribd*.

[11] William J. Clinton, "Remarks on Welfare Reform in Kansas City, Missouri, June 14, 1994," *American Presidency Project*.

don't think it is."[12] While Governor of Arkansas and Chairman of the National Governors Association, Clinton had successfully lobbied Congress in 1988 to pass the Family Support Act, which encouraged states to require recipients of benefits who were parents of young children to sign a contract committing themselves to job training at work.

Later, as a putative presidential candidate, Clinton coined the phrase that would define his approach to welfare policy. Clinton's "ending welfare as we know it" mantra made its rhetorical debut in a speech at Georgetown in October 1991. Enveloping the slogan in a quasi-religious package by invoking the Puritan notion of a "New Covenant" between people and government, Clinton promised to "erase the stigma of welfare for good by restoring a simple, dignified principle: no-one who can work can stay on welfare forever."[13] Under his embryonic proposals, entitlements would last for up to two years, before claimants would have to take a job in the private sector or undertake community service. According to Bruce Reed, Clinton's domestic policy advisor and author of the "end welfare" phrase, it was a new type of social bargain—the definitive combination of opportunity and responsibility—and it represented Clinton's biggest intellectual and philosophical contribution to the Democratic Party.[14] Of course, there was also an electoral dimension. By acting on welfare, Clinton could defuse the charge that conservatives had fired at Democrats for decades: that the benefit system was pampering the undeserving African American poor at the expense of the supposedly hardworking, White middle-class. By eliminating this line of attack from the right, Clinton, with the enthusiastic backing of his polling strategist Dick Morris, believed race could be neutralized as an election issue.[15] But within the Democratic Party, not everyone shared Clinton's zeal: old-style liberals and the Congressional Black Caucus (CBC) viewed welfare reform as an attack on the Great Society safety net that had lifted millions of Americans from poverty since the 1960s. Blue-collar unions feared the impact on jobs and wages of a new army of low-paid employees flooding the labor market. And despite enthusiasm for the broad principles of welfare reform, finding agreement from the Republican side of the aisle was just as challenging. Even for moderate

---

[12] Quoted in DeParle, *American Dream*, 113.

[13] Clinton, "The New Covenant Speech: Part One. October 23, 1991."

[14] Bruce Reed Interview, April 12, 2004, *Bill Clinton Presidential Oral History*.

[15] Morris, *Behind The Oval Office*, 159.

Republicans, Clinton's sketchy proposals, with their associated government-funded training programs, were unacceptably expensive. For those more conservative on social issues, including the Christian Right, the problem was a moral one: from their perspective, welfare cheques paid to unmarried mothers encouraged illegitimacy. High rates of non-marital births were the main source of society's ills, they claimed, especially poverty and crime. For the right-wing moralists, the solution was clear—abolish all welfare for single mothers. In this atmosphere, unsurprisingly, consensus was elusive.

That dynamic changed after the 1994 midterm elections. The Republican landslide created a philosophically attuned welfare alliance, between a New Democratic president and a Republican-controlled Congress, which significantly increased the prospects of legislation. Unencumbered by the prospect of congressional obstruction by his own divided party, Clinton recognized the changing circumstances. "[The Republicans] had spelled out a reform proposal…which had nastier budgetary offsets than our bill, but it was conceptually similar, [and] there was no Democratic leadership group to tell us not to do it anymore," recalls Reed.[16]

During the early months of 1995, the outlines of a Republican-backed Personal Responsibility Act emerged from the House, designed both to withstand attacks from the Christian Right (so keeping the Republicans united), while also making concessions to Clinton's demands for a safety net for the most vulnerable. Responsibility for welfare was to be handed to individual states, whose block grants would fund aid to dependent children. Claimants would have to get a job within two years and would be limited to no more than five years of assistance in their lifetime. All immigrants, legal or illegal, would be ineligible for welfare, and funding for Medicaid and food stamps would be dramatically reduced.

With the bill heading to the Senate, Clinton made his views clear. Some elements were still too tough on the poor. The work incentives were insufficient and there was the possibility that millions of unsupported children could be plunged into poverty: as it stood, Clinton was prepared to veto it.[17] But equally, he was uneasy about seeing one of his major policy goals drift unresolved into reelection year—he still hoped senators would

---

[16] Reed interview.
[17] Reed interview.

address these concerns and produce legislation he could sign. However, by late summer, even with some further concessions to the White House, it was clear that the Senate's version would be a hardline one: a states-run welfare program with capped funding and a lifetime limit for claimants.[18] With the Congressional arithmetic on the side of the Republicans, Clinton asked Morris to investigate whether the public could be persuaded that a presidential veto on welfare reform was justified. On August 10, Morris came back with an answer: voters overwhelmingly favored an overhaul of entitlements that required benefit recipients to work, and Clinton should "never, never" use his veto. Instead, Clinton should try to "increase identification" with welfare reform.[19] Less than a month later Cal Ripken Jr. would give him that opportunity.

On September 6, the day of Ripken's record-breaking game in Baltimore, Clinton sent a letter to the Senate majority and minority leaders calling on them to work together on fresh legislation which had been put before senators that day. The Work First Bill contained time limits to benefits and tough work requirements. It would, Clinton wrote, put work, responsibility, and family first: "[They] are not Republican values or Democratic values. They are American values—and no child in America should ever have to grow up without them."[20] Hours later Cal Ripken Jr. took center stage. The American hero who most embodied those values was at the end of his thirteen-year quest for the Gehrig record. This connection was captured in a White House speechwriter's contemporaneous note about that evening's game, which Clinton was due to attend. It began with the words: "I'm here as just one more fan of BB [baseball]," and went on to reflect on Ripken's qualities, echoing the dominant themes of the congressional letter.

> It is esp[ecially] great to be here because Cal is such a good model for young peop[le]. Respons[ibility], work hard & persevere. [The] kind of thing I've tried to promote as president—these values—hard work,

---

[18] Haskins, *Work Over Welfare*, 194–226.

[19] "Agenda for Meeting with the President on Aug 10," Item 3.1 reproduced in: Morris, *Behind The Oval Office*, 466–67.

[20] William J. Clinton, "Letter to Congressional Leaders on Welfare Reform September 6, 1995," *Public Papers of the Presidents of the United States: William J. Clinton; 1995, Book II, July 1 to December 31, 1995* (Washington, DC: Government Publishing Office, 1996), 1313–14.

devotion to fam[ily] + com[munity are] at [the] core of what we have to do as a nation to move forward in times of change.[21]

Here was the opportunity for Clinton to associate himself with the qualities that Ripken represented: love of country and community; devotion to family; and belief in the inherent dignity of a day's toil, a principle embedded in the founding of the nation. Clinton was now ready to join the public in a national sporting celebration and appropriate Ripken's story by applying it to the welfare debate.

Constructing Cal—a Blue-Collar Icon

In September 1995, millions of Americans were well versed in the significance of the sporting drama that was now advancing towards its climax. For years it had been a particular obsession of the baseball-writing press, but in recent months Cal Ripken Jr.'s relentless focus on Lou Gehrig's record had emerged from its sporting silo into the general media space—the stuff of profiles, commentaries, and television programs aimed at much wider audiences. Even though the assault on the record hardly counted as breaking news (*Sports Illustrated* called it "the least dramatic record run of all time"), on nine occasions over five days in early September, Ripken featured on the evening news broadcasts of the major networks.[22] On September 6, ABC scheduled a half-hour *Nightline Special* devoted to Ripken with Clinton himself contributing to the program.[23] And what attracted television executives, journalists, politicians, and viewers to a sports story that entirely lacked competitive jeopardy was the cultural resonance associated with Ripken's feat. While it was primarily a story of remarkable physical endurance, with an all-American backstory that embraced more than a splash of pathos, it also drew immense cultural power from its easily

---

[21] Note, OA/ID 10894 Folder: 9-13-95 National Family Partnership Event. Elridge, MD [1], Terry Edmonds, Speechwriting, *Clinton Presidential Records*. There is no official record of precisely when Clinton delivered these words, although press reports of his remarks when he met Ripken in the Orioles locker room prior to the game include at least one of the phrases.

[22] Richard Hoffer, "Hand it to Cal," *Sports Illustrated*, December 18, 1995.

[23] Between September 4 and September 9, the Ripken 'Streak' was covered four times by ABC, three times by CBS and twice by NBC. "September 1995 Broadcast Index," *Vanderbilt Television News Archive*.

transferrable meaning—a fascination with the simple virtue of turning up for work.

The national spotlight, so sharply fixed on Ripken in the late summer of 1995, was a far cry from how the journey to the record had begun, on May 30, 1982 in front of 21,632 fans, when, as a twenty-one-year-old in his second season with the Baltimore Orioles, he was selected to bat eighth in the lineup against the Toronto Blue Jays. From that day onwards, without interruption, Ripken would slowly chip-away at a number—2,130—long sanctified in the annals of American sports. The figure represented Lou Gehrig's unbroken sequence of major league appearances—a feat that spanned almost fourteen years of baseball's 'Golden Era' of the 1920s and 1930s. It was not only the record, but also the record-holder, which accounted for its iconic status. Gehrig's career had fused heroism and tragedy in an era of unprecedented celebrity for America's athletes, when sports spectatorship emerged as a new and exciting activity for an increasingly leisure-focused population. And Gehrig's memory had hardly dimmed in the national imagination in the subsequent six decades.

At the top of the celebrity tree in the interwar years had been Gehrig's New York Yankee teammate Babe Ruth, whose fame was built on his astonishing record of big hitting and a matching extravagant lifestyle. But not far behind was Gehrig, whose reputation relied on a distinct set of attributes: his discipline and determination in compiling a consecutive game run which earned him the nickname 'Iron Horse.' In August 1933, the *New York Times*, described Gehrig as a man of "sturdy virtues" who lived by "copy-book maxims": "He does not drink. He goes to bed early and gets up early. He is straightforward and upstanding. He has worked hard and he has prospered."[24]

Gehrig's unbroken streak had begun on June 1, 1925. It ended on May 2, 1939, when he finally sat out a game, unsteady on his feet, unable to time his swing, stricken by the symptoms of a neuromuscular disorder which would prove fatal two years later. The debilitating condition, amyotrophic lateral sclerosis, became known as Lou Gehrig's Disease, and his battle against its effects, alongside his farewell speech at Yankee Stadium, in which he declared himself, "the luckiest man on the face of the Earth," secured a place for Gehrig in the roll call of American heroes

---

[24] John Kieran, "The Man Who Is Known as Lou," *New York Times*, August 13, 1933.

and earned his record a special status in the public memory.[25] "He stood for something finer than merely a baseball player," declared the *Herald Tribune* in praising the modesty and courage of Gehrig's words. "He stood for everything that makes sport important in the American scene."[26] So important that Hollywood crafted a movie out of the story of his life and death, and Gary Cooper, playing Gehrig, was nominated for an Academy Award. More than eighty years later, Gehrig's "luckiest man" speech was still revered in the *New York Times* as "Baseball's Gettysburg Address," invoking one of the canonical texts of American civil religion.[27] It was to this standard that Ripken had found himself held by the media, as season-by-season, day-by-day, he advanced on Gehrig's record. By the early 1990s the two ballplayers' personalities, playing styles, and achievements were constantly compared, mostly favorably, and in similarly hallowed terms. Collectively they were the "Iron Horse" of New York and the "Iron Man" of Baltimore. With his small-town background, itinerant youth, blue-collar persona, and one-club career, Ripken fulfilled a baseball creed that had existed since the mid-nineteenth century: that it was an indigenous sport, originating in the countryside, and that when brought to the cities, baseball imposed order and inculcated idealized American values of self-reliance, loyalty, and community pride on a messy urban world.

Indeed, by the summer of 1995, when Ripken-mania really cemented its grip, Ripken's quest was no longer just a nostalgic reenactment of Gehrig's feat; it was celebrated by commentators as the embodiment of wider values upon which harmonious societal relationships depended at the close of the twentieth century. "No other record in sports better exemplifies the most enduring of American values: hard work, steadiness and loyalty. There's no flash and dash to Ripken, no swagger, no earrings. He's just there, every day, doing his job," wrote Steven Roberts in *US News & World Report*.[28] In the *Washington Post*, eulogies to Ripken bridged ideological differences: "What makes [Ripken] extraordinary is the way he does the ordinary," enthused the conservative commentator Charles

---

[25] Lou Gehrig, "Farewell to Baseball Address: 4th July, 1939," *American Rhetoric*.

[26] Quoted in Eig, *Luckiest Man*, 318.

[27] Richard Sandomir, "Eighty Years Ago, 'The Luckiest Man' Took the Field One Last Time," *New York Times*, July 4, 2019.

[28] Steven Roberts, "Remember, Baseball Is a Great Game," *US News and World Report*, August 14, 1995.

Krauthammer, while the same newspaper's liberal voice, E. J. Dionne, shared similar sentiments, hailing "the magnificent achievement of ordinary virtue" and the "heroism of steady work." "Ripken's message is that working hard doesn't make you a chump...that the act of meeting ordinary daily demands can transform itself into extraordinary achievement."[29]

According to those around him, Clinton was caught up in this adulation of the ordinary. Benjamin Barber, a political theorist and occasional presidential advisor, noted that Ripken had become "an exemplary text for Clinton's frequent paeans on behalf of persistence and reliability, which Clinton saw as underrated moral values."[30] The historian Taylor Branch, summoned to the White House to be the unofficial chronicler of his presidency, observed that Clinton saw in Ripken, "a paragon example of renewed workhorse excellence."[31] The White House Press Secretary, Mike McCurry, detected some self-absorption in Clinton's enthusiasm for the Ripken story: "Clinton saw parallels between what it takes to go day-in and day-out to be a professional athlete doing your job and what he felt like he was doing, doing his job as president." Ripken was someone "who really toughed it out, sometimes under hard circumstances," just as Clinton himself had turned up, day after day "to work for America" during his own travails.[32]

On the newspaper and magazine features pages journalists were equally assiduous in the process of mythmaking, propagating a sentimentalized Ripken family backstory that contributed to the creation of a blue-collar icon. According to the *Christian Science Monitor*, as an infant Cal Jr. had been "lulled to sleep by his father's tales of life in baseball's minor leagues."[33] In the summer months of his childhood, Cal Jr. was constantly on the move, trailing along with the family to whichever small-town club his ballplaying father, Cal Sr., had been assigned. In a nostalgic recollection of an itinerant family life recounted in *Time* magazine, Cal Jr.'s mother, Violet, was portrayed as "the matriarch of the clan," summoning

---

[29] Charles Krauthammer, "One for the Book: Consummate Prose," *Washington Post*, September 6, 1995; E. J. Dionne, "Baseball's Ordinary Hero," *Washington Post*, September 5, 1995.

[30] Barber, *The Truth of Power*, 247.

[31] Branch, *The Clinton Tapes*, 232.

[32] McCurry, interview by author.

[33] Peter Grier, "In a Game of Tradition and Myths, Ripken Is a Genuine Icon," *Christian Science Monitor*, September 5, 1995.

her offspring to dinner where the old-school father, Cal Sr., insisted on old-school manners and a strict dress code—clean hands, clean shirt, combed hair, no jeans. "He's a blue-collar man and proud of it," explained Cal Jr.[34] Press admiration for the instilling of traditional values through active parenting was echoed in a best-selling 1995 biography in which Cal Sr. and Violet were rendered as the throw-back parents of a more innocent era: "They taught their children always to ally themselves with what is right, to value the importance of family life and to believe in themselves doing the best at everything they did."[35] According to Thomas Boswell in the *Washington Post*, the Ripken family represented the small-town values of rural Maryland: "For [Cal Jr.,] the 60s and 70s might as well have been the 40s and 50s—when America was productive, self-confident, simplistic, and not too hip to have heroes."[36] By uncoupling the Ripkens from a worldview which millions of Americans had inherited from the sixties, Boswell effectively removed them from the front line of battles over sexuality, race, popular culture, and morality which divided nineties America.

In the retelling of the Ripken family saga, Cal Jr.'s work ethic was inherited from his father, who set a tireless example by doubling-up doing multiple jobs around the minor league ballparks where he played, managed, and coached. "I think that's where I first picked up my work ethic," recalled Cal Jr. "My dad did everything."[37] When Cal Jr. was in his teens, Cal Sr. secured a position as the bullpen coach at the big-league club in Baltimore and, at the age of eighteen, the young Ripken joined him in the Orioles organization. Three seasons later Cal Jr. played his first game of major league baseball. By 1983, Cal Ripken Jr. was playing shortstop for a World Series winning team. He was already a consistently strong hitter, but his acute positional sense also made him highly dependable on defense, despite a six-foot, four-inch frame which was unusual in a shortstop—a position that customarily puts a high premium on speed and agility. That year Ripken added the American League MVP title to his World Series ring and was chosen for the MLB All-Star team for the first time. He would be an All-Star in every one of the next eighteen years, also picking

---

[34] Steve Wulf, "Iron Bird," *Time*, September 3, 1995; also, Ripken Jr. and Bryan, *The Only Way I Know*, 13, 24.

[35] Rosenfeld, *Iron Man*, 4.

[36] Thomas Boswell, "Focused on Greatness," *Washington Post Magazine*, March 22, 1992.

[37] Quoted in Wulf, "Iron Bird."

up eight Silver Slugger awards for his batting and two Golden Gloves for his fielding. In 1999 Ripken was voted onto the MLB All-Century Team, putting his name alongside the greats of the game—Babe Ruth, Lou Gehrig, Joe DiMaggio, Ted Williams, Jackie Robinson, Mickey Mantle, and Hank Aaron.

But it was his unbroken run of consecutive appearances upon which the Ripken myth was built. By 1987, Ripken was into his sixth season without missing a game, and the themes of his indefatigable work ethic and unrelenting reliability, combined with the traditional 'all-American' dynamics of the Ripken family, were embedded in the media narratives of his career. Cal Sr. had been promoted from third-base coach to manager of the Orioles; Cal Jr. was an established star; and younger brother Billy had also signed for Baltimore, prompting *Sports Illustrated* to devote its cover to "The Ripken Gang," and inside to run a five-page feature about how the members of this one family were the saviors of a ballclub that, in the years after the 1983 World Series success, had fallen on sporting hard times. In the two-dimensional pen-portraits typical of sports journalism, Cal Sr. was the gruff taskmaster "first-to-come-last-to-leave"; Young Billy "The Kid" was labelled the prankster; and Cal Jr. was summed up as "milk drinking and clean living."[38] These were humble virtues directly handed down from the Gehrig era.

As the streak continued, the nostalgic renditions of Ripken's life that routinely filled the sporting press sometimes spilled into the general media space. In May 1993, the men's lifestyle magazine *GQ* featured "Iron Cal" on its cover, the accompanying story presenting Ripken as the hero of Baltimore—a place once notorious as the nation's murder capital now scrubbed up as "a blue-collar, brick-built city, quilted in marble row houses, a town where people take particular pride in doing their job." The film director, John Waters, a Baltimore native, explained Ripken's appeal: "[Baltimore] has a low tolerance for pretension. It just doesn't work when you try to be chic in a blue-collar town."[39] It was common for Ripken's self-reflection to be colored by this blue-collar lens through which his life and family were presented: "I'm sure that whatever I am as a man and as a

---

[38] Hank Hersch, "One Rip Roaring Family Affair," *Sports Illustrated*, March 9, 1987.

[39] Peter Richmond, "Local Hero," *GQ*, May, 1993.

ballplayer comes from the way I was raised," he told *Sports Illustrated*.[40] The Orioles trainer, Richie Bancells, noted: "He equated playing shortstop every day to being a welder who went to work every day, or a guy punching a clock at a factory."[41] Mike Lupica, writing in *Esquire*, emphasized the impact this had on Ripken's popularity: "Baseball fans identify with Ripken more than with the loud chest thumpers of sports because he is like them in one crucial way. He goes to work every day."[42] Naming Ripken its "Sportsman of the Year" in 1995, *Sports Illustrated* gushed: "In an era of slouching gods, this devotion to duty was a curative.... He just kept coming to work because—why wouldn't you?"[43]

This unpretentious depiction of a multimillionaire sports star may have been an exaggeration, but it was a representation that the media seized upon with enthusiasm, elevating Ripken's superficially dull persona of industriousness, duty, and modesty into a model of American manhood and a pillar for national life. In the *Washington Post*, Boswell wrote: "Tell Ripken he's dull and it makes his day. He still thinks doggedness is his trump card in life."[44] The best-selling book *Men at Work*, which claimed on its cover blurb to "get to the root of the game we all love," devoted sixty admiring pages to Ripken. Its author, George Will, noted: "He is a difficult man to see depths in, but they are there. His passions are submerged beneath his public self, which is steadiness personified."[45] This unassuming profile appealed to advertisers who recognized marketing value in a six-million-dollars-a-year athlete with a 'regular guy' image. "Cal's lack of flamboyance is one of the most attractive things about him," admitted Kurt Rittner, an executive with General Motors, who were looking for a celebrity to front an ad campaign for their equally unglamorous Chevrolet Trucks.[46] Unlike some teammates, Ripken turned down the opportunity to promote men's underwear, choosing to be the face of milk instead. "This would be a defining moment for me in the public eye," Ripken explained

---

[40] Quoted in Ralph Wiley, "Second to One," *Sports Illustrated*, September 15, 1995.

[41] Quoted in Eisenberg, *The Streak*, 6.

[42] Mike Lupica, "Let's Play Two Thousand," *Esquire*, April 1995.

[43] Hoffer, "Hand it to Cal."

[44] Boswell, "Focused on Greatness."

[45] Will, *Men at Work*, 286.

[46] Raymond Serafin, "Cal Just a Short Stop From Making History," *Ad Age*, September 11, 1995.

in his autobiography. "I am a milk person both in substance and how I want to be seen."[47] Eventually Ripken also picked up national endorsement deals, but he always remained the familiar face of the Middle Atlantic Milk Marketing Association, appearing alongside his father as the all-American son.

Indeed, the myth of the Ripkens became a parable of family solidarity, a folk tale of devotion and hard work, and the setting for an expression of generational cultural transmission—the bonding of American fathers and sons through baseball. Ripken's father would summarize it in a paperback self-help guide, *The Ripken Way: A Manual For Baseball and Life*, which interlaced homespun wisdom on baseball and parenting, under sections with titles like, "The Work Ethic"; "Our Guiding Principle for Raising Children"; and "The Pride of Parenthood."[48] Adding to the mythology of a Ripken creed, such presentations merely confirmed the appeal of Ripken's virtues. "Hundreds of politicians talk about family values. This guy lives them," enthused David Broder, the *Washington Post's* political commentator, praising Ripken's respect for his parents who had taught him that "work is a value in itself."[49]

Thanks to press coverage like this, a composite hero of clichéd and contradictory national stereotypes had been constructed: a hardworking small-town American, a blue-collar champion, and the "Iron Man" representing the steel city of Baltimore. Ripken's story embodied the paradox that sustained baseball's myth: its revered place in the American chronicle relied on a synthesis of working-class urban progress and a memory of a rural past to establish its status as a crucible of American values. In a *New York Times* opinion piece, nominally addressed to Bill [Clinton], Bob [Dole], and Newt [Gingrich], the columnist R. W. Apple Jr. emphasized the point by adding an iconic American president's integrity to the roll call of Ripken's virtues: "Intelligent. Steadfast and self-effacing, as honest as Abe, the unashamed exemplar of the simple unadorned values of the American Sunday school."[50] Here was Ripken, the heroic individual in a team sport: a blue-collar icon who symbolized the Puritan-descended

---

[47] Ripken Jr., Bryan, *The Only Way I Know*, 113.

[48] Ripken Sr., *The Ripken Way*.

[49] David Broder, "Blue Collar Heroes: Ripken and Powell," *Washington Post*, September 11, 1995.

[50] R. W. Apple Jr., "Bill, Bob, Newt: Watch Cal," *New York Times*, September 8, 1995.

equation of work and godly virtue. It was the perfect avatar for Clinton to mobilize in his efforts to secure welfare reform.

Ripken Reaches "the Unreachable Star"

Cal Ripken Jr.'s first at bat of the 1995 regular season was on April 26, almost a month later than usual because of the disruption of the seven-month-long strike which had wiped out the end of the previous campaign and much of spring training. Despite the extra-long layoff, Ripken's sequence of 2,009 consecutive games was still considered officially alive, much to the delight of Major League Baseball which would now have the opportunity to indulge in some serious record-breaking hysteria. So, when Ripken took to the field in Kansas City—121 games short of Gehrig's mark—the four-and-a-half-month-long path from there to the record had been fully mapped-out. Unless Ripken was cut from the roster through injury or (even less likely) benched, he would equal Gehrig's total in Baltimore on September 5. The next night Gehrig's record would be history, and Ripken would stand alone.

With the September 6 date earmarked months in advance, the celebrations and ceremonies for the big night could be planned to the finest detail. The climactic finale would take place midway through the last game of a nine-game homestand, during a matchup against the California Angels. The setting was fitting for an event immersed in ruthlessly marketed nostalgia: the Orioles ballpark, Camden Yards, which stood a few blocks from Babe Ruth's birthplace, was the first of a new wave of retro-styled downtown ballparks built in the 1990s, which replaced the multipurpose, car-oriented, suburban stadia of the sixties and seventies. Located on the city's Inner Harbor, Camden Yards sat amid the architecture of urban regeneration, reflecting the industrial origins of the professional game. Looming over the outfield wall was the restored brick facade of the Baltimore & Ohio Railroad's freight warehouse, the longest building on the Eastern seaboard. In a tangle of apparent cultural contradictions, it was simultaneously a new ballpark with retro-twists and an already sacred venue: two years earlier the stadium had witnessed Maryland's largest ever naturalization ceremony when four thousand immigrants simultaneously swore the Oath of Allegiance. A month after the record-breaking night it was scheduled to host a Papal Mass conducted by John Paul II, on ground which the *New York Times* suggested was already "hallowed" because it was the home ballpark of the saintly Ripken.[51]

During the first week of September—labelled "Streak Week" by the media—this recently built temple to the national pastime was transformed into a venue for an extended expression of baseball as American civil religion and a celebration of civic pride. Patriotic red, white, and blue bunting adorned the outfield walls and four, ten-foot-high, orange and black banners (the colors of the Orioles) dominated the B & O warehouse, each displaying a digit to spell out the number of games played by Ripken. Elaborate rituals pointed to the civil religious significance of the occasion: jazz, the flag, the President, the family all weaved together in a symbolic opening. A grand piano was wheeled onto the field where Bruce Hornsby and the saxophonist, Branford Marsalis, improvised an instrumental version of the Star-Spangled Banner. Live television pictures mixed the fluttering Stars-and-Stripes with blurry images of the soon-to-be-surpassed number, 2,130, cutting between pictures of Ripken in the field and Clinton in a sky box, both holding their hand to heart, and Ripken's family sitting in the front row next to the Orioles dugout.[52] Highlighting the centrality of family to the occasion, Ripken's two children, Rachel and Ryan, threw opening pitches. "After each catch Cal returned the ball to his child and tenderly kissed them in front of God and 46,722," reported the *Washington Post*.[53] Ripken's family-oriented presentation would recur throughout the evening. "They are the greatest thing that has ever happened to me. I think kids are the secret to life," Ripken told one reporter.[54]

Among those impressed was the nonagenarian columnist for the *Washington Post*, Shirley Povich, whose career linked Ripken directly to Gehrig (he had reported on Gehrig's "luckiest man" speech in 1939). Povich praised the homespun style of the Iron Horse's successor:

---

[51] John Kifner, "The Pope's Visit: A Final Message; Pope Ends Tour Calling for Politics of Mercy," *New York Times*, October 9, 1995.

[52] ESPN, "Cal Ripken's 2131 Celebration w/HR - Original Broadcast," *YouTube*.

[53] Tony Kornheiser, "In Cal, We See a Picture of America," *Washington Post*, September 7, 1995.

[54] Quoted in Tim Kurkjian, "Man of Iron," *Sports Illustrated*, August 7, 1995.

"[Ripken] exemplifies the family values that politicos only talk about."[55] One politico doing plenty of talking was Clinton, who, in sharing the spotlight with fifteen-year-old Chelsea, also acknowledged the importance of family to the occasion. Al Gore was there too with his son, the Vice President's presence at the same event as the Commander in Chief representing a relaxation of the next-in-line security protocol which usually prevented the two being together at large-scale outdoor venues. Back in Washington, routine business took second place to Ripken. Roll call votes in the Senate were halted at 5:30 p.m. to give legislators a chance to get to Baltimore in time for the first pitch;[56] and at the White House, staffers were told that a long-planned shake-up in the meetings schedule had been put on hold "so as not to interfere with Cal's big week."[57] A few hours earlier, the President's spokesman had been asked why Clinton and Gore were both attending. "They want to take their kids like thousands of other fans," McCurry told the reporters. He was asked if the President would try to "get in on the act and go on the field." No, McCurry said the President just wanted to spend some time at the ballpark with his daughter, to experience a "historic moment that many followers of baseball thought impossible."[58]

But Clinton, like Ripken, was also at work, and there was substantial presidential performance on view. During a pregame visit to the clubhouse Ripken presented the President with a baseball jacket and an autographed bat. In return Clinton gave Ripken a signed copy of *Baseball: The Presidents' Game*, an illustrated history of presidential engagement with the

---

[55] Shirley Povich, "Beyond the Feat, Ripken Fills Gehrig's Shoes," *Washington Post*, September 8, 1995. Povich's original report on Gehrig's 'luckiest man' speech is reprinted at: "This Morning With Shirley Povich: 'Iron Horse' Breaks as Athletic Greats Meet in His Honor," *Washington Post*, August 27, 1995.

[56] 104th Congress, 1st Session: Vol. 141, No. 138 — Daily Edition, "Congratulating Cal Ripken Jr. on Breaking the Major League Baseball Record for Consecutive Games Played," S12754–56. *Congressional Record Online*.

[57] Email, Cheryl L. Sweitzer to White House Counsel Staff, "The first day of the rest of your life…." September 6, 1995, 16:26:42.97, Folder: [07/17/1995 – 09/15/1995], NLWJC-Kagan Emails Received, Automated Records Management System, *Clinton Presidential Records*.

[58] William J. Clinton, "Press Briefing by Mike McCurry, September 6, 1995," *American Presidency Project*.

sport.[59] The President then headed for the broadcast booths, first to ESPN, which that night attracted the cable channel's record ratings for a baseball game.[60] For an inning, Clinton bantered with the announcers, seamlessly blending the roles of the fan and father, with that of the politician and president. "These stands here are full of people who never get recognized but show up every day," Clinton remarked in presidential mode. "These are the people who make America. Cal Ripken, in a funny way, has made heroes of them."[61] And then, with ease, Clinton switched. The First Fan offered his opinion on a range of subjects: the fallout from the strike; the fashion for sideburns among players; his television-free childhood listening to Cardinals games on the radio. Clinton's nostalgic rhetoric was in full flow when the cameras suddenly cut to Chelsea, striding through the crowd. "That's my girl!" exclaimed the First Father, "having a great time....She loves baseball."[62] The First Daughter, who had notably appeared playing softball with her father in the 1992 campaign video, *The Man from Hope*, was again authenticating the baseball-derived, American family values of the First Fan and the First Family.[63]

A few minutes later, Clinton repeated the performance for the radio audience, sharing commentary with announcer Jon Miller, when Ripken hit a home run in the third inning. As Ripken launched the ball over the left field wall, Clinton seized control of the microphone, yelping, "Go! Go! Yeeees," laughing and clapping his hands.[64] "That was what made it so fun," Miller later recalled: "The President of the United States led the cheering."[65] While honoring McCurry's pledge to stay away from the on-field celebrations and official ceremonies, Clinton had played the role as

---

[59] Mead and Dickson, *Baseball: The Presidents' Game*.

[60] The game had an average 7.5 Nielsen rating, and peaked at 11.3 from 9:30 to 9:45 p.m. Richard Sandomir, "Numb and Numbers: 2,131 and Counting," *New York Times*, September 8, 1995.

[61] Quoted in Milton Kent, "Minimum of Words Gets Maximum Effect 2,131: Ripken Passes Gehrig," *Baltimore Sun*, September 7, 1995.

[62] ESPN, "President Clinton at Ripken's Record Breaking Game, 1995," *YouTube*.

[63] Geoffrey Tuchman, "The Man From Hope, 1992," *Media Burn Independent Video Archive*.

[64] MLB, "Clinton Calls Ripken Homer," *mlb.com*.

[65] *Candid Voices with Donny Baarns*, "Jon Miller on Bill Clinton's Reaction to Cal Ripken," *YouTube*.

national cheerleader and, via his broadcast appearances, reached an audience of millions. In doing so he had also placed himself at center stage in the public memory.

The symbolic climax of Streak Week came at 9:20 p.m., the midpoint of the fifth inning, the moment the game between the Orioles and the California Angels became "official" under baseball's rules, so adding another number to Ripken's unbroken sequence. With play paused, hundreds of balloons were released, a volley of fireworks blasted from the stadium roof, and the banner on the fourth digit on the B & O warehouse unfurled, revealing the new record number—2,131. Some in the crowd waved handmade signs: "We consider ourselves the luckiest fans on the face of the earth," referencing Gehrig's farewell speech, and in doing so demonstrating the fans' self-consciously nostalgic role. Clinton, now relieved of his broadcasting duties, was up in the stands behind a bulletproof screen, flanked by Chelsea and the Vice President, clenching both fists above his head in salute. Ripken climbed out of the dugout for a curtain call, waved a few times, then took off his hat and shirt and handed them to his children sitting in the front row. Underneath he wore a T-shirt printed with the words, "2,131 + hugs and kisses for Daddy." Six more curtain calls from the dugout followed, before Ripken embarked on a lap of honor, circling the stadium's dirt track beneath the outfield fence, touching the outstretched hands of fans, teammates, opponents, and security staff. The game had been suspended for more than twenty-two minutes before Ripken resumed his place in the dugout.

While tens of thousands inside Camden Yards witnessed the moment in person, a far greater number experienced it through the mediation of television, whether live or via the recycled images on network news bulletins and cable channels. Chris Berman, ESPN's announcer, was in hyperbolic mood: "Cal Ripken Jr. has reached the unreachable star," he declared before remaining silent for eighteen minutes, letting the images and sounds of the crowd carry the live coverage while Ripken circled the stadium—a production technique that added a layer of purity and reverence. The pictures largely concentrated on Ripken (one unbroken shot of Ripken lasted almost five minutes), pulling away occasionally to his family, the fans waving signs ("The Blue-Collars Salute You"), the warehouse banners displaying the new record, and baseball legends of the past applauding from the stands. Fourteen times the cameras cut to a tearful Joe DiMaggio, eighty years old and an enduring icon of twentieth-century

American popular culture, whose life as the symbol of a lost generation of American heroes had been lamented in song by Simon and Garfunkel. This was DiMaggio "the Yankee Clipper," the long-ago teammate of Lou Gehrig, the heartbroken husband of Marilyn Monroe, and the guardian of another of baseball's most sacred records.[66] This was Joltin' Joe, the throwback to a more innocent era, acting as a vessel for the transmission of simple American values, publicly endorsing his successor, Cal Ripken Jr.

Once Ripken had completed his lap, ESPN's Berman broke his silence: "a moment that will live for 2,131 years," he said with solemnity, implying the feat would be remembered for a period longer than the history of Christianity itself.[67] Wrapping Ripken's achievements in a quasi-religious shroud was common. An umpire had once likened ejecting Ripken from a game to "throwing God out of church."[68] Earlier in Streak Week an aircraft had flown over Camden Yards during a game trailing a banner: "God Bless Cal."[69] Journalists routinely referred to Ripken as baseball's "Messiah" for restoring faith in the national pastime and bringing back the fans after the previous winter's strike. The broadcast blimp hovering above Camden Yards lit up with the words "Cal is #1." A sign was held aloft in the crowd: "Thank you Cal for saving baseball." The next day the front page of the *Baltimore Sun* hailed "Immortal Cal," and the *New York Daily News* carried the capitalized page one headline "HOLY CAL!"[70] Through this secularization of sacred language, the press endowed the events of the evening with civil religious meaning: the virtues of the work ethic; the ritual of the celebrations; and Ripken as the anointed saint.

When the game finished, after three-and-a-half hours, more formal ceremonies began. First, the bestowing of offerings to the hero, a ritual long associated with record-breaking in baseball, with Ripken accepting

---

[66] DiMaggio's fifty-six consecutive games in 1941 in which he hit safely to reach first base is regarded as one of baseball's greatest achievements.

[67] ESPN, "Cal Ripken's 2131 Celebration w/HR - Original Broadcast."

[68] Wulf, "Iron Bird."

[69] Ross Newhan, "Fans, Players Are Backdrop for Ripken," *Los Angeles Times*, September 5, 1995.

[70] "Holy Cal! Fans Go Wild as Ripken Tops Gehrig Record," *New York Daily News*, September 7, 1995; "Immortal Cal," *Baltimore Sun*, September 7, 1995.

gifts from the club and teammates. Then came a few words from the Orioles owner, Peter Angelos, and a brief speech by DiMaggio: "Wherever my former teammate Lou Gehrig is today I am sure he's tipping his cap to you Cal Ripken."[71] When Ripken took the microphone it was after midnight, but thousands remained in their seats. In a ten-minute speech, Ripken reinforced the abstracted images that had been the refrain of the media for months: a hardworking, family-oriented son, father, and husband. He thanked his father, for teaching him the importance of "being there for your team and to be counted on by your team-mates," and his mother, "the glue that held the family together." Embracing his wife, Kelly, Ripken declared, "You, Rachel, and Ryan, you are my life." Twice he called baseball "the great American game." And he ended by placing his own name in a roll call of the national pastime's greats: "Whether your name is Gehrig or Ripken, DiMaggio or Robinson, or that of some youngster who picks up his bat or puts on his glove, you are challenged by the game of baseball to do your very best day-in and day-out. And that's all I've ever tried to do."[72] It was a statement of quasi-religious intent, pledging himself to the credo of the national pastime: the saints of the past, the generational transmission, the constant struggle for improvement. It was a commitment to keeping American values alive.

In the following days, media coverage emphasized the cultural significance of Ripken's achievement, surrounding the streak with a homespun and nostalgic halo which jarred with the perceived social anxieties so often reported in the pages of newspapers. In an editorial comment headlined "Cal Ripken, Regular Guy," *National Catholic Reporter* offered him as the balm to a country "battered by seemingly irresolvable arguments."[73] Ken Rosenthal, in the *Baltimore Sun*, praised Ripken's "simple virtue," noting, "in this harried age, simple can be remarkable."[74] In the *Washington Post*, Kornheiser offered a larger cultural landscape on which to locate Ripken's deeds. He called the celebration of Ripken "the fanfare for the common man," detecting universal American values in a "working-class hero" and

---

[71] MLB, "CAL@BAL: DiMaggio Speaks at Ripken's 2,131," *YouTube*.

[72] MLB, "Ripken Speaks After 2,131st Consecutive Game," *YouTube*.

[73] National Catholic Reporter Editorial Board, "Cal Ripken, Regular Guy," *National Catholic Reporter*, September 15, 1995.

[74] Ken Rosenthal, "Immortal Cal: He Touches Home With Victory Lap," *Baltimore Sun*, September 7, 1995.

"the rhythms of America" in his achievement. "Providing for our family like our fathers did before us is something we can all relate to....In the country that invented the work ethic, going to work is as American as, well, baseball"[75] At a campaign fundraiser on September 7, Clinton echoed this common-man theme. Most of those in the crowd, he said, were just like Ripken: "They work when they don't feel good. They work when the weather is bad. They work to earn money to do right by their children. They are the people that keep this country going."[76] The Ripken parable would remain a thread in presidential rhetoric for months to come: on New Year's Eve, reflecting on his personal highlights of his year, Clinton singled out his visit to Camden Yards, again praising Ripken's "old fashioned" virtue in "showing up for work every day," and his one-club loyalty which had resisted the "consumer culture" of professional athletics.[77]

Equally eager to leave their imprint on events were the legislators who had travelled to Camden Yards and who presented a resolution of congratulations to Ripken in the Senate. Maryland's Barbara Mikulski spoke of "masculine virtue, honor and integrity." Patrick Leahy of Vermont, who sat with Clinton during the game, said the occasion reflected on everyone who got up each day and went out to work: "Whether it is the nurse who is there for the evening shift on a weekend, the person who shows up at the police department and goes to work to protect all of us, the teacher who is there teaching our children."[78] The Virginia Senator Mark Warner said Ripken represented the essence of what it meant to be American: "a

---

[75] Tony Kornheiser, "In Cal, We See a Picture of America," *Washington Post*, September 7, 1995.

[76] William J. Clinton, "Remarks at Clinton/Gore '96 Dinner, September 7th, 1995," *American Presidency Project*, 1995.

[77] White House Internal Transcript, "Remarks by the President at Renaissance Weekend Dinner, December 31, 1995" OA/ID 10983, Folder: 1-15-96 MLK Day Atlanta, GA [2}, Terry Edmonds, Speechwriting, *Clinton Presidential Records*.

[78] 104th Congress, 1st Session: Vol. 141, No. 145 — Daily Edition, "Tribute to Cal Ripken, Jr.," S13704, *Congressional Record Online*.

modest hero, a humble role model, a decent citizen, a caring father, a loving husband."[79]

If these values exemplified by Ripken and espoused by politicians were viewed as being quintessentially American, in their mediation they were also often presented as intrinsically White. The work and welfare discourse had long been racialized in American political culture not least through the tropes of the work-shy African American father and the Chicago 'welfare queen.' Now, with Ripken embodying a White, Puritan-inherited American work ethic, the post-streak media cacophony presented another stigmatized African American trope as its sinister counterpoint: the violent, ill-disciplined, lazy African American athlete. The coded overtones were barely concealed in Max Boot's commentary in the *Wall Street Journal* in which he compared one-club Ripken, a "throwback to the days of heroes," to the Black NFL player Deion Sanders, a flashy "hired-gun passing through town." The contrast, according to Boot, highlighted a set of broader challenges confronting society: "a land of alienated individuals bouncing from place to place without ever putting down roots, a country locked in an endless and unavailing search for self-gratification."[80] Boot was by no means alone in assigning pejorative labels to Black athletes. The *Christian Science Monitor* presented supposed examples of laziness and frailty drawn from the ranks of African American athletes as the inverse of Ripken's virtues. "Ricky Henderson sat down because he wasn't 'mentally prepared' to play....Deion Sanders missed two games because of a headache," the newspaper asserted. "Where Ripken comes from you need better excuses than those to miss work."[81] And where did Ripken come from? The solid White stock of small-town America. Jim Murray of the *Los Angeles Times,* also saw a values crisis in sports as a metaphor for a broken America: "You know what I'm talking about:...basketball players who make millions and don't show up for team practices and make magazine covers, scofflaws whose very criminality gives them celebrity, the whole,

---

[79] 104th Congress, 1st Session: Vol. 141, No. 138 — Daily Edition, "Congratulating Cal Ripken Jr. on Breaking the Major League Baseball Record for Consecutive Games Played," *Congressional Record Online.*

[80] Max Boot, "Cal, Deion - and Us," *Wall Street Journal,* September 13, 1995.

[81] Grier, "In a Game of Tradition and Myths, Ripken Is a Genuine Icon."

sorry sick, panoply of sports in the '90s."[82] It hardly needed pointing out that the majority of professional basketball players were Black, as was the one man whose celebrity and identity was anchored by sport, his race, and his alleged criminality, and whose media presence in 1995 eclipsed even that of Cal Ripken Jr.—O. J. Simpson.

The trial of Simpson for the murder of his ex-wife Nicole and her friend Ron Goodman, ran from January to October 1995, spanning the whole of Ripken's triumphant season. Preceding Ripken as the holder of the unofficial title of 'America's favorite sports star,' Simpson had risen to the heights of celebrity as the easygoing African American athlete turned actor, a ubiquitous presence on television and in film, whose popularity appeared to embody the apparent color blindness of nineties multicultural America. But live television coverage of the trial, and the seemingly compelling evidence against him, fueled a national debate about Simpson's guilt, with public opinion dividing along race lines.[83] As Ripken's streak edged toward its climax, the ballplayer and the ex-footballer were sharing the front page, albeit presenting sharply contrasting visions of the direction in which American society appeared to be travelling. This was especially apparent in the scenes which played out on the opposite sides of the country on September 6, Ripken's record-breaking day. While in Baltimore, tens of thousands of baseball fans, and millions watching on television, celebrated a moment which appeared to project a heroic reaffirmation of enduring American ideals, demonstrating anew, according to *Sports Illustrated*, "that positive values can leak from sports into the greater part of our culture," two-and-a half-thousand miles away, hundreds of mainly African American supporters of Simpson surrounded the Los Angeles County Superior Courthouse demanding his acquittal after the prosecution's most important witness, a racially compromised police detective, took the Fifth Amendment to protect himself from self-incrimination.[84] As James Wellworth of *Time* reported that day, "the chanting from the crowd outside seemed like an ominous threat that unless O. J. walked there would be

---

[82] Jim Murray, "The Old School Is Just Fine, Thank You," *Los Angeles Times*, August 31, 1995.

[83] Hunt, *O. J. Simpson Facts and Fictions*, Table 1, 19.

[84] Hoffer, "Hand It To Cal."

more race riots in Los Angeles."[85] It was a prospect of violence that the Clinton Administration took seriously, with the Justice Department putting together emergency contingency plans in consultation with the Los Angeles Police Department and African American community leaders.[86] Thus, at the very moment that a White, meticulously constructed, blue-collar cultural throwback was judged in the media to be renewing a sense of traditional family values, a once transcendent African American sporting figure in America's multicultural landscape appeared to have edged the country to the brink of racial conflict. "Not even the Los Angeles riots, horrifying though they had been, seemed as discouraging to people who had hoped for a closing of the racial divide in America," recalled the historian James Patterson.[87] Simpson's once celebrated presence in the pantheon of American sporting heroes now appeared to be an aberration. Thank goodness, it seemed, that America had someone else to turn to: solid, dependable Cal. Cal could again play the role of savior—the son, the father, the husband, the inheritor of Gehrig's mantle, the upholder of old-style American virtues. And in Baltimore the celebration of Ripken and his virtues continued. Less than twelve hours after the final speeches at Camden Yards, Ripken was carried through the thronged streets of inner-city Baltimore on a float constructed from 2,131 baseballs, before getting ready to head to Cleveland and game 2,132.

On the same day at the White House, Clinton met Morris to discuss welfare reform. The pollster brought with him mixed news: the public still doubted Clinton's commitment to overhauling welfare and those doubts were making it harder "to insist on our version of reform."[88] The next morning, with a Senate vote a little over a week away, Clinton spoke at the religious leaders breakfast about the need to build consensus: "what worked for…Cal Ripken? Showing up for work, having the right attitude, working for the team, working for tomorrow, that's what works." It was

---

[85] James Wellworth, "Fuhrman Takes the Fifth," *Time.com*, September 6, 1995.

[86] Stephanopoulos, *All Too Human*, 302.

[87] Patterson, *Restless Giant*, 310.

[88] "Agenda for Meeting with the President on Sept 7, Item II. A2," reproduced in Morris, *Behind The Oval Office*, 469.

not surprising that voters had a low opinion of Washington, Clinton concluded, if all they ever saw was fighting.[89] It was a clear expression of the President's belief that partisan conflict over welfare should end. In his weekly radio address, Clinton indicated that he was prepared to compromise—for the first time he would endorse a Republican welfare bill. "Real reform, first and foremost, must be about work," he said, and the "values Americans hold most dear." He urged legislators to put aside political differences and called for a new system based on "independence, work, responsibility, and family"—the refrains most dominant in the mediation of Ripken's streak.[90]

The breakthrough came a few days later: the Democrats wanted more money for childcare, and the Republicans now offered three billion dollars over five years. The sum was enough for the White House, and Clinton's aides set about persuading Democratic senators to accept the compromise. By September 15, a bipartisan agreement was in place. Soon after, the Senate passed the bill by 87–12. Clinton praised the Senate's "wisdom and courage" in getting to grips with "one of the most fundamental social problems of our time."[91] It had been nine days since he had led the cheering to celebrate the work ethic of a baseball hero, and Clinton appeared to be within striking distance of forcing through one of his signature policies—a work-oriented welfare system.

Welfare Reform Finally Passes: The Streak Finally Ends

Although symbolically important, the September 1995 Senate vote was to prove a false dawn. Within weeks, attempts to reconcile the Senate bill with a version from the House were derailed by the looming row over the federal budget and the December 1995 government shutdown. Concerned about proposed cuts in Medicaid and by Republican attempts to tie welfare reform to broader budget cuts, Clinton twice used his veto. It took another eight months, and the pressure of an election campaign, before the White

---

[89] Clinton, "Remarks at a Breakfast With Religious Leaders, September 8, 1995."

[90] William J. Clinton, "The President's Radio Address, September 9, 1995," *American Presidency Project*.

[91] William J. Clinton, "The President's Radio Address, September 16, 1995," *American Presidency Project*.

House and the Republicans would again put together a deal over welfare reform—and then only in the face of opposition from many in Clinton's inner circle who argued that it would lead to a sharp increase in poverty.

Clinton's internal critics notwithstanding, on August 22, 1996, the President signed the Personal Responsibility and Work Opportunity Reconciliation Act into law, transferring swathes of responsibility on welfare to the states, and scrapping Aid to Families with Dependent Children (AFDC), the sixty-one-year-old federal program which provided financial support to children of families on low income: "From now on our nation's answer to this great social challenge will no longer be a never ending cycle of welfare, it will be the dignity, the power and the ethic of work," Clinton declared.[92] Three senior health officials in his administration resigned in protest. Not without controversy and with the long-term impact unknowable, the fundamentals of the American welfare state had been upended, from benefit entitlement to an expectation of work. This legislative landmark had been delivered with baseball deployed as part of a rhetorical framework which reinforced the sanctity of the work ethic. Ripken's example had contributed to presidential rhetoric and performance around the breaking of Gehrig's record; it had elicited Congressional motions in praise of the "Iron Man of Baltimore"; and seen the media construct and then deify a blue-collar icon for revitalizing the meaning of work in American society.

The long journey of welfare reform, across the political battlefields of Washington and through the legislative machinery of Congress, had reached a climax, but Ripken's relentless demonstration of the American work ethic still had more than two years to run. In this period Clinton would have two more gameday encounters with Ripken: on Opening Day in 1996 when he described the ballplayer's constancy in the Orioles jersey as "reassuring to the American people,"[93] and in July 1997 when he hailed Ripken's "hard work and discipline," appearing alongside him for the

---

[92] William J. Clinton, "Remarks on Signing the Personal Responsibility and Work Opportunity Reconciliation Act of 1996 and an Exchange With Reporters," *American Presidency Project*.

[93] William J. Clinton, "Interview With Mel Proctor, Jim Palmer and Mike Flanagan of Home Team Sports in Baltimore, April 2, 1996," *American Presidency Project*.

launch of a public service film which urged parents to get more involved in their children's education.[94]

The Streak finally came to an end on September 20, 1998, after 2,632 consecutive games when, at the age of thirty-eight, Ripken volunteered to sit out the Orioles last home game of the season. The end of Ripken's streak prompted another burst of values-laden reflection, much centered on the events in Baltimore in 1995, and the celebration of traditional ideals that it had inspired. The trademark Ripken characteristics of humility, determination, and reliability, again constituted the dominant themes. "He will always be revered," wrote a columnist for the *Hartford Courant*, "as a man with an extraordinary work-ethic."[95] David Cone, the opposing pitcher on the night Ripken stood down, revived the common-man imagery: "A lot of people who go to work every day can identify with Cal. The Streak supersedes baseball."[96] In *Sports Illustrated*, Tom Verducci presented Ripken's story as American allegory, with all the tropes associated with him again emerging in discourses on what it meant to be American: "The Streak wasn't just his identity; it was ours too. This was America the way we wish it to be—blue-collar, reliable, built on an honest day's work, one day after another."[97] No longer was the nostalgia centered on Gehrig, the sepia-tinted Yankee of half-a-century earlier, but on Ripken and his streak, which, in Verducci's lament, was already referred to in the past tense—now itself history. With the country engulfed in political, moral, and cultural mayhem over Clinton's relationship with Monica Lewinsky, the timing of Ripken's decision to stand down added to a sense of nostalgic loss. The following day the President's video-taped evidence to a grand jury, in which he confessed to "inappropriate sexual contact" with Lewinsky, was broadcast on all the major television networks—four hours of excruciating embarrassment and presidential evasion about his sexual

---

[94] William J. Clinton, "Remarks on Behalf of the Public Service Campaign for Educational Excellence in Baltimore, Maryland, July 2, 1997," *American Presidency Project*.

[95] Jack O'Connell, "Ripken Ends Streak At 2,632 Games," *Hartford Courant*, September 21, 1998.

[96] Quoted in J. A. Adande, "Ripken Gave Baseball, Fans, Renewed Vigor," *Los Angeles Times*, September 21, 1998.

[97] Tom Verducci, "Endgame," *Sports Illustrated*, September 28, 1998.

tastes, witnessed by millions of Americans.[98] That morning Ripken's name had been missing from Orioles' box score on the sports pages for the first time since 1982, breaking the continuity with what already felt like a more innocent era. It seemed fitting that the end of The Streak appeared to have extinguished not only a folktale of individual endurance but also a sixteen-year narrative of American virtue.

---

[98] C-SPAN, "President Bill Clinton - Grand Jury Testimony, August 17, 1998," *YouTube*.

Chapter Four

Bill Clinton, Affirmative Action, and the Jackie Robinson Myth

1997: Celebrating Jackie Robinson

On April 15, 1947, more than a year before President Harry Truman signed an executive order integrating the military, more than seven years before the courts ordered the desegregation of public schools and colleges, and a decade-and-a-half before segregation in public places and racial discrimination in employment were banned by law, White Americans for the first time in the twentieth century, allowed a Black American to play the national pastime at the highest professional level. Fifty-years later, the moment when Jackie Robinson trotted out to take up his position at first base at Ebbets Field in Brooklyn was celebrated by the President of the United States, by those who administered and played professional baseball, by the media, and by millions of Americans who memorialized it as a supposed turning point—an important stepping stone in the postwar struggle against racial injustice. In appearing to demonstrate that talent counted for more than skin color, Robinson had supplied "the blueprint for the integration of the nation," wrote his biographer, Johnathan Eig.[1] It was a story which, as the distinguished chronicler of baseball's integration Jules Tygiel noted, had become to Americans what the Passover story was to Jews: "it must be told to every generation so that we must never forget."[2] By translating this assertion into multiple symbols and performances, the celebration of the fiftieth anniversary of Robinson's major league debut strengthened baseball's claim to being an expression of America's civil religion in that it appeared to realize the promise of the African American Jeremiad—despite its multiple sins on matters of race, eventually American society

---

[1] Eig, *Opening Day*, 5.
[2] Tygiel, *Baseball's Great Experiment*, 345. Tygiel credited this analogy to the historian Steven Riess.

will redeem itself and complete its prophetic mission to chosen nation status. In doing so, it would rely on the myth that the national pastime had, in 1947, cast aside its shameful record on race to resume its inevitable ascendant narrative of American virtue.

Throughout 1997 the institutions of national, civic, corporate, and cultural life played their parts in disseminating this myth by producing a broad array of outputs which appeared to confirm baseball as a civil religious force for progress and redemption: the United States Mint struck Robinson's image onto two hundred thousand silver dollars and one hundred thousand five-dollar gold coins—the first time an African American had featured on a US Mint gold coin.[3] In Washington, an exhibition opened at the National Museum of American History on The Mall, saluting Robinson's "historical significance in spawning racial integration in American sports."[4] The guardian of America's mainstream cultural legacy, the Smithsonian Institution, staged a Robinson-themed lecture series: "the impact of Robinson's breakthrough was so profound that Americans began to see themselves, and their favorite sport in a new light," declared the promotional material. "From this time on, Americans would realize that heroes come in all colors."[5] The national pastime's own sacred place, the National Baseball Hall of Fame, followed suit, unveiling *Pride and Passion: The African-American Baseball Experience*, an exhibit which showcased relics from Robinson's career and presented baseball as a "catalyst for change throughout America."[6] Robinson appeared on Wheaties cereal boxes and in multiple forms of marketing for quintessential American brands including Coca-Cola, McDonald's, and Nike. The anniversary was celebrated on baseball caps worn by the President, on trading cards, in books, and on other memorabilia. In New York, a five-mile stretch of

---

[3] United States Mint Press Release, "US Mint Announces Jackie Robinson 'Legacy Set,'" *usmint.gov*, June 13, 1997.

[4] Smithsonian Institution, "Jackie Robinson and the Integration of Major League Baseball," *si.edu*, 1997.

[5] "Forum on American Life: Jackie Robinson: Barrier Breaker," *The Smithsonian Campus on the Mall*, 10, supplement to *The Smithsonian Associate*, February 1997.

[6] National Baseball Hall of Fame, "Pride and Passion: The African-American Baseball Experience," *baseballhall.org*.

highway linking Brooklyn and Queens was renamed in Robinson's honor. At the University of Massachusetts Amherst, hundreds of students signed up for two newly introduced courses which examined the Robinson legacy. Numerous tributes were paid on Capitol Hill. California senator Diane Feinstein said Robinson represented "everything that was great with [sic] America."[7] Rep. Carrie Meek said his historic breakthrough was what America was about: "equal opportunity for all."[8] Meanwhile baseball's acting commissioner, Bud Selig, announced that Robinson's jersey number, forty-two, would be retired in perpetuity across all major league clubs in recognition of the fact that he was the only player who was "bigger than the game."[9] And at the conclusion of this outpouring of civil religious production, the President of the United States stood at home plate on a major league ballpark, with Robinson's widow at his side, and declared that Jackie had "changed the face of baseball and the face of America forever."[10] Taken together, the celebrations of Robinson's fiftieth anniversary were, according to the cultural critic, Gerald Early, "one of the most pronounced and prolonged ever held in the history of our Republic in memory of a Black man or of an athlete."[11]

But the inheritance affirmed by this array of artifacts and symbolic performances had little connection with the White, turn-of-the-century, Protestant creed of honor and purity embodied by Cal Ripken Jr., which Clinton had embraced so enthusiastically two years earlier. Nor was it reflected in the idealized outpourings of numerous purveyors of a romanticized baseball history, such as Bart Giamatti, who had written of the sport

---

[7] 105th Congress, 1st Session: Vol. 143, No. 41—Daily Edition, "Commemorating the 50th Anniversary of Jackie Robinson's Debut in Professional Baseball," S2950, *Congressional Record Online*.

[8] 105th Congress, 1st Session: Vol. 143, No. 44—Daily Edition, "Tribute to the Memory of Jackie Roosevelt Robinson," H1516–20, Congressional Record Online.

[9] Smith, "A Grand Tribute to Robinson and His Moment."

[10] William J. Clinton, "Remarks in Queens Celebrating the 50th Anniversary of Jackie Robinson's Integration of Major League Baseball, April 15, 1997," *American Presidency Project*.

[11] Gerald Early, "Performance and Reality: Race, Sports and the Modern World," *The Nation*, August 10, 1998.

embracing "all classes, conditions and regions" as America "opened up her arms to the foreign born and healed the wounds of the war."[12] On the contrary, Robinson, as an African American cultural icon, supplied a different baseball legacy—one which challenged the sport's sentimentalized past and civil religious sanctimony. For African Americans, the supposed purity of America's game was fictional, banned as they were from competing as players in the White-only major leagues until the middle of the twentieth century and forced as spectators to sit in segregated stadiums. Black professional baseball had instead developed and thrived in the Negro Leagues—institutions which were the sporting illustration of W.E.B. Du Bois' double consciousness: they both sought to serve their communities' own cultural needs and to win respectability and acceptance within broader, White-dominated society.[13] When finally allowed to play the game professionally outside the Negro Leagues, Robinson and other Black players remained oppressed by Jim Crow, often forced to stay in separate accommodation from their White teammates and abused by opposing players and fans. And it was not only in the South: not until 1959 did the Boston Red Sox add an African American to their roster, by which time Robinson had retired from the game.

For his part, President Clinton acknowledged the "almost insurmountable obstacle of racism" that had confronted Robinson but nevertheless embraced the romanticized reading of the myth, molding it to his familiar framework of opportunity, responsibility, and community. Robinson was, according to Clinton, "the embodiment of the American Dream—the idea that if you work hard, you can succeed in this country."[14] Furthermore, Clinton effectively enlisted the fiftieth anniversary celebrations to endorse a comforting proposition—that the integration of baseball had been the first, largely successful, affirmative action program in

---

[12] Giamatti, "Baseball and the American Character," in *A Great and Glorious Game*, 55–56.

[13] Tygiel, "Unreconciled Strivings," in *Past Time: Baseball as History*, 117; Du Bois, *The Souls of Black Folk*.

[14] Transcript, 'Videotaped Remarks by the President in Tribute to Jackie Robinson for ESPN Documentary', OA/ID 10988, Folder: Jackie Robinson [1], Terry Edmonds, Speechwriting, *Clinton Presidential Records*.

American history.[15] The success of Robinson's "remarkable career" on the field of play, Clinton said, was a reason to embed affirmative action more deeply into American corporate life.[16] Those that ran the national pastime were no doubt content with this reading, suggesting, as it did, that Major League Baseball, the self-styled premier equal opportunity employer in America, had led the way—a narrative that aligned with Tygiel's assessment that "to black America, Robinson appeared as a savior, a Moses leading his people out of the wilderness."[17]

But of the many racial components which contributed to the fracturing of American society in the nineties, affirmative action was among the most conflict-ridden: supported by some in the growing African American middle class but dismissed by many African Americans as a symbolic program that failed to address the structural causes of Black poverty; and disliked by many Whites as a denial of a level playing field in employment and educational selection. By the beginning of the Clinton administration, the passions in the political and legal arenas aroused by affirmative action had, according to one scholar, "reached a boiling point."[18] When, in April 1995, *Newsweek* headlined an article about affirmative action, "Race and Rage," the rage to which the writer referred was not the fury of Black victims of racial discrimination but the resentment of White suburbanites at the perceived unfairness of what they saw as the reverse discrimination promoted by affirmative action.[19] Examples like this, of the entrenched reluctance of White America to recognize a need to address past racial injustices, led many to suggest Robinson's elevation to civil rights sainthood, alongside Rosa Parks and Martin Luther King, privileged a White version of baseball's integration that minimized controversy and mirrored American society's painfully slow advance toward meaningful racial equality. It is an analysis Robinson would have recognized. As the public intellectual Cornel West pointed out, at the time of Robinson's death in 1972,

---

[15] Pratkanis and Turner, "Nine Principles of Successful Affirmative Action," in *Out of the Shadows*, ed. Kirwen, 194–222.

[16] Clinton, "Remarks in Queens Celebrating the 50th Anniversary of Jackie Robinson's Integration of Major League Baseball, April 15, 1997."

[17] Tygiel, *Baseball's Great Experiment*, 196.

[18] Carter, *Brother Bill*, 135.

[19] Howard Fineman, "Race and Rage," *Newsweek*, April 2, 1995.

this "great American hero," a "transracial figure beloved by blacks and whites," would neither salute the flag, nor sing the national anthem, nor engage in the "empty gestures of country-worship." Such was his disillusion with the bigotry and prejudice he still encountered both within baseball and in society at large.[20] For Jackie Robinson and his African American teammates, the national pastime was neither civil nor religious.

This chapter explores the intersection of baseball, race, and the presidency where metaphors of sports, especially baseball, were deployed as components of presidential rhetoric and performance in efforts to address fears of a fragmenting America in the closing years of the twentieth century. Its focus is on the contested meaning of the Robinson myth through its presence in the 1990s debates over affirmative action and the broader discourse over racial justice that marked the Clinton years. Thanks to the zeal of the country's most prominent African American political campaigner, Jesse Jackson, the President and the national pastime were drawn together in these debates, exposing baseball's handling of the Robinson inheritance to intense scrutiny and testing Clinton's commitment from the outset of his presidency to policies that were critical links to his African American supporters.

The Schott Affair, Jesse Jackson, and the Opening Day Pitch

It was no accident that issues of civil rights and racial equality had only occasionally surfaced in Clinton's 1992 presidential election campaign: as the sign in his Little Rock campaign headquarters proclaimed, it was "the economy, stupid."[21] By early 1992, America had been in recession for twenty months, the country was struggling with the tax-cut-defense-spending induced deficit inherited from the Reagan era, and unemployment was at a ten-year high. As a result, Clinton's campaign focused on Republican economic mismanagement and health-care reform. In response, President Bush attacked Clinton's character, vaunted his own foreign policy credentials as the victorious leader in the Cold War and Gulf War, and allowed the religious right to seize the platform at the

---

[20] West, "Introduction," in Robinson, *I Never Had It Made*, xii.
[21] Greenberg, *Dispatches from the War Room*.

Republican National Convention with talk of a "cultural war for the soul of America."[22]

However, when riots erupted in Los Angles in late April after the acquittal by an all-White jury of four police officers accused of assaulting an African American, Rodney King, race had inevitably surfaced as an issue. Visiting the rubble-strewn streets of South Central Los Angeles, Clinton acknowledged the importance of increasing investment in urban infrastructure but also spoke of the need to end a culture of dependency: the poor needed to take responsibility for their own lives.[23] The message was crafted to appeal to White middle-class voters suspicious of government solutions to urban social problems. Clinton reinforced it with his criticism of a rapper, Sister Souljah, who, in an interview with the *Washington Post* in the wake of the Los Angeles riots, mused, "if you're a gang member and you would normally be killing someone, why not kill a white person?"[24] On June 12, Sister Souljah was invited onto the platform at the national convention of Jesse Jackson's Rainbow Coalition. The next day Clinton addressed the same gathering. Seizing the moment to condemn the rapper, Clinton told the audience that her comments had been "filled with a kind of hatred you do not honor."[25] Clinton appeared to be signaling to White voters and the media that the days of instinctive Democratic deference to Jackson were over. Clinton had demonstrated he was tough enough to govern. Similar signals had been sent in January when Clinton interrupted his primary campaign to return to Arkansas to oversee the execution of Rickey Ray Rector, a mentally impaired African American on death row. "He put someone to death who only had part of a brain. You can't find them any tougher than that," noted the political consultant David Garth.[26]

---

[22] Patrick J. Buchanan, "The Cultural War For The Soul of America, September 14, 1992," *Patrick J. Buchanan Official Website*.

[23] Robert Pear, "Riots in Los Angeles: The Democrats; Clinton Tours City's Damaged Areas and Chides Bush," *New York Times*, May 5, 1992.

[24] David Mills, "Sister Souljah's Call To Arms," *Washington Post*, May 13, 1992.

[25] William J. Clinton, "Remarks of Governor Bill Clinton, Rainbow Coalition National Convention, Washington Sheraton Hotel, Washington DC, June 13, 1992," *ibiblio*.

[26] Quoted in Annas, *American Bioethics*, 70.

With the media focus on Los Angeles inevitably dwindling as the news cycle moved on, so race and civil rights issues attracted diminishing attention in the election campaign. One member of the CBC complained that Clinton deliberately put Black issues "on the backburner," so concerned was he to appeal to White, Reagan-Democrats.[27] However, the Democratic convention platform did make a simple statement in support of affirmative action, accompanied by a broad pledge to continue "the fight to ensure that no American suffers discrimination."[28] Clinton promised to appoint a cabinet that "reflects America," and in his nomination speech spoke of a "common community" to heal the country. "There is no Them, there is only Us," he said, urging Americans to look beyond the stereotypical portrayals of minorities.[29] In *Putting People First*, the campaign book co-authored with his running mate Al Gore, a chapter on civil rights emphasized economic empowerment for minorities via the mantra of work, family, individual responsibility, and community. In a section entitled "Protect Rights for All," there was a commitment to prohibit discrimination in federal employment, contracts, and government services and a pledge to enforce the 1991 Civil Rights Act to ensure "workplace fairness rules for all Americans." But the term "affirmative action" was conspicuous by its absence. Instead, the Clinton-Gore ticket promised to "oppose racial quotas," thus ruling out setting specific targets for minorities in certain job categories, the most controversial component of affirmative action programs.[30] This pledge on quotas matched Bush's position, again neutralizing the issue among potential White swing-voters. For Clinton, the strategy of courting Whites carried little apparent risk: African American voters had nowhere else to go given they were unlikely to support a Republican party whose religious-right platform routinely attacked welfare recipients and socially liberal lifestyles.[31] So it proved: in November,

---

[27] Gwen Ifill, "Clinton Waves at Blacks as He Rushes By," *New York Times*, September 20, 1992.

[28] Democratic Party Platforms, "The 1992 Democratic Party Platform, July 13, 1992," *American Presidency Project*.

[29] William J. Clinton, "Address Accepting the Presidential Nomination at the Democratic National Convention in New York, July 16, 1992," *American Presidency Project*.

[30] Clinton and Gore, *Putting People First*, 63–66.

[31] Andrew Rosenthal, "Issues -- 'Family Values'; Bush Tries to Recoup From Harsh Tone on 'Values,'" *New York Times*, September 21, 1992.

Clinton lost the popular vote among Whites narrowly, by thirty-nine to forty-one percent, but secured eighty-three percent of African American votes. Although this figure was lower than the previous two Democratic presidential nominees had achieved, it was more than enough to contribute to a comfortable Electoral College victory.

Race as a mainstream issue may have been downplayed during the campaign, but within days of Clinton's 1992 victory a scandal in professional baseball erupted onto the national stage which highlighted the game's continuing struggle to address the problem of race. It centered around remarks made by the owner of the Cincinnati Reds, Marge Schott, whose description of two of the team's players as "million-dollar niggers" emerged in a lawsuit brought by a former executive who claimed he had been fired because he disapproved of Schott's racial slurs and her failure to hire minorities for front-office jobs. Challenged about her remarks, Schott denied abusing her players, but in a legal deposition she acknowledged she may have used terms such as "nigger," "Japs," and "money-grabbing Jews." "But if, and when, I've used them it was only kiddingly," Schott told reporters.[32] However, further evidence of her bigotry surfaced during a conference call with fellow baseball executives when Schott reportedly said: "I'd rather have a trained monkey working for me than a nigger."[33] When her remarks were leaked, the indecisive response from MLB exposed a reluctance to acknowledge evidence of institutional racism in the sport. The press played its part by presenting Schott not so much as a malignant presence in baseball but as an eccentric, almost comical, outlier: only the second woman owner in history, a *grande dame* of "rough-hewn charm," as the New York Times described her, who took her dogs to the ballgame and allowed them to soil the field, who was a collector of stuffed animals and Nazi memorabilia and who admitted to having little knowledge of the sport itself.[34] The initial response of fellow owners was muted, reflecting a reluctance to intervene in a case which they believed merely demonstrated Schott's idiosyncrasies and personal failings. It took until February for MLB's Executive Council, and then only after pressure from Jackson, to act: they found Schott guilty of using "offensive and unacceptable

---

[32] Quoted in Ira Berkow, "Marge Schott: Baseball's Big Red Headache," *New York Times*, November 29, 1992.

[33] Quoted in Murray Chass, "Ex-A's Employee Cites Schott Racial Remarks," *New York Times*, November 26, 1992.

[34] Chass, "Ex-A's Employee Cites Schott Racial Remarks."

language." But the punishment was lenient: Schott was fined twenty-five thousand dollars, suspended from day-to-day operations for a year, forbidden to sit in her usual field-level seat in Riverfront Stadium, and ordered to complete multicultural awareness training. However, she was not forced to divest herself of her ownership interest: she could still attend games and make major policy decisions. Hank Aaron, one of only a handful of African Americans in leadership roles in baseball, was fiercely critical: "It sends out a message—that we are still living in a captivity world where Blacks are treated no better than twenty or thirty years ago....It's a country club."[35] In a comment by the editorial board headlined "Winking at Baseball's Racism," the *New York Times* now adopted a more critical tone: the sanctions on Schott were "feeble," falling "far short of the declaration of racial justice the nation deserves to hear." Racism in baseball went far deeper than Schott, the paper asserted: "The Marge Schott affair is yet another reminder of how far baseball's cramped reality lags behind its self-promotional puffery."[36] In an opinion piece for the *Los Angeles Times*, the scholar Neal Gabler framed the Schott affair as an apostasy—a threat to the legitimacy of baseball's idealized American values; of heroes who "ascend directly from the playing field to the Heavens"; and of its celebration of American identity and spirit. "Can the faith of a believer survive these troubled times?" Gabler asked. "Marge Schott and the others will have to answer for that. They will have to answer for the destruction of the Church of Baseball."[37] The deployment of civil religious metaphor—baseball as "The Church," the fans following a faith, the summoning of notions of collective memory of an idealized past, the lament for an imagined purity, and the sense of impending loss of a defining symbol of American virtue—all foreshadowed the outpouring of cynicism toward baseball's stakeholders which would be a feature of the players strike two years later.

Meanwhile, with attention focused on Schott's incendiary language another aspect of baseball's pervasive racism exposed by the case—MLB's poor record of employing minorities in front-office, executive, and leadership positions—was largely ignored. Only one member of Schott's forty-

---

[35] Quoted in Marty Noble, "Ban: Schott Out For a Year, Aaron Hammers Judgment," *Newsday*, February 4, 1993.
[36] New York Times Editorial Board, "Winking at Baseball's Racism," *New York Times*, February 5, 1993.
[37] Neal Gabler, "A Time of Mourning for the Church of Baseball," *Los Angeles Times*, December 6, 1992.

five front-office staff was Black, and none were Hispanic. This glaring lack of diversity, which was mirrored in many other major league franchises, received far less media attention than Schott's punishment for her racist diatribes. It was a collective lapse noted by one writer with the *New York Times*, Claire Smith, an African American baseball reporter who had broken into the White, male-dominated world of sports journalism. Smith suggested the owners had "applied a Band-Aid to their most recently exposed racial sore and ignored all the others."[38] Schott's own admission, that she had no specific plans to hire more racial minorities ("I don't think that's fair," she told ABC.), also played second fiddle in press coverage, overshadowed by her insistence that she herself had been the victim of a witch hunt because she was a woman.[39]

While many failed to follow up on the employment injustices which lurked behind the more obvious headline-grabbing aspects of the Schott affair, Jackson did not. On January 12, 1993, eight days before Clinton's inauguration, Jackson announced he would organize a boycott of MLB by fans and players unless all teams committed themselves to affirmative action programs for the forthcoming season—and fully aware of the symbolism of what he was about to do, he devised a way in which to draw the incoming president into the controversy. The focus of his protest would be the presidential pitch, traditionally thrown on Opening Day of the new baseball season. By constructing Opening Day as the potential flashpoint, with race as the contentious issue, Jackson was challenging one of the tenets of American civil religion—the national pastime as a tool of social cohesion.

By 1993, the ritual of the president throwing baseball's Opening Day pitch had accumulated more than eighty years of precedent. With the exception of Jimmy Carter, every occupant of the White House since William Howard Taft in 1910 had performed it at least once during their term in office. For seven decades the brief ceremony involved the president tossing a ball onto the field from the stands, but in 1984, Ronald Reagan, broke with tradition to take to the diamond for his pitch. In 1989, his successor, George H. W. Bush went further, becoming the first president to attempt a throw the full distance from the pitcher's mound. It was now

---

[38] Claire Smith, "Just Another Swing and Miss," *New York Times*, February 5, 1993.

[39] Associated Press, "Schott Says She's Victim of 'Witch Hunt', Blames Media," *Colorado Springs Gazette Telegraph*, February 12, 1993.

a more overtly masculine performance—with the president donning the uniforms of players, and the competence of the throw (distance, power, and direction) becoming a media proxy for presidential manhood. It also took on a civil religious dimension: it underscored the role of President as First Fan, living out the dream of millions of baseball followers by pitching on the sacred field of play. This was the symbolic expression of commitment to the national pastime, due to be embraced by a rookie president, which Jackson threatened to disrupt.

The vehicle for Jackson's campaign was the Rainbow Commission for Fairness in Athletics, established in December 1992 as an offshoot of the Rainbow Coalition in the wake of Schott's racist outburst. As well as demanding Schott be "removed and rehabilitated" for her "grave injury to our society and baseball," Jackson orchestrated a series of well-publicized statements and meetings with owners, in which he pointed out that less than four percent of professional baseball's executive decision-makers and less than eight percent of front-office employees were Black.[40] MLB disputed the figures, but Jackson was undeterred. His case, he argued, had an undeniable moral imperative: minorities were due a bigger share of the White-dominated eighty billion dollar American sports industry in all its facets, whether it was ownership, front-office roles, or jobs in the support industries, broadcasting, and the media: "We say that forty-six years after Jackie Robinson, it's time for a change," Jackson told the winter meeting of baseball owners.[41] He outlined his plan for an Opening Day boycott at the turnstiles unless every MLB team introduced an affirmative action program. Furthermore, he threatened to raise the issue with Congress and lobby public hearings in cities in which baseball clubs were seeking municipal support for stadium development. Jackson called it community resistance: "I look up and down the list, and I see zero, zero, zero when it comes to key management positions. Those zeros do not refer to our intelligence, but to institutionalized racism that has locked us out."[42] And if change was not forthcoming, he would demand that Clinton support the boycotts and protests by refusing to throw out the Opening Day pitch on April 5.

---

[40] Danny Robbins, "Jackson Outlines Boycott: Baseball," *Los Angeles Times*, January 13, 1993.

[41] Quoted in Rabun, "Jackson Threatens Baseball Boycott."

[42] Quoted in William C. Rhoden, "Jackson Is Setting Focus on Sport," *New York Times*, January 13, 1993.

In the post-Schott climate, Jackson's campaign gathered momentum: the managing partner of the Texas Rangers and future president, George W. Bush, was sympathetic: "I think we need to tell Jesse 'hey here is what we are doing in baseball, but it's not enough. How can you help us?'"[43] In Los Angeles, at the symbolic setting of a Martin Luther King Day speech, Jackson invoked the language of civil rights to urge Clinton not to cross any Opening Day picket line. "Challenge baseball, challenge Schott to do justice," Jackson said, in remarks directed at the President-elect just four days before his inauguration.[44]

A few weeks later, a two-day symposium in Washington convened by the Rainbow Commission was attended by several MLB owners, the NFL Commissioner, prominent athletes, and representatives from the Justice Department, the Equal Employment Opportunity Commission (EEOC), and the Civil Rights Commission (CRC). Jerry Reinsdorf, the Chicago White Sox owner, admitted that Schott was an embarrassment but insisted MLB teams were on the same side as Jackson: "We want to talk and discuss and arrive at a place where there is fairness and dignity in baseball."[45] Jackson, however, wanted more specificity: he called for individual employment goals, targets, and timetables. To some it looked like a demand for quotas—the most controversial aspect of affirmative action which had been rejected by Clinton in 1992. An infuriated reader wrote to a Pennsylvania newspaper complaining of what he called Jackson's hypocrisy: "They tell us we need to live in a color-blind society....Then they turn around and threaten to boycott Opening Day games unless the baseball establishment creates a plan to hire a certain number of African Americans, Hispanics, and women."[46] Baseball was clearly embroiled in the debate on race which was raging around affirmative action and quotas. But accusations of hypocrisy against Jackson in this case were difficult to justify. His Rainbow Coalition had long advocated race-conscious measures which sought to ensure minority groups got their 'fair share,' in contrast to the color-blind policies adopted from the rhetoric of sixties civil rights

---

[43] Quoted in Danny Robbins, "Jackson Outlines Boycott."

[44] Quoted in Amy Wallace, "Jackson Renews Call for Boycott of Baseball," *Los Angeles Times*, January 17, 1993.

[45] Quoted in Leonard Shapiro, "Jackson Again Asks Baseball For a Plan," *Washington Post*, February 27, 1993.

[46] Letter from Joseph J. Sedler, "A Hypocritical Focus on Race," *Morning Call*, January 24, 1993.

activism, which were increasingly embraced by conservatives opposed to preference programs. While Jackson was clear that he was talking about affirmative action, he insisted he was not talking about quotas: "The only quota we are aware of," he wrote in a comment for the *New York Times*, "is baseball's quota of zero in virtually every power position."[47] Jackson added to the pressure by raising the prospect of public hearings into baseball's employment practices on Capitol Hill.[48] The Chairman of the CRC, Arthur Fletcher, said he was sympathetic to the idea.[49]

Jackson's campaign also brought increased scrutiny of individual clubs, exposing a deep-seated complacency on issues of race. Joe Molloy, the General Partner of the Yankees, insisted his team was "very oriented" to hiring minorities but confessed he did not know precise numbers because the club operated over two separate sites in New York and Florida.[50] At the end of March, MLB responded to Jackson's initiative with a multipoint plan which it claimed would help it become "the premier equal opportunity employer in America": minority candidates would be included in consideration for jobs "within a reasonable time frame"; clubs would aim for appropriate minority representation on their boards; they would try to use more minority-owned contractors and insist that all stadium vendors be equal opportunity employers; there would be new efforts to attract minority fans; multicultural awareness training would be introduced "unless clearly unnecessary"; and there would be increased community and charitable activity. Jackson dismissed the plan for its lack of detail, its conditionality, and its failure to propose a team-by-team plan of affirmative action. Baseball, he said, had failed to recognize the nature and size of the problem. With seven days until Opening Day, he insisted he had no alternative but to lead a campaign of direct action.[51]

---

[47] Jesse Jackson and Richard Lapchick, "Equality in Baseball Is Still Somewhere Over the Rainbow," *New York Times*, April 4, 1993.

[48] Leonard Shapiro, "Jackson Again Asks Baseball For a Plan." Washington Post, February 27, 1993.

[49] "Jackson Convenes Commission to Discuss Fairness in Sport," *Jet*, March 22, 1993.

[50] Claire Smith, "No Prejudice Within the Pinstripes, Say Yankees," *New York Times*, February 26, 1993.

[51] Ross Newhan, "Baseball Approves Minority Initiatives," *Los Angeles Times*, March 30, 1993; Jerry Bembry, "'Take Me Out to the Ole' Ballgame.' A Strike-out for Blacks?" *Crisis* 100, no. 4 (1993), 12–14.

Although Jackson maintained the MLB owners were the primary target of his protests, the White House knew the focus would inevitably be on the President's scheduled appearance in Baltimore for the first Orioles game of the season. At a press conference four days before Opening Day, Jackson had taken aim not only at MLB but also at the President by contrasting Clinton's criticism of Sister Souljah to his silence on Marge Schott: "It's the President's decision whether he chooses to focus on Sister Souljah or Sister Schott."[52] Jackson demanded a "clear unequivocal commitment to affirmative action" from the President to end institutional racism in baseball and warned that he would encounter a picket outside the stadium, where fans would be leafletted about unjust hiring practices. However, on the same day as Jackson's press conference, Clinton's spokesperson, George Stephanopoulos, confirmed the President's participation in the Opening Day ceremonies. Although Stephanopoulos acknowledged that Jackson had raised serious questions and conceded that baseball had not made enough progress in addressing them, Clinton was still going to the ballgame.[53]

On the morning of Opening Day, Jackson made one final appeal, sending Clinton a letter urging him to use the opportunity provided by his presence in Baltimore to "say something meaningful about equal opportunity, racial justice, and gender equality."[54] The eight-page letter was supplemented by a bulky appendix listing the race and gender of every member of the Baltimore Orioles organization, the media corps that covered their games and the coaching, administrative and media staff of four of the country's most prominent college basketball programs, to illustrate that this was more than just a baseball problem. Jackson attached forty-five pages of tables containing hundreds of names with "White" next to virtually every non-playing position—clear evidence, he said, of institutional racism. The astonishing scarcity of Black umpires elicited a particularly painful lament: "between 1947 and 1993, 46 years, fair people would have thought that MLB could have found, trained, and given experience to more than two black umpires." Unsurprisingly, the hometown team was

---

[52] Quoted in Robert McG. Thomas Jr., "Camden Yards Opener: Rainbow Protest Leaflets," *New York Times*, April 1, 1993.

[53] Mark Asher, "Camden Pickets Planned," *Washington Post*, April 1, 1993.

[54] Letter, Reverend Jesse Jackson to Bill Clinton, April 5, 1993, OA/ID 23338, Folder: HU012, Subject Files, Records Management, *Clinton Presidential Records*.

the focus of Jackson's ire: he pointed out that in a majority-Black city, whose taxpayers had subsidized the building of the spectacular Camden Yards ballpark, only eight percent of those on the payroll were minorities and the figure for concessionaires and vendors was less than two percent. It was the same in the front-office, on the board, in the broadcast booth, and in the press box. Jackson also crafted a personal message for Clinton, recalling the President's commitment to addressing the "race flaw that continues to plague our nation and mar its character" and reminding him that it was one of the reasons he had chosen a life in public service. Jackson continued: "now that we have the laws on the books; and now that we have affirmative action as a matter of law, these laws deserve and require enforcement by the President." Jackson called for a reinvigorated CRC and EEOC and a beefing up of civil rights enforcement by the Justice Department. At the end of the letter he drew the threads of his argument together by combining two emblems of America's civil religion—the memory of Martin Luther King and the President's ceremonial pitch. Pointing out that Opening Day fell just a day after the twenty-fifth anniversary of King's assassination, Jackson called on Clinton to send a signal to "all Americans about where this administration stands and how it intends to deal with the monitoring and enforcement of civil rights and affirmative action laws." Jackson had framed Clinton's obligations toward progress in racial equality in explicitly civil religious terms by invoking the martyr of the civil rights movement and focusing on the opportunity provided by the sacred setting of Opening Day. "Seize this moment," Jackson urged.

As it was, Clinton seized the moment with a performance that played-on his role as First Fan, while also alluding to the racial justice issues at the core of Jackson's campaign. He did so through crafted symbolic actions and choreographed photo-opportunities. At the White House briefing that morning, Stephanopoulos said the President had read Jackson's letter. Nevertheless, as he had already indicated, the President would be going to the game—and Stephanopoulos revealed that he would be travelling from Washington by suburban train, a new president, on his first Opening Day, heading to the ballpark using public transportation, mixing with ordinary fans.[55] During the hour-long journey from Washington, a baseball-jacketed and cap-wearing Clinton mingled with other passengers

---

[55] William J. Clinton, "Press Briefing by George Stephanopolous, April 5, 1993," *American Presidency Project*.

and the press. He praised Jackson for raising what he said was a "legitimate issue" and described the picket he expected to encounter outside the stadium as "a good thing."[56] When he arrived in Baltimore, Clinton was greeted by about three hundred pickets (several hundred short of Jackson's prediction), who had gathered around two entrances at Camden Yards chanting, "don't believe the hype, baseball ain't white." Before the demonstration, in a performance rooted in the civil rights religious tradition, the protestors linked hands in prayer, asking for God's blessing for their picketing, "because we know there's some unfairness going on, we know there's injustice going on and we are here in your stead."[57] Then they raised placards, including some that read, "Forty-Six Years After Jackie Robinson. Twenty-Five Years After Martin Luther King and One Year After Rodney. Now We Have Marge Schott."[58] Others displayed the words, "I Am a Man," the slogan of the striking refuse workers who King had been supporting when he was shot dead in Memphis in April 1968.[59] "We have not forgotten the dream. We are going to keep the dream alive," one demonstrator told a television crew, referencing King's most famous speech.[60] Indeed the significance of the King anniversary and its role in national memory was seeded throughout the demonstrations, with the protestors articulating the jeremiad of African American civil religion that King himself had voiced—past promises had only led to current failure, but eventually they would be fulfilled.[61]

---

[56] William J. Clinton, "Exchange With Reporters En Route to Opening Day Baseball Game in Baltimore, Maryland, April 5, 1993," *American Presidency Project*.

[57] Black History Cinema, "Jesse Jackson On Injustice in Baseball, 1993," *YouTube*.

[58] Bembry, "'Take Me Out to the Ole' Ballgame.' A Strike-out for Blacks?"

[59] Alex Dominguez, "Sports News," *Associated Press*, April 6, 1993.

[60] Black History Cinema, "Jesse Jackson on Injustice in Baseball, 1993."

[61] Jana Weiss, "Remember, Celebrate and Forget? Martin Luther King Day and the Pitfalls of Civil Religion," *Journal of American Studies* 53, no. 2 (2019): 428–48; 434.

As he made his way into Camden Yards, Clinton made no direct attempt to engage with Jackson, nor any of the pickets. Instead, pictures captured the President entering the stadium carrying a baseball glove, cap, and ball and flanked by two prominent Black politicians, the CBC Chairman, Kweisi Mfume, and the Mayor of Baltimore, Kurt Schmoke. It was a performance that projected Clinton's fusion of the two threads of civil religion at work that afternoon: the mitt and ball represented the tradition of Opening Day, while simultaneously the President appeared alongside respected African American politicians, establishment figures in the battle for civil rights, who were prepared to honor the national pastime even as some of their brothers and sisters in the civil rights movement were declaring it a vehicle for institutional racism.

While Clinton used that image to symbolically absolve himself of criticism, it also demonstrated his skill at exploiting the tension facing Black political leaders—the pull between their institutional roles as elected politicians and their community roles as race leaders. Certainly Jackson felt betrayed by Mfume, who had initially supported the protest but had now "violated us for a photo opportunity" with the President.[62] Beyond a broad acceptance that Jackson had a valid case which needed addressing, Clinton offered no full-throated support that day for the application of affirmative action in baseball or any specific encouragement on employment practices. As for the ceremonial pitch, Clinton played out the ritual to the full, with the attendant trappings of masculine performance. Dressed in an Orioles warm-up jacket and cap (the uniform of an organization that Jackson had described as "racist and sexist" in his letter only that morning), the President threw from just in front of the pitcher's mound to shorten the distance to the catcher, so reducing the chances that he would suffer the unfortunate pitching fate of his underperforming predecessor.[63] "Seeming to float through the air as soft and large as a down-filled pillow, the ball described a gentle arc to land safely, if unexcitingly, in the glove of the Orioles catcher," reported the *New York Times*.[64]

---

[62] Jackson's spokesman quoted in Courtland Milloy, "Choosing a Game Plan for Protest," *Washington Post*, April 7, 1993.

[63] John E. Yang, "Pardon His Pitch: Bush Strikes Dirt," *Washington Post*, April 7, 1992.

[64] Michael Kelly, "Baseball; Arkansas Rookie Makes Debut," *New York Times*, April 6, 1993.

Later Clinton made his way to the broadcast booth to lend his hand at television commentary—a talent which he would hone with considerable skill during his presidency. Clinton's on-air demonstration of his knowledge of the batting lineups certainly impressed Bill Nicholls, a White House reporter with *USA Today*. "Clinton appeared to know what he was talking about," he enthused.[65] Thus, in his dual civil religious roles, Clinton had excelled: as the head of America's civil religion he had performed the Opening Day ritual with the apparent endorsement of moderate African American leaders, successfully disentangling himself from Jackson's criticisms and pointing to an inclusive, cohesive, and multicultural civil religion; and as First Fan he had fulfilled his sacred duty of performance on behalf of the ordinary fan.

Five hundred miles to the west of Baltimore, however, the performance, symbolism and ritual of baseball's Opening Day carried a different meaning. At the Cincinnati Reds first game of the season Marge Schott watched from her exiled position in the stands, banned from her usual seat at field-level by the MLB sanctions. But far from being an outcast, Reds fans had anointed Schott an Opening Day martyr, decorating her empty seat with black ribbons and a floral wreath. Mocking the baseball establishment that had punished her, Schott recorded a video message which was played on the giant scoreboard before the game, telling fans, "I love you. I miss you," prompting cheers from the crowd.[66] In Baltimore, Clinton had been keen to proffer a multicultural civil religious narrative for baseball, but it was clearly in conflict with the civil religion of the national pastime on display in Cincinnati, which was, culturally and institutionally, as White as ever.

While Jackson's campaign and his assertions of institutional racism generated significant media attention on Opening Day, once the season was up-and-running, press interest dwindled. With the presidential pitch now dispatched, there was little leverage with which Jackson could continue to use baseball to draw the White House into the debate, and the fans who attended games, the vast majority of whom were White, appeared to be indifferent to the issues he had raised. Midway through the season, Jackson returned to Baltimore, organizing a demonstration at the

---

[65] Bill Nichols, "Clinton Enjoys Day in The Sun," *USA Today*, April 6, 1993.
[66] Associated Press, "Bittersweet Opening Day for Schott," *New York Times*, April 6, 1993.

All-Star Game attended by Gore, to renew his demands for the application of affirmative action in MLB. The *Associated Press* reported that protestors carrying placards reading, "Jackie Robinson Didn't Give Up, Neither Will We," drew only slight curiosity from fans.[67] This time the owners countered Jackson's leafletting by distributing literature of their own, claiming that there had been an increase in minority hiring over recent years and blaming any sluggishness in the pace of change on low employee turnover. William Giles of the Philadelphia Phillies summarized the owners' case: baseball had been responsible for significant racial progress over the past few years, and while there were still issues, there were mitigating circumstances for a continued racial imbalance; the problems around minority hiring were complex and little understood.[68] This encapsulated the complacency surrounding efforts to end baseball's racial discrimination in employment. Robinson's breakthrough had set the country along a virtuous path, claimed MLB, but from here progress would inevitably be slow given the practical challenges. For the time being, the institutional mass of the national pastime—its ownership, its leadership, its fanbase, its mediation in the press—would remain quintessentially White.

Despite his symbolic actions, Clinton's reluctance to wholeheartedly back Jackson's cause reflected his cautious approach to affirmative action in the early part of his presidency. The Clinton-Gore campaign had sidestepped the issue in 1992, but in the first two years of the administration a slew of headline-grabbing cases alleging that Whites were victims of reverse discrimination fueled a conservative backlash against affirmative action, and especially quotas. Stephanopoulos called the sort of cases that drove this sentiment "killer anecdotes" that were virtually impossible to counter in the heat of political debate.[69] Affirmative action was already an electoral wedge issue, and the potential for it to damage Clinton's political agenda rose sharply after the Democratic defeat in the 1994 midterms. With his approval ratings low and the Republicans eager to dismantle the administration's civil rights policies, Clinton's reelection looked vulnerable to the mood of so-called 'Angry White Men,' a demographic identified by political scientists as one which was disoriented by globalization and the assignment of new employment rights to Blacks and minorities. For these

---

[67] Associated Press, "Baseball; Jackson Leads Demonstration," *New York Times*, July 13, 1993.

[68] John Roll, "Sports News," *Associated Press*, July 14, 1993.

[69] Stephanopoulos, *All Too Human*, 361.

middle-income White men, work had become a place where they were viewed by politically-correct America as "the illegitimate beneficiaries of a past patriarchal white order," and they had revolted.[70] Faced with this electorally damaging 'White anger,' Clinton's instinct, according to the historian of affirmative action, Terry Anderson, was to shy away from controversy by isolating himself from policy commitments over affirmative action and instead to address the individual conservative *causes célèbres* in narrowly legal terms.[71] At the same time, he focused on promoting diversity—the more abstract and less contested concept of harnessing the potential of all citizens, minorities and women, as a moral duty and a public good. Clinton's low-key response to Jackson's demands for prescriptive affirmative action in baseball clearly fit into the same framework: a commitment to a diverse society and a multicultural narrative combined with some notable symbolic actions—but an unwillingness to confront head-on professional baseball's institutional whiteness. Instead he responded to questions by saying he was encouraged by the example of those who had successfully made the breakthrough, such as Don Baylor, who became the fourth Black manager of an team when he was appointed by the Colorado Rockies in 1993.[72] It was the essence of Clinton's approach to race in his first term, viewed this time through the aperture of the national pastime: Major League Baseball, Marge Schott, Don Baylor, Sister Souljah, Angry White Men, and Jesse Jackson all set the boundaries, which Clinton negotiated with a skillful civil religious performance, promising social cohesion by carrying a baseball glove in one hand and with a moderate African American politician on each arm.

Clinton's Multicultural Double Play

The summer of 1995—the season of Cal Ripken's creeping assault on Lou Gehrig's record and Congressional wrangling over welfare reform—saw Clinton finally attempt to seize the initiative on affirmative action,

---

[70] Thomas B. Edsall, "Revolt of the Discontented," *Washington Post*, November 11, 1994.

[71] Anderson, *The Pursuit of Fairnes*, 226–27.

[72] Clinton, "Exchange With Reporters En Route to Opening Day Baseball Game in Baltimore, Maryland, April 5, 1993."

although, to a degree, his hand was forced by the increasingly frenzied tone of the debate in the political and public arenas. The newly elected congressional Republican majority had launched a barrage of attacks on affirmative action threatening to repeal all federal programs. Clinton's prospective presidential opponents joined the fray, calculating that it was a wedge issue with which to batter the incumbent and his party: Senator Bob Dole declared "the race-counting game has gone too far."[73] The Democrats, meanwhile, divided on the issue, with two wings "flying in different directions," according to Stephanopoulos, whom Clinton had asked to carry out a review of all government affirmative action programs.[74]

In California, momentum was growing for a ban on affirmative action in public employment to be put to a state-wide vote in 1996, and elsewhere, legal challenges to affirmative action continued to make their way through the courts. In June, in a ruling that confirmed a judicial trend to limit the scope of affirmative action, the Supreme Court deemed preferential programs constitutional only if they were narrowly tailored to specific circumstances and could withstand a "strict scrutiny" test.[75] With the Stephanopoulos review near completion, Jackson demanded the President give a clear statement of support for affirmative action, just as he had done on the eve of the 1993 baseball season. "Review and renew," Jackson urged.[76]

On July 19, 1995, two-and-a-half years into his presidency, Clinton laid out a coherent and detailed defense of affirmative action anchored in what he said were essential moral, historical, and economic truths.[77] He did so at the National Archives in Washington, where America's canonical civil religious texts—the Constitution, the Declaration of Independence, and the Bill of Rights—were the physical backdrop for his speech. In the symbolic setting of the Rotunda for the Charters of Freedom, Clinton called the founding documents "the bedrocks of our common ground" and

---

[73] 104th Congress, 1st Session: Vol. 141, No. 48 — Daily Edition, "Affirmative Action." S3929. *Congressional Record Online.*

[74] Stephanopoulos, *All Too Human,* 361–65.

[75] US Supreme Court, "Adarand Constructors, Inc. v. Peña, 515 US 200 (1995)," *Justia.com.*

[76] Quoted in Valerie J. Macmillan, "Jackson Defends Affirmative Action," *Havard Crimson,* April 24, 1995.

[77] William J. Clinton, "Remarks on Affirmative Action at the National Archive and Records, July 19, 1995," *American Presidency Project.*

the nation's "crown jewels"; and invoking the legacies of slavery, segregation, and the civil rights movement, he argued that the task of ending discrimination was not over. This was a speech outlining Clinton's vision of a multicultural American civil religion. Even though his analysis remained embedded in the mantra of opportunity, responsibility and community, Clinton insisted there was a role for government in giving people the tools to overcome discrimination: "We need all hands on-deck, and some of those hands, need a helping hand."[78] Carolyn Curiel, the White House writer who drafted Clinton's words that day, recalls it as "a speech of conscience"; "after losing the midterms we had to appeal to peoples' sense of honor and dignity for all."[79] For the first time Clinton was ready to depart from his previous public caution by suggesting the solution to White perceptions of unfairness associated with affirmative action was to "mend it, don't end it," a phrase honed by Curiel to address the reservations of affirmative action's critics. Her thinking at the time was: "It's not perfect, we still have work to do, but this has to be our starting point." In practical terms affirmative action would stay, but Clinton promised new executive orders that would eliminate quotas and ensure that federal programs did not give preference to unqualified job applicants or operate any form of reverse discrimination.

While the timing had an element of political expediency, it also sprung from Clinton's sensitivity to racial inequality grounded in his Arkansas upbringing, where racism was a daily part of life, his experience of governing a poor southern state in the late-seventies and eighties, and a principled vision about what was the right course for America. His approach, according to Curiel, was informed by a sense of community and fairness that was imbued in him as a child: "he truly felt he had a home in the black community."[80] To Clinton, the logic of affirmative action was simple and inescapable: divisions within society were simply not in the national interest. It was a formulation he returned to in his 1996 campaign book, *Between Hope and History*, in which he wrote, "when we work together, America always wins."[81] In these terms, affirmative action was not a purely moral imperative but also the basis for exploiting the economic

---

[78] Clinton, "Remarks on Affirmative Action at the National Archive and Records, July 19, 1995."

[79] Curiel, interview by author.

[80] Curiel, interview by author.

[81] Clinton, *Between Hope and History*, 114.

opportunities of a global economy—it was "both spiritually and materially productive."[82]

Three months after his National Archives speech, Clinton united the civil religion of race and the civil religion of baseball to demonstrate the degree to which this fusion of morality and economic self-interest fit into his vision of a multicultural America. In his weekly radio address, delivered to welcome back the World Series after its cancellation the previous year, Clinton spoke of baseball's "simple virtues" helping to hold the country together.

> We can look at the green grass of the outfield, or feel the worn leather of an old glove, or watch a Latino shortstop scoop the ball to a Black second baseman, who then throws it to a White first baseman in a perfect double play, and say, yes, this sure is America. This is who we are.[83]

By combining nostalgic imaginations—the sentimentalized pastoral setting and the battered mitt passed across the generations—with the slickly-functioning, multicultural unit of infield players working in harness, Team America successfully executes a double play. The team wins. The American community wins. America wins.[84] Clinton would repeat this formulation at a White House ceremony for the 1997 World Series-winning Florida Marlins, who had a multiracial team and a largely Hispanic fan base. Clinton said the Marlins, many of whom were new immigrants, proved that people of different ethnic backgrounds could play together and win.[85] Just as it had been a hundred years earlier, baseball was a force for assimilation, a route to becoming a successful American.

Clinton had also executed his own double play. As the seasoned Clinton-watcher Joe Klein observed, he had given liberal Democrats affirmative action and New Democrats welfare reform, successfully negotiating

---

[82] Sullivan and Goldzwig, "Seven Lessons From President Clinton's Race Initiative, " in *Images, Scandal, and Communication Strategies of the Clinton Presidency*, ed. Denton and Holloway,

[83] Clinton, "The President's Radio Address: October 21, 1995."

[84] In an early draft, a Japanese pitcher was also included in the imagined double-play lineup: Draft of baseball radio address with notes, 10/20/97 10:00 A.M. OA/ID 10705, Folder: Baseball Radio Address, David Shipley, Speechwriting, *Clinton Presidential Records*.

[85] Clinton, "Remarks to the 1997 World Series Champion Florida Marlins, February 17, 1998."

the party's ideological divisions, and protecting his own electoral fortunes.[86] In both policy areas he had articulated a vision of American virtue and multiculturalism through the rhetoric of baseball, allowing the national pastime, with all its contentious cultural baggage, to be successfully embedded into his own narrative of national renewal. The events of 1997, including the celebration of Robinson's fiftieth anniversary, would give him the opportunity to try to do so once more.

Baseball and 'One America'

"The one thing everyone knew," observed Michael Waldman, reflecting on his role as a White House speechwriter for the *President's Initiative on Race*, "was that the President was at his most eloquent, most persuasive, most morally commanding when it came to race."[87] In the months immediately following his 1996 reelection, Clinton was to use his rhetorical skills and passion more than at any other time during his administration to address what he called "the divide of race" that had been "America's constant curse."[88] The intent to address racial division in his second term had been apparent during the campaign, when Clinton spoke of coming together "black and white alike to smother the flames of hatred and kindle the flames of faith and hope."[89] And certainly there were those within the White House, such as speechwriter David Shipley, who felt a substantive presidential intervention on race was long overdue. In the wake of the acquittal of O. J. Simpson, Shipley had circulated a memo (deploying a familiar baseball metaphor) which urged Clinton to speak out at what he felt was a "defining moment" for the administration: "If he does not step-up to the plate, it will be seen as an abdication of leadership. If he does step-up to the plate but does nothing but fall back on the dated elixir of 'opportunity and responsibility' then the effort will fall flat, and we will have missed a terrific opportunity to show leadership."[90]

---

[86] Klein, *The Natural*, 150.

[87] Waldman, *POTUS Speaks*, 167.

[88] William J. Clinton, "Inaugural Address, January 20, 1997," *American Presidency Project*.

[89] Clinton, *Between Hope and History*, 141.

[90] Memorandum, David Shipley, OA/ID 10985, Folder: Quotes, Jokes, Stories [2], Terry Edmonds, Speechwriting, *Clinton Presidential Records*.

With reelection secured, Clinton did indeed respond in substance. Beyond a defense of affirmative action, a much broader landscape of racial justice appeared to be on Clinton's mind. In his Second Inaugural Address, he acknowledged the forces of "prejudice and contempt" which still plagued America, calling on them to be replaced "with the generous spirit of a people who feel at home with one another."[91] Addressing Congress two weeks later, Clinton developed the theme, insisting that diversity was America's greatest strength and that a national mission should be to build a common future as "One America," that would give all its citizens an opportunity to achieve their own greatness.[92] Why Clinton chose this moment for his rhetorical pivot toward addressing the race issue is a matter of debate: some suggest Clinton's stirring comments about healing racial divisions had tested well in private polling; with widespread public acceptance of multicultural rhetoric, there were now fewer political risks.[93] Furthermore, the Los Angeles riots had receded in the public consciousness—they had become a distant symbol of the failed Bush presidency. Even O. J. Simpson's acquittal had not led to the social unrest or the White backlash that so many had predicted. Others point to a genuinely-held idealistic vision for a multicultural America. Sidney Blumenthal, a presidential advisor, notes how the notion of inclusion was at the root of Clinton's idea of the country: "The private President was even more adamant about this theme than the public one."[94] Even those who suspected that political instinct rather than idealism was the driving force accepted that Clinton cared deeply about the issue and that it was possible to deploy both idealism and political self-interest to positive effect.

However multifaceted his rationale, Clinton's "One America" rhetoric located him in the ideological space under the broad canopy of "soft multiculturalism"—a formulation which sought to celebrate diversity at the same time as promoting a set of common American ideals to which citizens should aspire. Among the proponents of this approach was Gordon Wood, one of a network of historians and intellectuals whose views

---

[91] Clinton, "Inaugural Address, January 20, 1997."

[92] William J. Clinton, "Address Before a Joint Session of Congress on the State of the Union, February 4, 1997," *American Presidency Project.*

[93] Claire Jean Kim, "Clinton's Race Initiative: Recasting the American Dilemma," *Polity* 33, no. 2 (2000): 175–97; 191.

[94] Blumenthal, *The Clinton Wars,* 278.

Clinton sought ahead of big speeches.[95] In November 1994, in an article for *New Republic*, Wood lamented the rise of identity politics and the growing influence of ethnocentricity among educationalists critical of the Eurocentricity of American mainstream culture. For Wood, this "hard multiculturalism" was breaking the nation into antagonistic and irreconcilable fragments. What was preferable, Wood argued, was a "soft multiculturalism," where distinctive ethnicity was celebrated within the context of an assumed process of assimilation. In this way an ethnic identity and an American identity could be concurrently constructed.[96]

Wood was contributing to intellectual debates about multiculturalism upon which Clinton was well-briefed: in 1991 the historian, Arthur Schlesinger Jr., a frequent Clinton correspondent and White House guest, argued in *The Disuniting of America*, that the notion of a unifying American identity was threatened by a multiethnic dogma which had replaced assimilation with fragmentation, and integration with separatism. The heterogeneity of the United States, asserted JFK's former special advisor, made "the quest for unifying ideals and a common culture all the more urgent."[97] Another influential historian of the nineties, David Hollinger, saw the embrace of a fluid cosmopolitanism as a solution to these tensions, but nevertheless defended the notion of a national culture as "an adhesive," enabling diverse Americans to see themselves as sufficiently "in it together" to act on problems that are genuinely common.[98] In December 1996, Sheldon Hackney, the historian whom Clinton had appointed to the chairmanship of the National Endowment for the Humanities, wrote to the President about the need for a more inclusive society "with as little tribalism as possible." The American Dream, he argued, was not just about economic opportunity: "It is also, and perhaps more importantly about

---

[95] Memorandum, Ricki Seidman to Don Baer, Bill Galston, April 20, 1994. OA/ID 10138, Folder: Scholars Meeting, Don Baer, Communications, *Clinton Presidential Records*.
[96] Wood, "Truth in History," in *The Purpose of the Past*, 142–43.
[97] Schlesinger, *The Disuniting of America*, 21–24.
[98] Hollinger, *Postethnic America*, 14–15.

belonging [his emphasis]."[99] Amid these overlapping perspectives, a common thread emerged—the desire to identify shared cultural bonds where it was perceived that ethnicity was contributing to societal fragmentation. So it is not surprising that the national pastime would reemerge as a cohesive force, especially in this particular year when the inherent institutional whiteness of baseball could be offset in the public arena by the myth of Jackie Robinson, enabling the game's symbolic status to carry at least a measure of multicultural legitimacy.

In the early months of 1997, the mythologized version of Robinson's contribution to the American civil rights narrative which would feature so strongly in that year's cultural output was already gathering momentum. On February 13, a week after Clinton delivered his "One America" speech to Congress, the comic actor Bill Cosby led a thirteen-minute tribute to Robinson at the *ESPY* awards in New York, the sporting equivalent of the Oscars.[100] Cosby was an appropriate choice as host, not just because he was arguably the country's most prominent African American comedian. Like Robinson, he was hugely popular with both White and Black audiences: his hit series, *The Cosby Show*, appeared to celebrate universal American values and to challenge racial stereotypes by presenting a successful Black family, the Huxtables, in a prosperous socioeconomic setting. White media commentators were eager to shower Cosby, and his comforting picture of upwardly mobile African American life, with praise for breaking down racial divisions. But just as there were those who asserted that Robinson's contribution to racial equality should be viewed in the context of baseball's lingering racial inequality, there was a similarly alternative reading of *The Cosby Show*—that it concealed a complacency toward the racial injustice and institutional racism that existed outside the cozy confines of the Huxtable household.

Such readings of the racial landscape were reflected in the *ESPY* ceremony, where the multiple honoring of elite African American athletes and the presentation of a special award to an infirm Mohammed Ali by

---

[99] Letter, Sheldon Hackney to Bill Clinton, December 18, 1996, Folder: 012, NLWJC [Elena] Kagan, Ideas-Other, Domestic Policy Council, *Clinton Presidential Records*.

[100] ESPN, "1997 ESPY Awards," *YouTube*.

the veteran Oscar-winning actor Sidney Poitier, for "fighting for what was right" and standing up for racial pride in an "age of discrimination," carried the implicit message that such battles were a thing of the past. Clinton made his own contribution to the evening, recording a video tribute to Robinson in which he said it was impossible to imagine America without a hero who had taught that the divisions of race "don't just keep us apart, they hold us back."[101] Clinton's brief eulogy was followed by a film about Robinson's career interspersed with comments from former players and civil rights leaders, among them Jackson. Then, in a moment which resembled an evangelical revival meeting, four male sports stars—three Black and one White—were invited onto the stage, each picked-out by a single spotlight to give personal witness to the influence of Jackie Robinson on their lives. The segment was rounded off with a brief speech by Robinson's widow, Rachel, who called on everyone to "rededicate themselves to the struggle for equal opportunity."

Clinton made further contributions to the expanding canon of Robinson celebratory content with an interview for a television documentary which aired in late February in which he said Robinson was an inspiration to "break down those barriers wherever we find them—in our institutions, our businesses, and in our hearts."[102] But Clinton's main contribution came two months later on April 15, when MLB celebrated the Robinson fiftieth anniversary with a ceremony halfway through a game at New York's Shea Stadium between the Mets and the Los Angeles Dodgers, the inheritors of Robinson's Brooklyn franchise. Terry Edmonds, the first African American speechwriter to be appointed to the White House staff, was assigned to compose Clinton's remarks. Among those whose input was sought was the legal historian Paul Finkelman, who laid out in an email to White House speechwriters, how he believed Robinson's integration should be framed in terms of the affirmative action debate.

---

[101] Transcript, "Videotaped Remarks by the President in Tribute to Jackie Robinson at ESPN Award Ceremony," OA/ID 10988, Folder: Jackie Robinson [1], Terry Edmonds, Speechwriting, *Clinton Presidential Records*.

[102] Transcript, "Videotaped Remarks by the President in Tribute to Jackie Robinson for ESPN Documentary."

> [The] integration of baseball made teams better because it increased the talent pool....In that sense it was an issue of economic entrepreneurship. All that great talent was out there for the taking. And it made baseball a better game. That is the affirmative action argument. Overcome your doubts...and you tap into a huge supply of good labor (workers, hitters, fielders, etc.) that is not being utilized well.[103]

In this way the Robinson metaphor could be deployed to energize an argument that Clinton had already been making in defense of affirmative action: alongside moral and social considerations, there was an equally compelling economic case.

If the celebration at Shea Stadium on April 15 was intended to convey the emotional weight and imagery which had made Cal Ripken's lap of glory around Camden Yards such an intense occasion almost two years earlier, then it did not fully live up to expectations. As in Baltimore, the game was temporarily halted after five innings, only this time the interruption was not led by a spontaneous outburst from the fans, but a carefully orchestrated ceremony, again broadcast live on cable television, in which Clinton was at the center of the official tributes. However, in the absence of a symbolic moment of achievement or record breaking, the atmosphere was subdued, lacking the fervor of Ripken's big night. And unlike Camden Yards, Shea Stadium was not full, despite the presence of fourteen thousand children who had been given free tickets. Both celebrations were sacred, but this occasion was reserved rather than ardent in its expression of civil religion. The *New York Times* observed that the fans were "uncharacteristically well-mannered," talking in earnest tones and walking to the stadium "with a kind of ritual patience as though they were about to witness a ceremony rather than a ballgame."[104] The components of the occasion were indeed ritualistic: Robinson's grandson, Jesse Robinson Simms, threw out the first pitch, acknowledging the generational transmission at the heart of baseball's myth. Clinton, as was now routine for his presidency, visited the commentary booth for his First Fan performance,

---

[103] Emails, hard copies with notes, Prof. Paul Finkelman to Jordan Tamagni, April 7th, 1997, and April 8th, 1997, OA/ID Number 10988, Folder: Jackie Robinson [1], Terry Edmonds, Speechwriting, *Clinton Presidential Records*.

[104] Bruce Weber, "Celebration Stirs Up Memories in Stands," *New York Times*, April 16, 1997.

reminiscing with ESPN's Chris Berman (the same announcer who had described Ripken's sacred night) about watching Robinson on television as a child, supplementing his personal memories with reflections on Robinson's place in the national collective memory.

> Clinton: It made a very real difference to the way people thought about race. I think that's more important than the fact that he was a great baseball player....This was a huge deal. Most Americans now can't imagine how big a deal it was. This was the year before President Truman signed the order to integrate the army. This was a huge deal.
>
> Berman: It was really fifteen years plus before marches in the sixties. I mean it was so far ahead of its time.
>
> Clinton: Almost a decade before Rosa Parks. And it was baseball, so it was a statement about America. Anything you said about baseball in the forties and the early fifties, it was a statement about America.
>
> Berman: By the way, Olerud is at first base, with a single, one out. But Bernard Gilkey is up.
>
> Clinton: He's doing better in New York, isn't he?...He's hitting well again and it's good. It's been a good move for him.[105]

This was the essence of Clinton's civil religious performance: seamlessly and instantly switching between two civil religious personas—the pastor, preaching on Rosa Parks and Jackie Robinson, sainted heroes of American multicultural civil religion, and, moments later, the First Fan effortlessly and expertly exchanging details about the game unfolding in front of him. Clinton's capacity to embrace both roles so convincingly was one source of his compelling civil religious presentation.

The more formal elements of the celebration came during the fifth-inning pause. Standing close to the dugouts, the African American singer Tevin Campbell performed the Broadway hit, *The Impossible Dream*, as the giant video screen projected images of Robinson's career and civil rights activism, while the director of the live television coverage picked out shots of Black Mets players. President Clinton, Rachel Robinson, and Bud Selig, MLB's acting commissioner, then emerged from the stands and walked to home plate for the speeches. Selig was up first, declaring

---

[105] William J. Clinton, "Interview With Chris Berman of ESPN in Queens, April 15, 1997," *American Presidency Project*.

integration baseball's "proudest moment," before announcing that Robinson's uniform number, forty-two, would be permanently retired from the game.[106] Clinton hailed Robinson for "changing the face of America forever" and recalling the themes of his One America speech, he said, "America is a better, stronger, richer country when we all work together and give everyone a chance." Equality had been reached on the playing field—the next step was to equalize the boardrooms of baseball and corporate America.[107] The President also made a point of honoring the golfer Tiger Woods, Robinson's "brilliant successor," who, with his victory in the Masters in Augusta the previous weekend, had become the first minority winner of a golf major, although Woods had turned-down an invitation to be Clinton's guest at Shea Stadium that evening. Rachel Robinson echoed Clinton's sentiments, expressing the hope that this "heady environment of unity" would result in a more equitable society. As soon as the game resumed, after the thirty-five-minute interruption, most of the crowd, including the President, drifted away, their work done. In unifying the past, present, and future they had paid homage to a saint of the national pastime and embraced a future of supposed racial justice.

The press, meanwhile, used the occasion to pick apart the meaning of these symbolic events. Two years earlier, media commentators had positively embraced the Cal Ripken parable of hard work and reliability, but this time the Jackie Robinson parable of race and integration exposed more contested mediations. While the man himself was lionized and the historical nature of the moment acknowledged, the sense that MLB was more content to wallow in a self-congratulatory haze than to address current race issues in the sport and wider society was a common theme, echoing many of the arguments of Jackson's Opening Day campaign of 1993. "Everything about Jackie Robinson's life has two sharp edges," observed Thomas Boswell: "one that cuts away any illusions about how bad the past really was. And the other that jabs its point into our conscience in the present."[108] Broader perspectives were everywhere. On anniversary day, a *Washington Post* front-page story highlighted the *de facto* segregation of

---

[106] ESPN, "Dignitaries Remember Jackie's First Game, April 15, 1997," *YouTube*.

[107] Clinton, "Remarks in Queens Celebrating the 50th Anniversary of Jackie Robinson's Integration of Major League Baseball, April 15, 1997."

[108] Thomas Boswell, "By Bringing Us Together, He Made All the Difference in the World," *Washington Post*, April 16, 1997.

parts of Brooklyn where Robinson spent his playing career. The newspaper described tensions between African Americans and Hasidic Jewish residents, the segregation of schools, playgrounds, and restaurants, and the reality that baseball itself was "an alien concept" for most inner-city youths.[109] Other commentators again focused on the persistent lack of minorities in MLB's upper echelons. The *Atlanta Journal-Constitution* called the Robinson celebrations "an absolute joke" in suggesting that baseball had repented its sins.[110] A *Kansas City Star* comment piece labelled the slow progress in minority hiring "insulting," accusing Selig of muttering the "same drivel the white majority has uttered for years," so projecting baseball's racial hypocrisy into society in general.[111]

After months in which the White House agonized over how to take forward Clinton's desire to address the challenges of diversity and race relations, *One America in the 21st Century – the President's Initiative on Race* was launched by Clinton on June 14, 1997, a few weeks after the Robinson anniversary, in a speech in California—the state where the politics of education had been cleaved by conflict over affirmative action for much of his presidency. Addressing students at UC San Diego, the President declared his intention to open a national dialogue to educate Americans about racial divisions. Clinton said he himself would play a leading role in the conversations through speeches and televised town hall meetings: he would be advised throughout by a seven-member board of scholars and public figures which would convene meetings, conduct investigations, and propose concrete policy actions. "Can we be one America, respecting, even celebrating our differences, but embracing even more what we have in common?" Clinton asked. Not surprisingly, some of the dilemmas aired by Clinton echoed the discourse surrounding baseball's integration: "Remember…in spite of the persistence of prejudice, we are more integrated than ever," Clinton declared.[112] Waldman expressed this presidential

---

[109] Marc Fisher, "50 Years Later, Jackie's Mark Fades for Many," *Washington Post*, April 15, 1997.

[110] Terrence Moore, "Robinson's Tribute Underlines Baseball's Foot Dragging," *Atlanta Journal and Constitution*, April 20, 1997.

[111] L. E. Neal, "Instead of Retiring a Number, Raise One: Hire Minorities," *Kansas City Star*, April 20, 1997.

[112] William J. Clinton, "Commencement Address at the University of California San Diego in La Jolla, California, June 14, 1997," *American Presidency Project*.

ambivalence another way—when it came to racial justice, was America's glass half full or half empty?[113] It was the same unanswered question that chipped away at the national pastime's claim to virtue.

As was commonplace in the Clinton Administration, the presidential race initiative which finally emerged was the result of an unwieldy process of outreach, lobbying, and internal meetings. Ideas came from all sides—political allies and aides, scholars, and civil rights activists. The White House had been swamped with proposals and policy papers by various interest groups—the problem was more how to construct anything solid out of the deluge. One early proposal which caught Clinton's attention suggested using the Robinson anniversary as the launchpad for a *President's Council on Racial Reconciliation* modelled on President Kennedy's *Council on Physical Fitness* which had aimed to energize a sedentary nation in the 1960s. The proposal's sponsor was Clinton's friend, William Winter, the former Governor of Mississippi, who wrote to him about the need to "put the expression of racist attitudes and behavior outside the realm of permissible conduct in our society," attaching a fifteen-page briefing note on how such an ambition might be achieved.[114] The author of the accompanying note was Michael Wenger, an official with the Appalachian Regional Commission and a passionate baseball fan whose childhood hero had been Jackie Robinson. In his paper, Wenger proposed putting the Robinson anniversary at the center of an elaborate outreach program with the overriding conceit that all citizens were members of "The American Team."[115] He believed baseball was in a unique position as a visible national institution which "illustrated every day the significance of racial reconciliation."[116] In his document, Wenger suggested promoting the shared values of The American Team in television commercials during baseball games, establishing partnerships between major league clubs and community organizations, producing American Team billboards and baseball cards and

---

[113] Waldman, *POTUS Speaks*, 170.

[114] Letter, William F. Winter to Bill Clinton, on Proposal for Council on Racial Reconciliation, January 24, 1997, Folder 12, NLWJC – Kagan, Race Commission [3], Domestic Policy Council, *Clinton Presidential Records*.

[115] Paper by Michael R. Wenger on Proposal for "President's Council on Racial Reconciliation," January 3, 1997, Folder 12, NLWJC – Kagan Race Commission [3], Domestic Policy Council, *Clinton Presidential Records*.

[116] Michael Wenger, Interview by Author, Washington, DC, September 13, 2019.

launching a national essay-writing competition on "what it means to be in the America Team" with trips to the World Series and the White House as prizes. Clinton added a handwritten comment to Winter's correspondence: "I'll think about this. It might work." The Wenger document was widely circulated and became the basis for a series of meetings in the West Wing during March 1997 attended by Winter, Wenger, senior White House Officials, academics and, on one occasion, the President and Vice President. Although baseball had been integral to the original proposal, according to Wenger two other issues dominated discussions: whether the initiative should focus solely on race or should encompass other oppressions; and whether it should spend time and resources researching attitudes toward race or be more action-oriented to achieve quantifiable outcomes. By mid-April, Robinson's fiftieth anniversary had come and gone with the shape of the President's initiative still largely undecided.

With the passing of the anniversary, the direction of the conversation veered away from Robinson and baseball to encompass the broader intersection of race and sports, with baseball as just one, albeit important, element to be exploited in televised events involving the President. "Sports has a long history of successes and failures with integration and can be used as a microcosm for the rest of the country," wrote the White House official charged in early 1998 with planning one of the race initiative's televised presidential town hall meetings: "I believe the President can facilitate a dialogue using sports as the starting point and then relating discussions to society at large."[117] It was an attractive proposition because a sports-focused televised event had the potential to reach a demographic who were unlikely to otherwise engage directly with the race initiative. With ESPN as the proposed broadcast partner, their predominantly White, male, middle-class viewership made an enticing target audience. "They may not feel they have anything to learn from or contribute to the race discussion and this is our opportunity to connect with them through a vehicle they would be open to and tuned-into," suggested a briefing note written for Clinton.[118]

---

[117] Memorandum, Jon P. Jennings, Town Hall Working Group, February 12, 1998, OA/ID 40140, Folder: ESPN Town Hall Info, Meetings, President's Advisory Board on Race, *Clinton Presidential Records*.

[118] Briefing Note, "A Conversation with the President, Race and Sports: Running in Place?" April 13, 1998, OA/ID 40140, Folder: ESPN Town Hall Info, Meetings, President's Advisory Board on Race, *Clinton Presidential Records*.

Some in the civil rights community expressed concern that an initiative which had hitherto concentrated on heavyweight social issues such as poverty, unemployment, and education, would be trivialized by a focus on sports—and there was also a fear that racial stereotypes of the African American athlete would be perpetuated.[119] But with the previous televised presidential events criticized for being dull, the allure of a potentially new audience and the likely publicity impact of contributions by major sports stars made the ESPN collaboration appealing to the White House. To ease apprehensions, the Executive Director of the One America initiative, Judith Winston, struck a reassuring tone in a note to members of the President's Advisory Board, pointing out that the event would specifically address issues relating to sport which had broader applications to society at large. It would, she argued, "allow us to look at sports as a 'laboratory' for race relations—where it has been successful, and what are the shortcomings?"[120] And although a comprehensive Robinson tie-in had now been dropped in favor of this broader approach, the White House nevertheless circulated a series of talking points for use in media appearances which highlighted Clinton's participation in the fiftieth anniversary commemoration as an example of his commitment to racial healing and unity.[121] Once again the debate about the direction in which American society was heading at the end of the twentieth century was being framed by the Clinton White House through the metaphor of sport.

A Conversation with the President: Sports and Race: Running in Place? was broadcast live from Houston on ESPN at 7:00 p.m. on April 14, 1998, the eve of the fifty-first anniversary of Jackie Robinson's integration of the major leagues. Scheduled for an hour-and-a-half, the broadcast overran by

---

[119] Memorandum, Judith Winston, "Assessment of Proposals for Next Presidential Conversation on Race," February 24, 1998, OA/ID 40140, Folder: ESPN Town Hall Notes, Meetings, President's Advisory Board on Race, *Clinton Presidential Records.*

[120] Briefing Note, Judith Winston to the Advisory Board of the President's Initiative on Race, April 10, 1998, OA/ID 40135, Folder: ESPN Background Information, Meetings, Transcripts and Background; President's Advisory Board on Race, *Clinton Presidential Records.*

[121] Talking Points, Michael Waldman, OA/ID 14439, Folder: Talking Points, Michael Waldman, Office of Speechwriting, *Clinton Presidential Records.*

fifteen minutes to squeeze in extra questions from the floor. Alongside the President, a panel of ten, including athletes, former athletes, broadcasters, coaches, and executives, took questions from the moderator, Jim Ley, and members of the audience of about eight hundred. The MLB Commissioner's Office declined to provide a panelist, so a perspective on baseball was offered by Joe Morgan, the African American former second baseman for the Cincinnati Reds, turned TV analyst, and John Moores, the White owner of the San Diego Padres, who accepted a personal invitation to appear. Clinton opened proceedings, identifying sport as "a metaphor for what Americans are as a people," which had provided opportunities for all races but faced continuing challenges. In language drawn from his speeches on affirmative action, he spoke of the importance of "getting a fair chance" and "closing the opportunity gaps that have existed historically between the races"—an issue with larger implications for society as a whole.[122] Thereafter Clinton largely took a back seat as the discussion bounced around familiar issues: low levels of minority hiring to senior positions, the closed business networks and power structures which prevented Black ownership of sports franchises, the media stereotyping of Black athletes, the dwindling number of African American players in professional baseball, and the lack of sports facilities for inner-city youth.[123] The next day's *Washington Post* judged there had been few initiatives on offer.[124] Instead the most revealing moment of the evening came during a discussion prompted by Morgan about the failure of baseball to recruit minority youngsters from inner cities. When Moores was asked directly whether he had any African Americans on his scouting staff, he replied lamely that he did not know. It seemed that in the five years since Jackson had so publicly drawn a new president into the discourse on the institutional whiteness of the national pastime, and exactly a year after Jackie

---

[122] William J. Clinton, "Remarks at the ESPN Townhall Meeting on Race in Houston, April 14, 1998," *American Presidency Project*.

[123] Transcript attached to Email, hard copy, Elizabeth R. Newman, April 15, 1998, 08:22:37, 4-4-19 ESPN Town Hall, full transcript, OA/ID 40140, Folder: ESPN Town Hall Notes, Meetings, President's Advisory Board on Race, *Clinton Presidential Records*.

[124] Leonard Shapiro, "Race, Sports: Too Many Unanswered Questions," *Washington Post*, April 16, 1998.

Robinson's contribution to the fight for racial equality had been so enthusiastically embraced with apparent virtuous intent, nothing had changed.

Jackie Robinson: A Collective Memory Frozen in Time

The racial fault line that ran through baseball's history—and which resurfaced during the Clinton years at the intersection of the national pastime, civil religion, and the presidency—was, as the documentary maker Ken Burns had observed in his landmark 1994 television series, one of the sport's mythic contradictions. By defining baseball's integration as a precursor to the civil rights movement, the Robinson myth spoke powerfully to both Black and White audiences of a faith in American civil religion. But the tension in baseball between its sentimentalized, quasi-religious portrayal as a vessel for enduring American democratic values and its contrasting record, first of racial exclusion and then of pitifully slow progress toward racial equality, exposed a more complex narrative. Indeed, in the 1970s Robinson wrote of baseball "posing as a sacred institution dedicated to the public good" while systematically denying Blacks opportunities "with a ruthlessness that many big businesses would never think of displaying."[125] More than twenty years later, by participating in the civil religious performances around baseball, the President himself was drawn into the baseball-race discourse and the ensuing debates that it triggered on broader race issues. The presidential involvement was not entirely of Clinton's own choosing. Jesse Jackson had made a direct link between baseball's institutional racism and affirmative action—perhaps the most divisive race issue of the decade—in a challenge which inevitably demanded some sort of presidential response because Jackson associated the national pastime with symbolic articulations of American civil religious values. Just as Martin Luther King had framed his call for racial justice in the values espoused by the "magnificent words of the Constitution and Declaration of Independence," while condemning the "manacles of segregation and the chains of discrimination," so Jackson, himself a former baseball minor league prospect, spoke in reverential terms of "America's pastime" and "the great game we all love," while in the next breath condemning its institutional

---

[125] Robinson, *I Never Had It Made*, 261–62.

racism and sexism.[126] By constructing Opening Day as the flashpoint for his affirmative action campaign, Jackson pitted one symbol of civil religion—the presidential Opening Day Pitch—against another—the legacy of Jackie Robinson. Clinton's delicate negotiation of this event reflected his own political and ideological priorities at the time: his desire to engage with sacred rituals and symbols, of which the presidential first pitch was an example, to project a 'common community'; his eagerness to include the traditional Black leadership in these rituals; and his reluctance early in his presidency to embroil himself in the heated affirmative action debate or to be seen in any way to be reestablishing a submissive relationship with Jackson. Clinton successfully negotiated a potentially perilous encounter without political damage, in fact with a sense of his symbolic authority enhanced. Baseball, meanwhile, was spared the presidential pressure to deliver rapid and meaningful change.

Four years later the political sands had shifted. A reelected and emboldened president spoke with a new voice to articulate a "lifelong obsession" with racial justice.[127] In promising to "mend it, not end it," he had defined how he intended to defend affirmative action and was looking to build "One America" based on racial reconciliation and opportunity. In taking part in the ceremonies and performances marking the fiftieth anniversary of baseball's integration, Clinton believed he could fuse his declared aspiration for racial justice with the myth of Jackie Robinson: his legacy, said Clinton, should be "a grand slam society," in which everyone had a chance to work together and make a better life for their children.[128] Clinton was in search of sources of national cohesion, and baseball appeared to offer an example. The media embraced the anniversary, reminding the public of Robinson's early role in the civil rights struggle, thus bestowing on the celebrations a civil religious authenticity.

But this enriching narrative of integration once again provided a platform for a discussion of the continuing deficiencies in MLB's record on

---

[126] Letter, Jackson to Clinton, April 5, 1993; also, Martin Luther King Jr., "'I Have a Dream…': Speech by Rev. Martin Luther King at the 'March on Washington,'" *American Rhetoric*.

[127] William J. Clinton, "Remarks on the 40th Anniversary of the Desegregation of Central High School in Little Rock, Arkansas, September 25, 1997," *American Presidency Project*.

[128] Clinton, "Remarks in Queens Celebrating the 50th Anniversary of Jackie Robinson's Integration of Major League Baseball, April 15, 1997."

minority hiring—as it had in 1993—and one that linked it to broader issues of racial justice. Critics could point to Robinson's own words, written shortly before his death in 1972, in which he despaired of a country still plagued by racism where his African American brothers and sisters were "hungry, inadequately housed, insufficiently clothed, denied their dignity as they live in slums or barely exist on welfare," and justifiably ask what had changed?[129] Baseball as civil religion had been usefully appropriated by Clinton in the case of Ripken to mobilize America's White middle class in the welfare debate, but among Black Americans, the civil religion of baseball and the Robinson myth were problematic. By almost all measures, in 1997 baseball remained defiantly, culturally White. The numbers of African Americans on the rosters of major league clubs were in gradual decline, even if those of Hispanic and Asian heritage were on the increase.[130] The fans and the managers were overwhelmingly White, and in the long-term the proportion of White managers would grow; the majority owners and CEOs of major league franchises were all White. In 2003, Arte Moreno finally became the first minority owner in MLB when he purchased the Anaheim Angels, but it would not be until 2017 that an African American would reach the highest executive level when the former New York Yankee, Derek Jeter, became part-owner and CEO of the Miami Marlins. And this reflected networks in society as a whole—decades after supposed democratic equality had been achieved, the country was still scarred by racially defined economic inequality. In an observation reflecting the diminishing returns of some iconic historical narratives, the civil rights historian Jacquelyn Dowd Hall suggests that the collective memory of Martin Luther King was frozen in 1963: his endlessly reproduced and selectively quoted speeches had retained "their majesty but lost their political bite."[131] In the case of Robinson, something similar was at work—a collective memory frozen in 1947. There was a compelling majesty for all Americans in the grainy black-and-white television footage of a magnificent athlete stealing home; and there was emotional power in the retold stories of Robinson's stoicism in the face of racist taunts. But this emphasis

---

[129] Robinson, *I Never Had It Made*, 268–69.

[130] Mark Armour and Daniel R. Levitt, "Baseball Demographics, 1947–2016," *Society For American Baseball Research.*.

[131] Jacquelyn Dowd Hall, "The Long Civil Rights Movement and the Political Uses of the Past," *Journal of American History* 91, no. 4 (2005): 1233–63; 1234.

on myth and civil religious symbolism had obscured Robinson's critique of American society and his call for radical social change. Ultimately, the surge of Robinson-related civil religious output in 1997, which the President had embraced to his political advantage, only served to mask baseball and America's continuing racial divide. It was a tension that would become apparent again during the record-breaking drama of the following season's home run race.

Chapter Five

The Summer of '98
Presidential Scandal and the Home Run Race

Record Breaking News

On September 8, 1998, at 8:18 p.m. Central Daylight Time, Mark McGwire, the first baseman for the St. Louis Cardinals, hit his sixty-second home run of the season, breaking one of baseball's most sacred records and instantly propelling himself into American popular mythology.[1] More than forty-three million people, including the President of the United States, watched FOX's live television coverage as McGwire set a new mark for home runs in a single season to take a record once held by Babe Ruth, a figure with an unrivalled place in the American sporting imagination. In a sign of the significance of the moment, all the other major television networks interrupted their prime-time programming to pass on to viewers the breaking news from St. Louis. With one "mighty swing," the *Washington Post* reported the next morning, McGwire had "completed an amazing and wonderful journey into baseball history" finishing a mission that had "captivated a nation, revived a sport and constructed a legend."[2] In *Sports Illustrated*, Tom Verducci made a bold civil religious declaration: "America is a Baseball Nation again, and McGwire is its Head of State."[3]

In fact, for a man whose towering blasts had been likened by Verducci to some of the greatest manifestations of American scale—the Empire State Building, Hoover Dam, Mount Rushmore—McGwire's record-breaking hit was not a particularly mighty swing: staying airborne for only 341 feet, it was shorter than each of the sixty-one home runs McGwire had already hit that summer, barely carrying over the left field fence and

---

[1] FOX, "Mark MGwire's 62nd Home Run," *YouTube*.
[2] Richard Justice, "McGwire Surpasses Maris With 62nd Home Run," *Washington Post*, September 9, 1998.
[3] Tom Verducci, "Making His Mark," *Sports Illustrated*, September 14, 1998.

failing to reach any of the fifty thousand spectators who filled Busch Stadium, many equipped with mitts to snare the record-breaking ball and so claim the million-dollar bounty reportedly being offered by memorabilia dealers. Instead, the most valuable piece of cowhide that the game had ever known fell into a penned off area used to store batting equipment. Sprinting to get to the ball first was Tim Forneris, by day a computer programmer, by night a member of the Cardinals ground crew, whose job was to open the gate onto the field for visiting pitchers, and who had been patrolling the left field wall when the million-dollar missile fell from the sky. Scooping it up, he delivered it to the stadium security office where it was locked in a safe. There the precious object would rest until its authenticity could be verified by shining infrared light on invisible markings which had been imprinted, with the help of the US Treasury, on each ball pitched to McGwire that evening. A few hours later, McGwire would take a telephone call from an embattled President Clinton congratulating him on behalf of the American people. But for the time being, as he set off on his home run confirming journey around the bases, this was a personal triumph for McGwire which he wanted to share with Matt, his ten-year-old son.

Three days later, with the country and the media still agog from McGwire's achievement, Congress released onto the internet Kenneth Starr's report into the President's sexual relationship with Monica Lewinsky. In the full, 445-page document, the Office of Independent Counsel outlined eleven grounds for the President's impeachment, among them perjury, witness tampering, obstruction of justice, and abuse of power. It also described in clinical terms the ten sexual encounters at the White House between Clinton and Lewinsky between November 1995 and March 1997. Within hours of its release a vast swathe of the American public had a detailed knowledge of their president's sexual preferences. Within days, paperback books of the entire report were on sale, allowing all those not online to lap up every salacious detail. Some professed boredom with the latest twist in a scandal that had already dominated the news agenda for more than seven months: "Who wants to read hundreds of pages online? I'd rather check and see whether McGwire hit number 63," opined one contributor to the *Wall Street Journal*.[4] But the reality was a

---

[4] Bart Ziegler, Thomas E. Weber, and Michael W. Miller, "A Wildfire Transforms the Global Village," *Wall Street Journal*, September 14, 1998.

huge appetite for the details: twenty million read the report within forty-eight hours of its release.[5] Eleven days later, Clinton's videotaped grand jury evidence, in which he had been questioned about his affair with Lewinsky, was also released by Congress and immediately broadcast by all the major television and cable news networks. In the four-hour session, Clinton repeatedly parried questions about his sexual preferences, complaining that he was being subjected to indignities no previous president ever faced: "And during the whole of this time, I have tried as best I could to keep my mind on the job the American people gave me."[6] It was in this climate of political crisis, with television, newspapers, and the World Wide Web feasting on what the *Houston Chronicle* called a "Super Bowl of sordidness," that baseball once again exerted its cultural force as an emblem of American values.[7] "At a time in American life when we all would feel as if a law had been passed requiring us to look through some White House peephole at Bill Clinton and Monica Lewinsky in a charming little study off the Oval Office, baseball would feel as if it were saving not just the country, but the whole world," reflected the sportswriter Mike Lupica.[8]

This chapter explores how the cultural meaning of an iconic event in American sports—the 1998 home run battle between Mark McGwire and Sammy Sosa—became entangled with the political, constitutional, and moral crisis precipitated by the Clinton-Lewinsky sex scandal. It argues that a heroic baseball rivalry became a contested narrative—its meaning fought over between a president under siege, his opponents who sought his overthrow, and a media hungry for an uplifting story. All claimed that the American ideals represented in the summer-long duel between two baseball players pointed to the possibility of better things for a fractured society and a broken political culture. But each did so to support their own political or cultural interests: for Bill Clinton it was a matter of survival, tying his own personal redemption to the national redemption offered by the heroes of the national pastime; for his partisan opponents, the

---

[5] David Kravets, "Sept. 11, 1998: Starr Report Showcases Net's Speed," *Wired*, September 11, 2009.

[6] Office of Independent Council, Referral to the United States House of Representatives, Pursuant to Title 28, United States Code 595 c, Document Supplement A, Tab 16, 4353–628 (626), *govinfo.gov*.

[7] "The Editorials; Excerpts on Newspaper Judgments on Clinton," *New York Times*, August 19, 1998.

[8] Lupica, *Summer of '98*, 10.

ballplayers' apparent moral excellence could be weaponized against a sinful president; and for the media it offered an appealing and wholesome narrative for readers and viewers—a counterpoint to a summer of sleaze which they believed had witnessed the death throes of virtue in American public life.

Baseball's "World of Moral Sanity"

While the record-breaking ball hit by McGwire that night in St. Louis required the authentication of the US Treasury, the feat itself did not. The race for the record had captivated America for much of the summer; for months fans had been instructed on the home run's grip on the American psyche, a hero-hungry media offering it as an enduring symbol of a national myth. "The home run is America," declared Verducci, "appealing to its roots of rugged individualism and its fascination with grand scale." It was all the more totemic because McGwire was chasing a mark that had stood for thirty-seven years—a record immortalised by Babe Ruth and thought untouchable until Roger Maris took the Babe's crown in 1961. It was, wrote Verducci, a "godly" number.[9] The celebrity sports agent Tom Reich summarized the historical context in a page-one quote for the *New York Times*: "It's all tied up in Babe Ruth....McGwire reminds people of that Ruthian mythology."[10] Now he had surpassed both the Ruth and Maris marks, and watching his shot clear the fence, McGwire embarked on his victory trot around the bases to assure the legitimacy of the run. Momentarily distracted by the enormity of his achievement, the new record holder forgot to touch first base, only retracing his steps after a Cardinals coach pointed out his mistake. Not wishing to repeat the error McGwire purposefully planted his right foot as he passed second and third bases, slowing each time to accept the congratulations of the opposition fielders with a handshake or high five, his opponents just as keen to imprint their own presence on a transcendent moment. Above center field, the giant scoreboard flashed "The Legend of Mark McGwire Continues." At home plate the continuing Legend was greeted by his teammates and his son Matt, dressed like Dad in a Cardinals uniform. The image of a caring, sensitive father had been common to many of the glowing media profiles

---

[9] Verducci, "Making His Mark."
[10] Quoted in Murray Chass, "Ultimate Sports Goal Lures McGwire and Sosa Fans," *New York Times*, September 4, 1998.

written in anticipation of McGwire's achievement. Here he was, in his first act as the home run king, fulfilling that paternal prophecy—hoisting his son into the air, so cementing the notions of generational transmission that were the foundation of baseball's fabled virtues.

Among the throng of red-capped Cardinals surrounding McGwire, a single blue cap stood out: Sammy Sosa of the Chicago Cubs, McGwire's summer-long challenger for the home run crown, had jogged in from right field. For much of the season the two had dueled at distance, with each player progressing toward the record in separate ballparks. McGwire was the media's archetypical White, all-American hero: six-feet, five-inches, all muscle, dedicated father and son, from a family of five strapping boys from suburban Southern California—even his inevitable nickname, Big Mac, was an iconic emblem of American consumer culture. Sosa was a Black Hispanic immigrant from a humble family in the Dominican Republic, modest, devoted to his mother, always smiling, apparently grateful just to be part of the summer's plot. Tonight, thanks to a quirk of scheduling, the principal actors in the drama were sharing the same stage. Although stocky in build, Sosa was slight compared to McGwire, so it was the Cardinal who lifted the smaller player into the air—a White baseball player embracing his Black rival in a symbolic salute to racial equality in the national pastime, and by implication the country. Then each kissed the fingers on their right hand and tapped their hearts—a ritual initiated by Sosa earlier in the season and one he would reprise at the President's invitation a few months later, on the night of the State of the Union Address.

In this decisive act, the Cardinal had emerged victorious over the Cub, but both, in their daily displays of power, endeavour, good humor, and mutual respect, appeared to offer a commitment to traditional virtues in a new America, comfortable with its diversity. Their combined qualities represented two essential strands of the American myth: McGwire, the embodiment of the rugged individual; Sosa, the rags-to-riches immigrant exemplar of the American Dream. And it was through their record-breaking in baseball that these myths were being seeded in the national consciousness and propagated by a platoon of baseball-loving intellectuals. "The public's emotional involvement in this home run race encourages a kind of primitive solidarity among the population despite our diverse backgrounds," declared the sports historian Benjamin Radar in the *Christian Science Monitor*. "Our society has many forces that pull it apart. We don't have a king or a national church, but we do have a national sport. This is a tie that binds."[11]

This widely disseminated conviction in the moral excellence of the national pastime appeared even more compelling when set against the concurrent narrative of scandal engulfing the pinnacle of public life—amid what George Will called "the carpet-bombing cacophony of saturation journalism about people behaving badly."[12] Indeed, that morning, a letter published in the *New York Times* reflected a broader mood of resignation at the moral standards exhibited in the higher echelons of civic society: "We as a nation have been forced to reconcile the Presidency with the character of its tenant," lamented the correspondent.[13] In the stadium, Cardinals fans Ken and Sherry Irby, who had driven four hundred miles with their two children to be there, spoke to reporters about the direct link between the presidential scandal and baseball: "Good role models are few and far between for kids. The country's been kind of in the doldrums with the Lewinsky thing. We needed something to cheer."[14]

In the media, cheerleaders for the national pastime's moral superiority appeared everywhere. "Heroes in an Unheroic Time," shouted *USA Today's* front page, quoting Ken Burns. "The hyperbolic heavy breathing of the White House crisis won't cloud our memory of the great home run race. This is a time of joy, unalloyed joy in baseball."[15] For those seeking diversion from the seamy narrative emanating from the nation's capital, there was now clearly a choice. "Bill and Monica or Sammy and Mark?" asked the editorial board of the *New York Daily News*, suggesting the home run race was a "wholesome reminder" to politicians of "where we came from," where "the results are clear and final, where lawyers don't get to muck around with loopholes and where spin is what a curve does."[16] A

---

[11] Benjamin Radar, "A Ball and a Bat: Exclamation Point of Our Time," *Christian Science Monitor*, October 1, 1998.

[12] Will, *Bunts*, 338.

[13] George Hagen, "Would Repentance Help Clinton?," *New York Times*, September 8, 1998.

[14] Quoted in Ted Anthony, "An American Milestone—Baseball's Mark McGwire," *Associated Press*, September 9, 1998.

[15] Erik Brady, "Heroes in an Unheroic Time: Sosa, McGwire Stand Tall When the Nation Needs Them," *USA Today*, September 15, 1998.

[16] New York Daily News Editorial Board, "Bill & Monica or Sammy & Mark?," *New York Daily News*, September 26, 1998.

columnist in the same city's more august newspaper made a similar point: "It isn't Monica Lewinsky, it isn't Ken Starr and it isn't Bill Clinton—all bringing out the worst in us. It's just two nice guys bringing out the best in each other in a way that brings out the best in the country. Wouldn't it be nice if Democratic and Republican leaders treated the country with the same respect?"[17] The solution was offered by the students at Brigham Young University, whose daily newspaper asked: "How about a McGwire-Sosa ticket in 2000?"[18]

Back in the stadium, the FOX announcer, Jack Banner, described the scene to the millions of TV viewers, enthusing: "Folks, it couldn't have happened to a better man."[19] And, as if to prove his saintliness, McGwire plunged into the crowd to embrace the five Maris children whose late father's achievement he had just eclipsed. Whispering to them, he recalled how he had touched their father's bat earlier in the day—the one he had used to take the Babe's record—"I touched it with my heart," McGwire said.[20] A microphone connected to the stadium PA system was thrust into McGwire's hand, and looking mildly embarrassed, he thanked his family, his son, his teammates, Sosa, and his opponents—"Unbelievable. Class. Thank you St Louis"—before disappearing back into the darkness of the home dugout. After an eleven-minute interruption the game resumed.

When it finished after two hours and forty-seven minutes, McGwire returned to the field for fireworks, speeches, and presentations. Commissioner Selig led the ceremonies, calling it one of the sport's most historic nights: "There's something in the pursuit of records that only baseball can deliver," acknowledging the importance of the purity of the statistics in baseball's historic narrative.[21] McGwire, exhibiting the homespun modesty adored by the press, said he could barely remember his "sweet run" around the bases: "I was floating. I hope I didn't act foolish."[22] Meanwhile, the infrared beam had done its work. The ball was authenticated and

---

[17] Thomas Friedman, "Bringing Out the Best," *New York Times*, September 11, 1998.

[18] NewsNet Staff Writer, "In Our Opinion: McGwire/Sosa in 2000," *Daily Universe*, September 23, 1998.

[19] FOX, "Mark MGwire's 62nd Home Run," *YouTube*.

[20] Justice, "McGwire Surpasses Maris With 62nd Home Run."

[21] Quoted in Anthony, "An American Milestone."

[22] Quoted in Richard Justice, "A Mark for the Ages," *Washington Post*, September 9, 1998.

handed over to McGwire by its retriever, Tim Forneris. In the final public act of the evening, McGwire was presented with a '62 Corvette, and, cradling a specially created trophy adorned with a foot-long silver baseball bat, he was driven around Busch Stadium on a lap of honor. The following day the ball, McGwire's bat, his uniform, and his son's jersey would be transported with a police escort to the Hall of Fame in Cooperstown, the relics from a sacred day finding a resting place in the spiritual home of baseball's creation myth.

Eight hundred miles from St. Louis, in Washington, DC, Bill Clinton, like millions of Americans that evening, was following McGwire's exploits on television, though he had plenty of other claims for his attention. For the past week, amid global financial turmoil, Wall Street had taken a battering. The collapse of the Russian currency, the rouble, and contagion in the emerging markets of Asia and Latin America prompted *Fortune* magazine to warn, in its September 7 issue, that the world was facing its worst-ever financial crisis: "Never in the course of economic events—not even in the early years of the depression," the Nobel Prize-winning economist Paul Krugman wrote, "has so large a part of the world economy experienced so devastating a fall from grace."[23] Four days earlier, the Chairman of the Federal Reserve, Alan Greenspan, suggested this foreign-born crisis could soon be coming home: "It is just not credible that the United States can remain an oasis of prosperity unaffected by a world that is experiencing greatly increased stresses."[24] The Russian economy and Moscow's dysfunctional political structures were now threatening to undermine the five years of growth and low inflation enjoyed under Clinton. On a brief visit to Moscow the previous week, Clinton had urged his Kremlin counterpart, Boris Yeltsin, to accede to the conditions laid down by the International Monetary Fund for a bailout, which included fundamental reforms to tax and banking and an end to cronyism.

Returning to the White House on Saturday night after a stopover in Ireland, Clinton spent the rest of the long Labor Day weekend awaiting the markets' verdict on his international economic shuttle diplomacy. And when New York's traders returned from their late-summer break,

---

[23] Paul Krugman and Jeremy Khan, "Saving Asia," *Fortune,* September 7, 1998

[24] Alan Greenspan, "Remarks at the Haas Annual Business Faculty Research Dialogue, University of California Berkley September 4, 1998," *Federalreserve.gov.*

McGwire was not alone in rewriting the record books: the buyers were back in force. By the time the September 8 closing bell rang at the New York Stock Exchange—five hours before McGwire's million-dollar hit—the main market indexes had staged a spectacular rally, posting their best-ever one day gains. In a single session the Dow Jones Industrial Average added five percent to its value, wiping out all its losses of the previous week; the technology-based Nasdaq soared more than six percent. As Wall Street moved back into positive territory for the year, there was hope that the American economy could yet prove resilient in the face of the global buffeting. In Clinton's view it had always been "the economy, stupid," and he took comfort that the relative optimism of Wall Street would reflect well on his economic stewardship.

But even with the boost of a rebounding market, the President was still urgently in need of good news to shore up his authority, as the scandal which had dragged down his presidency throughout the summer appeared to be reaching its denouement. That afternoon, Clinton's lawyers had received a letter refusing them early sight of the OIC's report of its four-year investigation, led by Starr, into the President's financial dealings and private life.[25] The focus of the OIC's probe had been whether Clinton had lied about having sexual relations with a White House intern, Monica Lewinsky, in testimony in a sexual harassment civil case brought against him by Paula Jones, a former Arkansas state employee. Starr was convinced Clinton had lied under oath and obstructed justice to conceal his affair with Lewinsky, and in his report he laid out the evidence, testimony, and legal argument, which he considered constituted the grounds for the impeachment of the President. But he had no intention of handing the White House lawyers any public relations edge by letting them have a preview of his findings or his legal opinion before it was delivered to Congress. Starr's team informed the White House that the report would be sent directly to the House of Representatives the next day, September 9. Thereafter, members of the Republican-controlled House would decide what to do with it.

The related political outlook was just as gloomy for Clinton. Another letter in the *New York Times* that morning came from a professor of political science, Stanley Renshon, author of a book-length psychoanalysis of

---

[25] "Excerpts From Letters By Kendall and Starr," *New York Times*, September 9, 1998.

Clinton published in 1996.[26] He asked a simple question: "Can the President 'do contrition?'...Can he really appreciate the enormity of what he has done to us (and not just himself) and truly come to regret it?" On the basis of Clinton's performance three weeks earlier, Renshon was not optimistic about the answer.[27] In a televised statement on August 17, given immediately after his appearance before a grand jury, Clinton had at last publicly admitted to an "inappropriate relationship" with Lewinsky, after seven months of evasion and denial. In the four-and-a-half-minute address, Clinton initially expressed "deep regret" for misleading his wife and the country. But he also insisted his previous comments on the affair had been "legally accurate" and that he had never asked anyone to take any unlawful action. And halfway through any moderate hint of contrition disappeared altogether, as Clinton switched to an attack on Starr whom he accused of "hurting too many innocent people."[28] By also asserting that "even presidents have private lives," Clinton fueled the cynicism of critics—he had only confessed because he had been caught out by the forensic tests which had identified his semen on Lewinsky's blue dress.[29] Commentators were brutal about what they saw as a "non-apology apology." The *New York Times* used the words, "defiant," "unrepentant," and "bitter" in its page-one coverage. Michael Kelly in the *Washington Post* was scathing: "He made [it] quite clear he wasn't sorry, except, as all adolescents are, for getting caught."[30] Jonathan Alter of *Newsweek* said Clinton had "soiled his presidency"; ABC's Sam Donaldson accused him of "not coming clean."[31] As the constitutional scholar Akhil Reed Amar commented wryly: "He mouthed the words of contrition without really exhaling."[32] Judging by the polls, the public were equally unconvinced of the sincerity

---

[26] Renshon, *High Hopes*.

[27] Stanley Renshon, "Would Repentance Help Clinton?" *New York Times*, September 8, 1998.

[28] William J. Clinton, "Address to the Nation on Testimony Before the Independent Counsel's Grand Jury, August 17, 1998," *American Presidency Project*.

[29] OIC, *The Starr Report*, 17–18.

[30] Michael Kelly, "A Pathetic Speech and Untrue," *Washington Post*, August 19, 1998.

[31] Quoted in Howard Kurtz, "After the Speech, Instant Media Spin," *Washington Post*, August 18, 1998.

[32] Akhil Reed Amar, "Take Five: Why Clinton Should Consider a Sabbatical," *New Republic*, February 8, 1999.

of Clinton's remorse.[33] At the September 8 White House press briefing—the day of McGwire's record in St. Louis—journalists asked more than sixty questions about the affair and possible impeachment charges.[34]

Polls suggested the scandal had become increasingly important to the electorate as well, with moral and religious issues now among their top concerns.[35] With the Democratic Party facing midterm retribution for the President's lack of sexual self-control, Senator Joe Lieberman, chairman of the Democratic Leadership Council, condemned his "wrong and unacceptable" behavior and called for "some measure of public rebuke and accountability."[36] Other Democrats weighed-in: hours before McGwire's historic hit, Barbara Boxer, related to the Clinton family by marriage, called the President's actions "indefensible" and "immoral."[37] Fritz Hollings, the Democratic senator from South Carolina, declared, "we're fed up. The behaviour, the dishonesty of the President is unacceptable."[38] These were Democratic voices whose votes were needed if Clinton was to resist being forced from office.

But even as the legal and political problems associated with the threat of impeachment closed in on him, Clinton still had an important symbolic duty to perform in honoring a milestone in the national pastime. Ninety minutes after the ballgame, McGwire, who was still in the clubhouse, was told the White House was on the line. It was a moment, according to Richard Cohen of the *Washington Post*, when the fate of the President of the United States lay in the hands of a professional baseball player: "It says something about Bill Clinton's plight that had baseball's new home run king not taken the President's congratulatory phone call, Clinton would

---

[33] Busby, *Defending the American Presidency*, 202–3.

[34] William J. Clinton, "Press Briefing by Mike McCurry, September 8, 1998," *American Presidency Project*.

[35] Nancy Gibbs, "We, The Jury," *CNN.Com*, September 21, 1998.

[36] 105th Congress, 2nd Session: Vol. 144, No. 115 — Daily Edition, Senator Joe Lieberman, "The Ongoing Investigation of President Clinton," 59923–26, *Congressional Record Online*.

[37] 105th Congress, 2nd Session: Vol. 144, No. 117 — Daily Edition, Senator Barbara Boxer, "Private and Public Morality," 59950–51, *Congressional Record Online*.

[38] Quoted in CBS News Staff, "A Tough Tuesday for Clinton," *cbsnews.com*, September 8, 1998.

have been—in the word of the moment—toast," wrote Cohen.[39] McGwire's feat had placed him on a moral pedestal: he was an icon of American masculinity, a role model of integrity and modesty whose virtues were only magnified by the comparison with Clinton's perceived flaws. McGwire took the call and the two men spoke. The President said he had been watching at the White House: "It was really outstanding. America is really enjoying this," Clinton remarked, before also speaking to McGwire's son.[40] With these brief exchanges, baseball and the national political crisis of 1998 came together, and, not for the first time that summer, the sex scandal which accentuated the nation's partisan and cultural divisions was set against a sporting contest rich in the ritual and symbolism of the national pastime. It was this interface—of the impeachment crisis and the home run race—that, according to a contemporaneous commentary by the cultural critic Edward Said, reflected a public yearning for a compensatory process at a time of national trauma, an "attempt to see elsewhere in national life an alternative to Clinton's profanity and gracelessness."[41]

If some of the virtues of baseball's heroes espoused by the media—power, honesty, and masculinity—mirrored those celebrated during Cal Ripken Jr.'s historic streak three years earlier, this time the extraordinary circumstances of 1998 made the successful presidential appropriation of them a far more difficult proposition. Ever since the story of Clinton's affair with Lewinsky had first broken in mid-January, initially online in the *Drudge Report* and within days in the *Washington Post*, a discourse about personal morality and attitudes to extramarital sex became entangled with issues of public morality, behavior in high office, and legal questions about suborning perjury, making false statements, and obstructing

---

[39] Richard Cohen, "Two For The Record Books," *Washington Post*, September 10, 1998.

[40] The call is noted in William J. Clinton, *Public Papers of the Presidents of the United States; William J. Clinton 1998; Book II, July 1 to December 31, 1995* (Washington, DC: US Government Printing Office, 2002), 2226. However, Clinton's exact remarks are not recorded in any official document. It is McGwire's account of their brief conversation which was widely quoted in press reports. See Eisenbath, "For Mark McGwire, It Was the Culmination of a Season-Long Quest," in Peterson, *The St. Louis Baseball Reader*, 426.

[41] Said, "The President and the Baseball Player," *Cultural Critique*, 135.

justice.[42] "Clinton Accused of Urging Aid to Lie" was the headline above a page-one story in the *Washington Post* on January 21, which revealed that Starr's office had been investigating the President's relationship with Lewinsky.[43] Clinton's televised, finger-jabbing denial six days later that he "did not have sexual relations with that woman, Miss Lewinsky," defined the President's public position on the affair for the next seven months, but did nothing to stem the frenzy.[44] The First Lady went on national television to support her husband, complaining of a "vast right-wing conspiracy" against her family, just as some former Clinton allies spoke publicly about the possibility of impeachment.[45] The affair opened up a new front in ongoing cultural conflicts by resupplying the army of conservative critics already convinced of Clinton's moral depravity, while simultaneously summoning a legion of presidential defenders apparently outraged by what the Harvard law professor Alan Dershowitz characterized as "Sexual McCarthyism."[46] Reprising the themes of Gingrich's 1994 attacks on Clinton for being un-American, more than a hundred religious leaders signed a statement excoriating the President for creating moral confusion which they claimed threatened the foundations of civil society and the moral basis of the Constitution.[47] In the *Wall Street Journal*, Shelby Steele wrote of the corruption of the baby boomer generation, for whom personal responsibility had become separated from virtue, and which made it possible to have as President, a "much celebrated male feminist who also gropes and harasses women."[48] Christian conservatives expressed their outrage in jeremiad form, lamenting society's descent into decadence and suggesting the Clinton presidency was a form of divine punishment for a national moral

---

[42] Matt Drudge, "*Newsweek* Kills Story on White House Intern," *Drudge Report*, January 17, 1998.

[43] Susan Schmidt, Peter Baker, and Toni Locy, "Clinton Accused of Urging Aide to Lie," *Washington Post*, January 21, 1998.

[44] William J. Clinton, "Remarks on the After-School Child Care Initiative, January 26, 1998," *American Presidency Project*.

[45] Quoted in David Maraniss, "First Lady Launches Counterattack," *Washington Post*, January 28, 1998; Stephanopoulos, *All Too Human*, 434.

[46] Dershowitz, *Sexual McCarthyism*.

[47] "Declaration Concerning Religion, Ethics and the Crisis in the Clinton Presidency," in Gabriel Fackre, ed., *Judgment Day at the White House*, 1–3.

[48] Shelby Steele, "Baby-Boom Virtue," *Wall Street Journal*, September 25, 1998.

bankruptcy. "I cannot shake the thought that the widespread loss of outrage against this President's misconduct tells us something fundamentally important about our condition," wrote William Bennett, who had been Reagan's Education Secretary. "Our commitment to longstanding American ideals has been enervated. We desperately need to recover them and soon."[49] James Dobson, the founder of the Christian pressure group, *Focus On The Family*, noted that the greatest problem was not in the White House but "with the people of this land."[50]

For Clinton and his supporters, however, the problem was not the people but the partisan attempts to whip up a rage of moral indignation. Philip Roth, who was honored by Clinton in 1998 with the National Medal of Arts and Humanities, would set his next novel, *The Human Stain*, in that memorable summer when America was a country gorging itself on piety and the battle between two "home run gods," while in "Congress, in the press and on the networks, the righteous grandstanding creeps, crazy to blame, deplore and punish, were everywhere out moralizing to beat the band."[51] This was what the 'cultural warfare' identified in 1991 by the sociologist James Davison Hunter's actually looked like—battle lines of political and social hostility defined entirely by competing systems of moral understanding, with those on either side convinced that they represented fundamental American values.[52]

It was amid this contested cultural landscape that a narrative of baseball's home run gods as the exemplars of some kind of national moral revival began to emerge on multiple media platforms. "While the nation slogs through the Clinton scandal's scurrilous details," wrote Abraham McLaughlin in the *Christian Science Monitor*, "two middle-American cities [St. Louis and Chicago]—connected by the cornfields of the Heartland—have served up the saga of an immigrant and a dentist's son charging

---

[49] Bennett, *The Death of Outrage*, 129.
[50] Quoted in Laurie Goodstein, "Christian Coalition Laments Lack of Widespread Anger About Clinton's Behavior," *New York Times*, September 20, 1998.
[51] Roth, *The Human Stain*, 2–3.
[52] Hunter, *Culture Wars*, 42.

toward greatness with grace."[53] With attitudes toward the President's behavior accentuating America's cultural divide, two heroes of the national pastime now appeared to offer a framework of moral certainty which could still hold the country together. "They have brought the Golden Rule back to the United States of America," declared Mike Shannon, the Cardinals radio announcer: "They are pulling for one another."[54] In the five-dollar biographies of McGwire and Sosa which were rushed into the bookstores, baseball was now the primary source of national moral leadership: Sosa was a hero to be admired for his humility, his sportsmanship, and his humanity; McGwire was a role model for children.[55] "He showed how someone could withstand pressure, adversity and competition with skill and grace," gushed one pocket biography: "In his own way Mark challenged his fans to be strong moral citizens."[56] The point was picked up by the *Tampa Bay Times* columnist, Tad Bartimus. Beneath the headline, "Clinton, McGwire, Each Made Choices," Bartimus identified two Clinton priorities: "Don't get caught" and "If you do, lie about it." But in McGwire's moral universe the priorities were different: "Do your best" and "Share the credit and be grateful."[57] Rev. Richard John Neuhaus, who edited the conservative religious journal *First Things*, also emphasized the ethical framework of the home run race: "The world of Sosa and McGwire is a world of moral sanity.... There are rules, and everybody understands them."[58] *Grace, morality, humility, humanity*—through the language alone the home run race was effectively being sanctified.

One factor which propelled baseball's rediscovered virtues into the forefront of the national consciousness was the sheer scale of the media coverage devoted to the home run race, which even dwarfed that given to Ripken's record-breaking achievement. At the end of the year, when

---

[53] Abraham McLaughlin, "Sluggers' Saving Graces," *Christian Science Monitor*, September 20, 1998.

[54] Quoted in CBS News Staff, "62nd Ball Comes Back to McGwire," cbsnews.com, September 9, 1998.

[55] Guttman, *Sammy Sosa*, 144.

[56] Hall, *Mark McGwire*, 146–47.

[57] Ted Bartimus, "Clinton, McGwire, Each Made Choices," *Tampa Bay Times*, October 4, 1998.

[58] Quoted in McLaughlin, "Sluggers' Saving Graces."

Associated Press asked news executives to name the biggest stories of 1998, Clinton's scandal came first, but the McGwire-Sosa rivalry was a close runner-up. Editors clearly rated baseball as a more compelling narrative for their viewers and readers than any of the other major news events of the year, which included the international financial crisis, terror attacks on American embassies in Africa in which hundreds died, military action against multiple targets in the Middle East, and the first balanced federal budget for thirty years.[59] On many occasions, the baseball players shared page one with the latest on the scandal. Sometimes they eclipsed the President entirely, as McGwire himself noted in late August: "It's stunning when I'm beating Clinton to the front page," adding, "he probably likes it."[60] One survey found that McGwire's record-breaking home run was reported on the front page of ninety-eight percent of American newspapers. From small local publications to the newspapers of record of metropolitan America, the same impulse appeared to be at work: editors believed the home run race represented the best of America and matched the cultural preoccupations of their readers.[61] "It's like apple pie," McGwire remarked, drawing on the most familiar of cultural clichés, "that's why I think all Americans can relate to this sport."[62]

As Sosa and McGwire advanced on the record, television networks took the unusual step of rescheduling prime-time entertainment shows to make way for live broadcasts of baseball, maximizing the home run race's national reach. It was the culmination of weeks of near-saturation media coverage, which the cultural scholar Lisa Doris Alexander noted was of similar levels to a national election.[63] Every night Dan Rather, a veteran of many election night broadcasts, insisted that news of the latest at bats of McGwire and Sosa would always be the first item on his CBS *Evening News*, ahead of the day's developments in the presidential scandal, or,

---

[59] Associated Press, "Lists of the Top Stories of 1998," *AP News*, December 29, 1998.

[60] Quoted in Bernie Miklasz, "McGwire Conserves His Mental Strength Now That He's Home," *St. Louis Post-Dispatch*, August 26, 1998.

[61] Polumbaum, "News For the Culture," *Newspaper Research Journal*, 27–30.

[62] Quoted in Jack Curry, "Mark David McGwire; A Reluctant Home-Run Hitter, a Reluctant Hero," *New York Times*, September 9, 1998.

[63] Alexander, *When Baseball Isn't White, Straight and Male*, 13.

indeed, any other news story.[64] Rather reasoned that, in contrast to the heroic exploits of the home run rivals, sex stories about the President were "bad for the country."[65] It was a sentiment shared by the syndicated columnist Furman Bisher, who used the language of the ballpark to make his point: "There's no room on the front-page or the nightly news for a president with an 0–2 count against him. The home run takes precedence over philandering, and America is off chasing a new hero."[66]

And the cult of the baseball hero was just as pervasive on the internet, which offered fans new ways to follow the home run race at-bat-by-at-bat. Multiple websites reported record figures for baseball-related content, while a vote by users of AOL, the largest internet service provider at the time, named McGwire as its first "American of the Year" for "making the United States a better country" and "improving the quality of our lives." But even that salute from the online community could not escape association with the political crisis—the runner-up was Starr, while his prey, the President, ranked fourth.[67] The home run race and the presidential scandal were competing for space in this new, virtual public square.

It was the media's obsession with the contrasting rivalries at the center of the concurrent narratives of scandal and heroism which would make it awkward for Clinton to align himself successfully with baseball's heroes. In one drama, a flawed and compromised President was locked in conflict with Starr, the zealous prosecutor who appeared to be determined to secure Clinton's downfall whatever the cost to national life—a "mutual suicide" which left both men's reputation in tatters, according to the *New York Times*.[68] In the other, seemingly more virtuous drama, two sportsmen dueled—one Black, one White—proffering images of power, fair play, and

---

[64] Greg Bishop, "Souvenirs and Scars From '98 Home Run Chase," *New York Times*, July 5, 2009.

[65] Quoted in Howard Kurtz, "Public Disgusted With Frenzy Fed by Its Interest," *Washington Post*, February 12, 1998.

[66] Furman Bisher, "Mac Steps Up Just When We Need Him," *Atlanta Journal and Constitution*, September 10, 1998.

[67] AOL Press Release, "AOL Members Name Mark McGwire as the First Annual 'American of the Year,'" *Business Wire*, January 4, 1999.

[68] John Broder and Don Van Natta Jr., "Clinton And Starr, A Mutual Admonition Society," *New York Times*, September 20, 1998.

mutual respect in a contest rich in cultural symbolism. This contrast of the two narratives, which existed alongside their near-equivalent standing in the news hierarchy, was simultaneously and vividly on display—on magazine covers, in news coverage and commentary, and in the words of politicians. The McGwire-Sosa home run race was a "story about what America needs and ought to be," declared the Republican senator, John Ashcroft. "These two are opponents in most every way and in most every sense of the word. But my goodness they are not enemies."[69]

At the end of the year, the most widely read weekly news magazine, and its sports counterpart, published cover stories which illustrated the contrast. On the front of *Sports Illustrated*, the toga-clad, laurel-wreathed, muscle-rippling, "Sportsmen of the Year," McGwire and Sosa, stood side by side as Olympian gods, gazing toward a distant horizon of masculine virtue and baseball nirvana. McGwire and Sosa, according to *Sports Illustrated*, had given America a summer of "rivals embracing and gloves in the bleachers and adults turned into kids. A summer of Long Balls and Love." Furthermore, read the *Sports Illustrated* citation, "they went to such lengths to conduct the great home run race with dignity and sportsmanship, with a sense of joy and openness."[70] Seven days later, from the cover of *Time*, the somber artwork and shadowy faces of Clinton and Starr peered out at readers—the two men the ironic recipients of that magazine's "Men of the Year" award for "re-writing the book on crime and punishment, for putting prices on values we didn't want to rank, for fighting past all reason, a battle whose causalities will be counted for years." They were: "a faithless President and a fervent prosecutor, in a mortal embrace, lacking discretion, playing for keeps, both self-righteous, both condemned, Men of the Year."[71] In his 2019 memoir, Starr admitted it was tantamount to being awarded "Skunk of the Year."[72]

---

[69] 105th Congress, 2nd Session: Vol. 144, No. 118 — Daily Edition, Senator John Ashcroft, "Recognizing Mark McGwire of the St. Louis Cardinals for Breaking Historic Home Run Record," S10082, *Congressional Record Online*.

[70] Gary Smith, "Big Swingers Mark McGwire and Sammy Sosa Treated a Nation to a Home Run Race That Was as Refreshing As a Day at the Beach," *Sports Illustrated*, December 21, 1998.

[71] Nancy Gibbs, "Men of the Year," *Time*, December 28, 1998.

[72] Starr, *Contempt*, 296.

Elsewhere in the same issue of *Time*, McGwire was nominated "Hero of the Year," with the historian Daniel Okrent celebrating him and Sosa as "flawlessly scripted antagonists cast in the same play,...rapture vs. gravity, spontaneity vs. self-restraint, Latin brio vs. California cool." McGwire, wrote Okrent, "couldn't banish the stain of sleaze that leached through our public life, nor could he restore civility to our discourse," but "what balm he brought to a nation that seemed to spend the year flaying its flesh."[73] These were the two different characterizations of rivalry which steered a national conversation on morality in public life—one an enmity marked by fractious distrust driven by partisan hostility, the other a reconstruction of the virtues of the American Dream as demonstrated by the supposed purity of the national pastime.

With this uplifting tale of morality and virtue being shaped by the media, Clinton inserted himself into the narrative of the home run race. Seizing the opportunity to associate his own journey of personal redemption with that of the two baseball heroes who appeared to be carrying the country to national redemption, Clinton marked important batting milestones by telephoning each player twice during September—Sosa on the fifth and fifteenth, McGwire on the eighth and twenty-ninth. On the last call he invited McGwire and his son to visit the White House.[74] Other performances followed. With the ball whisked to the Hall of Fame in Cooperstown within hours of McGwire's hit, Clinton himself was unable to get close to the sacred object, so the White House engineered the next best thing—a meeting with Tim Forneris, the Cardinals employee who had retrieved the ball in Busch Stadium. In a photo opportunity facilitated by Walt Disney World in Florida, Clinton, who was on a midterm campaign trip to the state, was greeted by Forneris as he stepped off Air Force One at Orlando Airport. A Disney executive subsequently wrote to the

---

[73] Daniel Okrent, "Mark McGwire: A Mac For All Seasons," *Time*, December 28, 1998.

[74] Logan, *More Tales from the Cubs Dugout*, 159; Clinton, *Public Papers of the Presidents of the United States; William J. Clinton 1998; Book II, July 1 to December 31, 1995*, 2226; N. R. Kleinfield, "In New York, Solace and Signs of Opposition for the Man of the Moment at the Moment," *New York Times*, September 15, 1998.

White House claiming the stunt had achieved a "record breaking" amount of coverage in local and national media.[75]

Beyond these attempts at symbolic appropriation, Clinton tried to align himself with the ballplayers in other ways to bolster his fragile political position. With the press reporting that senior Democrats were openly speculating about whether he would be forced to resign, Clinton invoked McGwire's name to set out the case for staying in office for the remainder of his term. "How would you feel if Mark McGwire announced, 'well, I've been working real hard to do this all my life and if it's the same to you, I think I'll skip the last eighteen games?'," Clinton mused.[76] For McGwire—read Clinton. For McGwire's last eighteen games—read Clinton's final two years in office. Like McGwire, Clinton intended to carry on hitting home runs for America.

Two weeks later, with McGwire and Sosa tied on sixty-two home runs, Clinton revisited the analogy, attempting to apply it in an even more tortured way at an Illinois campaign event. With the Democrats increasingly nervous that their disillusioned supporters would stay away from the midterm polls, the home run race in Clinton's hands became a rhetorical tool for motivating the electorate: "If either Mark McGwire or Sammy Sosa announced that…sixty-five was enough…and they were just going to sit out the games, we would think they had lost it, wouldn't we?"[77] News reports took up Clinton's home run metaphors with gusto: "Clinton, Like McGwire, Up for a Slugfest," declared the headline in the *New York Daily News*, continuing, "an embattled President Clinton wants America to know that he and the home run king Mark McGwire plan to go the

---

[75] Letter, Kevin C. Young of Walt Disney Attractions Inc. to Bill Clinton, September 28, 1998, OA/ID 14108, Folder TR303, Subject Files, Records Management, *Clinton Presidential Records*.

[76] William J. Clinton, "Remarks at Hillcrest Elementary School in Orlando, Florida, September 9, 1998," *American Presidency Project*.

[77] William J. Clinton, "Remarks at a Luncheon for Gubernatorial Candidate Glenn Poshard in Chicago, September 25, 1998," *American Presidency Project*.

distance."[78] At a Boston fundraiser, Senator Edward Kennedy introduced Clinton and Gore as the "home run kings for working families."[79]

But the more common negative mediation of the Clinton-Starr conflict inevitably made Clinton's efforts to embrace baseball's virtues problematic, ridiculed by opponents, and widely dismissed by a cynical commentariat. In an article in the *Wall Street Journal* headlined "American Caligula," Peggy Noonan, a former Reagan speechwriter, was scathing about Clinton's self-referencing of the baseball players: "Would you want Mr. McGwire to give up now, he asked? But Mr. McGwire is a champion because he has shown himself the past 10 days to be what is now an amazing thing, a celebrity who is a good man. This is the exact opposite of what Mr. Clinton has shown."[80] Other commentators deployed the counternarrative of the home run race as a frame of reference for commenting on the presidential scandal, rendering the achievements of McGwire and Sosa in the legal language of the clash between Clinton and Starr. Thomas Friedman, in the *New York Times*, compared McGwire's openness with the press to the legalistic parsing in Clinton's testimony during his grand jury appearance of August 17: "[McGwire] could have said that even baseball superstars have private lives and therefore he does not have to answer any questions about muscle-building supplements, his divorce and his son, and no obligation to uphold the historic office of the home run king."[81] Some antihero actors in the scandal drama found their roles molded by journalists into the narrative of the home run race. In *Time* magazine, Okrent presented the trio of Linda Tripp,[82] Clinton, and Starr, each as the antithesis to the "near-perfect baseball player".

---

[78] Richard Sisk, "Clinton, Like McGwire, Up for a Slugfest," *New York Daily News*, September 10, 1998.

[79] Associated Press, "Ted Kennedy Errs on Sluggers' Names," *Associated Press*, September 18, 1998.

[80] Peggy Noonan, "American Caligula," *Wall Street Journal*, September 14, 1998.

[81] Friedman, "Bringing Out the Best."

[82] Tripp was the confidante of Lewinsky who secretly recorded their conversations about her relationship with Clinton and handed them over to Starr's office in return for immunity from prosecution.

Don't you think the McGwire we watched...would never surreptitiously tape conversations with a friend? Would never defend his behavior by retreating into the technical meaning of innocuous verbs? Couldn't possibly pursue his own fanatic agenda by rooting about in the private peccadilloes of another?[83]

While Clinton's appropriation of baseball was met with distaste by his detractors, some of those same critics acknowledged the national pastime's symbolic meaning by appropriating it themselves. Immediately after the publication of Starr's report, the *Weekly Standard*, one of the mainstays of conservative commentary, carried a front-cover cartoon of Starr, swinging a baseball bat like McGwire, the crowd cheering in the background and a document labelled '62' spilling from his briefcase. The image was an obvious rebuke to Clinton's claim to be hitting home runs for America; the headline, "STARR'S HOME RUN," suggested this was as much a historic moment for American conservatives as the home run race was for baseball fans. Starr had delivered a home run for Clinton's opponents, and the *Weekly Standard* rolled out the pages calling for immediate impeachment.[84]

The contextualization of the two dramas was clearly multilayered and complex, with the media deploying a variety of content genres to communicate those connections. Common treatments included news satire and comedy which engaged large new audiences via the internet, in addition to its traditional presence on television. For months, Clinton's troubles had offered an abundance of rich material for the opening monologues of television talk show hosts like Jay Leno, David Letterman, and Bill Maher. One survey found that more than a thousand Clinton-related jokes had been told on late-night TV in the first nine months of 1998.[85] Now, the two dominant news narratives merged in this cultural setting. "Do you folks have home run mania?" asked Letterman on his September 9 show, before cracking his first Clinton-McGwire one-liner of the evening. "The typical Mark McGwire home run takes off like Air Force One in a sex scandal," chortled the host, sweeping his arm skywards. Not letting up, Letterman's *Top Ten List*, a regular feature on the show, was devoted to "Least-Used Slang Terms for Hitting a Home Run" and included at

---

[83] Okrent, "Mark McGwire: A Mac For All Seasons."
[84] William Kristol, "Impeach Now," *Weekly Standard*, September 21, 1998.
[85] Maney, *Bill Clinton: New Gilded Age Presidency*, 201.

number six, "Impeaching President Baseball."[86] Two days later, Letterman's *Top Ten Signs You are About to be Impeached*, included: "When you call to congratulate Mark McGwire, he lets the machine get it."[87] Even White House staffers got in on the act, on September 15 sharing one of Letterman's jokes via email: "It turns out that President Clinton may have been involved with another intern," the joke read, "apparently Clinton was trying to break JFK's record of 61 in one season."[88] The following month, McGwire was Letterman's late-night guest. After an introductory segment which included a joke linking Clinton, the World Series, and phone sex, McGwire talked movingly about his son and reflected on what he and Sosa "had done for the country."[89] The juxtaposition in the same program clearly demonstrated the way in which baseball's virtues and Clinton's vices were linked in the national conversation.

On the ever-expanding and more anarchic World Wide Web, the entertainment was even more explicit. While producers of TV news shows agonized over what language was permissible to describe Clinton's sexual tastes, websites were free to bombard users with salacious, if largely fictitious, detail. Not surprisingly, jokes which united the Clinton-Lewinsky and baseball dramas appeared among the thousands of posts. "What do Bill Clinton and Mark McGwire have in common?" asked one. "They're both making front-page news with their whacker."[90] Another played on McGwire's record-breaking night in St Louis when he forgot to plant his foot on first base during his victory lap:

Q: How is Monica Lewinsky on a first date like Mark McGwire right after he hit his sixty-second home run?

A: They both get so excited they skip past first base.[91]

---

[86] CBS, "The Late Show with David Letterman September 9, 1998 Tim Forneris, Stephen Dorff, Wynonna," *YouTube*.

[87] Harry Levins, "People: From The Late Show With David Letterman," *St. Louis Post-Dispatch*, September 12, 1998.

[88] Email newsletter, Don Fitzpatrick "Shoptalk," September 15, 1998, Collection: 2019-0156-F, Automated Record Management System (EMAIL), *Clinton Presidential Records*.

[89] CBS, "The Late Show with David Letterman, October 19, 1998, Mark McGwire, Robert Benigni, Bruce Hornsby," *YouTube*.

[90] "Head Start," *reallyshortfunnyjokes.com*.

[91] "Ritiki's Place," *angelfire.com*.

Thus, on multiple platforms—newspapers, late-night television, web-based satire—the two narratives of the summer were sharing the same public arena, speaking a language that everyone understood, with each story infecting the other with its moral and ethical assumptions. The national pastime, traditionally a source of purity and high moral standards, was now itself contaminated by association with a president whose sexual tastes had become part of the national conversation. "What a story it would be if McGwire ran off with Lewinsky. Hey they're both available aren't they?" joked the *St. Louis Post-Dispatch* columnist Pat Gauen.[92]

In fact, baseball in the 1990s was hardly immune from what the sociologist Ari Adut identified as one of the hallmarks of discussion of the scandal: the "banality of sex-talk" in public spaces.[93] In tune with this cultural climate, major league ballparks—so long the self-styled venues of family values—were now the setting for new levels of sexualized language and imagery. The home run, it seemed, was nothing less than a celebration of sexualized masculine power. *Sports Illustrated* referred to the home run race as the pursuit of baseball's "sexiest record."[94] McGwire's postgame news conferences were reported with a breathless excitement, "fresh from the kill and reeking of testosterone."[95] "Everything about him [McGwire] is big," marveled Verducci.[96] Nike made a television advertisement with the tagline "Chicks Dig the Long Ball," which opened with two women gasping as McGwire smashes balls into the top deck.[97] Even the staid world of milk advertising, which had previously been so keen on capturing Cal Ripken's wholesomeness, now saw merit in exploiting McGwire's apparent eroticism. The ballplayer's rippling muscles, bulging in a sleeveless tank top, were featured in a milk ad campaign, shot by the celebrity photographer Annie Leibovitz.[98] The *Washington Post* reported the anguish of one parent whose children saw a newspaper cartoon depicting President Clinton and McGwire in a race for home runs, and having to explain to

---

[92] Pat Gauen, "Once Upon a Time There Was a Game," *St. Louis Post-Dispatch, (Illinois Post)*, September 14, 1998.

[93] Adut, *On Scandal*, 214–22.

[94] Tom Verducci, "Man on a Mission," *Sports Illustrated*, March 23, 1998.

[95] Paul Christopher Johnson, "The Fetish and McGwire's Balls," *Journal of the American Academy of Religion*, 68, no. 2 (2000): 243–64; 258–59.

[96] Verducci, "Man on a Mission."

[97] Nike, "Chicks Dig the Long Ball," *YouTube*.

[98] Annie Leibovitz, "1998 Milk Mustache Campaign," *Milkadman.com*.

them that the home run was a metaphor for sex.[99] When another baseball icon, Cal Ripken Jr., was invited to the White House in December, the *New York Times* framed it entirely in the context of sex and scandal: "This is how it is to be Bill Clinton these days....You give Cal Ripken and his wife and kids a tour of your treasured Oval Office on a bright Friday afternoon, while Congressmen a few blocks away debate precisely how—in those same rooms—you touched a woman not your wife."[100]

It was against this backdrop of the sexualization of two institutions of civil religion—the presidency and the national pastime—that contrasting presentations of 'the American father' emerged, presenting new versions of masculinity and challenging the assumptions that underpinned the idealized myth of the American family. As the President languished—both the architect of his own family breakdown and the source of national shame—it seemed that fatherhood and baseball's imminent glory offered an altogether more optimistic vision of the future to an American public which longed to see the return of morality at the pinnacle of public life.

Clinton and McGwire: America's Two Contrasting Fathers

"There is a place in us where our passionate commitments converge," suggested the author and educator, Jack Petrash, in a self-help paperback published as Clinton's presidency drew to a close, "and it is there that fathering and baseball intertwine."[101] Even in the late 1990s, a belief in the rites of passage which connected fathers, sons and (less often in cultural output) daughters through their mutual experience of the national pastime, remained a powerful cultural emblem, intrinsic to the American imagination. The generational transmission of rules and rituals was still mythologized in literature and film and had been threaded through Ken Burns' baseball-focused interpretation of American history. Now, at a time of acute public anxiety in the performance of the President—the father at the summit of national life—this idealized relationship between father and son emerged as a dominant motif in the mediation of the home run race. In

---

[99] Ann O'Hanlon, "Scandal Puts Parents On the Spot," *Washington Post*, September 13, 1998.

[100] James Bennett and Melinda Henneberger, "Clinton's Surreal Week," *New York Times*, December 12, 1998.

[101] Petrash, *Covering Home*, x.

doing so, the celebration of baseball and fatherhood inevitably spilled over into what James Davison Hunter considered "the most conspicuous field of conflict" of the culture war—the family. "If the symbolic significance of the family is that it is a microcosm of the larger society," he wrote, "then the task of defining what the American family *is* becomes integral to the very task of defining America [his italics]."[102] And in 1998 many in the media appeared to feel that McGwire's relationship with his son did indeed define the best of the American family.

For large parts of the summer of 1998, ten-year-old Matt McGwire seemed to be everywhere: batboy for the Cardinals, decked out in full uniform whenever his father went out to bat. When McGwire broke a midseason slump with two home runs, the relationship took on an almost mystical quality—McGwire credited his upsurge to his son who had kissed his bat before the game. "That's what it came down to," the kiss "was still on it," he told reporters.[103] Alongside portrayals like this, of the spiritual component of McGwire's fatherhood, were examples of a more materialistic paternal role—and they were just as celebrated by the media: the first national television advertisement to capitalize on McGwire's record featured him promising Matt a trip to Disneyworld. "The Superstar Slugger is a Big Hit With his Son," declared a headline in the *New York Daily News*.[104] It all perpetuated the myth of a civil religious holy trinity—Father-Son-Baseball.

On September 7, *Sports Illustrated* deployed this trinity on its front cover—Mark hugging Matt, both clad in Cardinals uniforms, the boy's face buried in his father's enormous chest. The strap read, "One Cool Daddy": the accompanying story was headlined "The Good Father."[105] For Clinton, it was a telling phrase, an unfortunate reminder of a label which had once applied to him. Back in 1996, the so-called 'Good Father' memo, written by his campaign managers, had sought to portray Clinton as the "comforting authority figure who builds and defends the family home."[106]

---

[102] Hunter, *Culture Wars*, 176–77.

[103] R. Fallstrom, "A Kiss For Good Luck," in *Home Run! The Year The Records Fell*, ed. Associated Press, 76.

[104] Bill Hutchinson, "The Superstar Slugger Is a Big Hit With His Son," *New York Daily News*, September 8, 1998.

[105] Rick Reilly, "The Good Father," *Sports Illustrated*, September 7, 1998.

[106] Eleanor Clift and Martha Brant, "Worrying About Women," *Newsweek*, February 12, 1996.

Two years later, McGwire represented an alternative version of the Good Father, built not around comfort but around heroism, redemption, and emotional sensitivity, all packaged into a new idealized myth for a modern American family.

In the reconstruction of the American family McGwire-style, it mattered little that the ballplayer was now a single father who had spent years on the road while his son grew up with his remarried ex-wife, from whom he separated when Matt was just a year old. For millions, such arrangements were the reality of American family life—complex and disjointed. Half of marriages in America in the late 1990s ended in divorce anyway. McGwire, it seemed, epitomized a reshaped male role within this fractured social architecture, and the press loved this inspiring example of how a divorced couple could happily raise a son. "Mac's a Hero For Parents Who Share Custody," read the headline in the *St. Louis Post-Dispatch*.[107]

It was not only the domestic unit that was reimagined and endorsed in the *Sports Illustrated* "Cool Daddy" cover feature, but also the idealised characteristics associated with the men in the family, as Ric Reilly's opening paragraph made clear: "Not until he allowed his emotions to show and his tears to flow, did he become what he really wanted to be. Huge men don't cry, but the McGwires do." McGwire's tears flowed through the article's five-and-a-half thousand words, with suppressed emotion a recurring theme as Reilly recounted the ballplayer's childhood, his divorce, his injuries, and his use of therapy to overcome depression. McGwire said he had only reached his full potential as a baseball player when he "discovered a missing father" in himself. "It took crying to make me realize who I am now. I am the Mark McGwire I am supposed to be..., an opinionated, understanding, communicative, sensitive...father."[108]

It was not the first time McGwire's tears had made national headlines. The previous summer he cried in front of reporters when announcing his one million dollar donation to launch a fund for abused children. The *New York Times* headlined the story, "McGwire Wears His Heart on 19-Inch Biceps," presenting a man whose emotional vulnerability and sensitivity seemed to be in perfect harmony with his physicality. In the *New York Times*, Claire Smith judged McGwire's tears as especially

---

[107] Susan Block, "Mac's a Hero For Parents Who Share Custody," *St. Louis Post-Dispatch*, September 29, 1998.

[108] Reilly, "The Good Father."

poignant because he was "so Herculean."[109] In *Time*, Okrent made the same association in admiring terms: "Revealed in his deep green eyes is a self-knowledge as imposing as his size and strength. I am what I am, what you see is what you get."[110] Here was the so-called 'new man' of the nineties revealed in the form of a professional baseball player. While the eighties had been the Rambo era of the muscle-bound, tough guy masculinity of Sylvester Stallone and Arnold Schwarzenegger, the nineties saw new sensitivities of vulnerability and emotional intelligence emerge in portrayals of American manhood. In the idealized 'new man,' these 'softer' manifestations of masculinity complemented and embellished the conventional masculine tropes of physical strength, competitiveness, and courage.[111] Most importantly, in the case of McGwire, it was packaged in the body of an elite athlete—"the leading definer of masculinity in mass culture."[112] "The biggest, strongest man in baseball is really a softy," swooned Verducci. "The giant is more sensitive than a sunburn."[113] To be sure, these so-called conflicted masculinities had to be negotiated, but McGwire appeared capable of doing just that: he could swat a ninety-five-mph fastball, carry his son on his shoulders and not just cry over the plight of abused children, but actually do something about it. In contrast to Clinton's faltering performance as both leader and father, McGwire projected this dual model of American masculine leadership, father of a young boy, but also of the nation: "Godzilla with a bat," declared the *New York Times*; "a 250-pound duplex with pillars for forearms," trumpeted *Sports Illustrated*, in suggesting that McGwire appeared to carry the weight of the whole country.[114] In a moral climate increasingly defined by the ballplayer's virtues, this idealized portrayal—of the single, new-man father, in a disrupted family unit—was in the ascendancy. In contrast, the family that had traditionally embodied an American domestic ideal to which the whole country could supposedly aspire—the First Family—now faced repudiation.

---

[109] Claire Smith, "McGwire Wears His Heart on 19-Inch Biceps," *New York Times*, December 27, 1997.

[110] Okrent, "A Mac For All Seasons."

[111] See Jeffords, *Hardbodies*.

[112] Connell, *Masculinities*, 54.

[113] Verducci, "Man on a Mission."

[114] Dave Anderson, "Baseball's Godzilla Has a Bat," *New York Times*, May 26, 1998; Reilly, "The Good Father."

In his history of presidential marriages, first published in 1997 with the waves of the Clinton-Lewinsky scandal yet to break, Gil Troy suggested Americans were living in an age of "growing balkanisation" in which the family in the White House offered the country, "a focal point—an inspiring standard or an inviting target."[115] By the late-summer of 1998 it was clear which type of focal point the Clinton family provided. Already buffeted by swirling accusations of ethical misdeeds involving sex, finance, and cronyism, the President, nominally the national archetype of authority and manliness, had now been exposed as a lying adulterer who for months had deceived his wife and daughter, his political allies, and the country. His behaviour had created a moral void at the heart of the nation's First Family, one unintentionally captured in a series of revealing television pictures and a famous *Time* magazine front cover. *Time's* August 31 edition carried an image of the First Family, caught as they strolled across the White House lawn—on the face of it a normative American family—husband, wife, teenage child—heading off on vacation. But the close up of their departure en route to Martha's Vineyard was published under the provocative headline, "It's Nobody's Business But Ours"—the defiant words Clinton had used in his televised address of August 17 in an effort to preserve his family's privacy after confessing to his relationship with Lewinsky.[116] Of course, it was never credible that the most scrutinised family in the country would be spared a media examination of their domestic agonies. This simple scene was dissected from multiple angles in newspapers and on television to reveal, it appeared, a splintered family held together not by the patriarch but by his daughter, Chelsea, who had learned of her father's infidelities less than twenty-four hours earlier. The eighteen-year-old walked between her parents, grasping their hands, and leaning slightly toward her mother, filling the emotional and physical vacuum between the First Couple.[117] Hillary, who for months had loyally performed as Clinton's principal defender, concealed her eyes behind dark glasses, a symbol of her victimhood. The *New York Times* called it a "televised tableau of family togetherness," but it appeared that Chelsea was the

---

[115] Troy, *Affairs of State*, 372–73.

[116] Clinton, "Address to the Nation on Testimony Before the Independent Counsel's Grand Jury, August 17, 1998."

[117] White House Television, August 18, 1998, Master Tape: #08856d, *Clinton Presidential Records*.

only cohesive element.[118] It would stand in stark contrast to the image of the McGwire family which adorned the cover of *Sports Illustrated* a few days later—the "Cool Daddy" of America's alternative First Family, upholding national virtue and smothering his son with love.

These comparisons were all the more damaging to Clinton because his public presidency was built around a paradigm of fatherhood of family and nation, sustaining the myth of president as the 'ordinary dad.' Clinton's strategists in 1992 had framed a heart-tugging backstory in terms of his fatherless childhood in the film, *The Man from Hope,* made for the Democratic National Convention. "I guess there will always be a sadness in me that I never heard the sound of my father's voice or felt his hand around mine," Clinton reflects to the camera.[119] With Chelsea the first child to live in the White House for two decades, Clinton's relationship with his daughter was central to his presidential performance, his public persona often constructed around images of fatherliness. Dick Morris had urged him to talk more about being a father: be seen helping with homework, go out camping with Chelsea. "The country craves fathers," Morris wrote in a memo in 1995, adding what would turn out to be an unfortunate coda: "women crave men who act responsibly."[120] Clinton projected himself as an involved parent, with photo opportunities of cycling, watching basketball, and playing softball with his daughter. He took Chelsea to Baltimore on the night of Ripken's record, allowing him to claim he had witnessed the historic event "through the eyes of children."[121] To the world they were as in tune as any First Family father and daughter could be.

There was a policy dimension as well. In 1995 Clinton launched the *Presidential National Fatherhood Initiative,* a series of executive orders mandating federal agencies to support the role of fathers within the family. "Without a father to help guide, without a father to care, without a father to teach boys to be men and to teach girls to expect respect from men, it's

---

[118] John Broder, "On an Island Retreat, A Time for Healing," *New York Times,* August 19, 1998.

[119] Tuchman, "The Man From Hope."

[120] "Agenda For Meeting With the President on October 11, 1995," published in Morris, *Behind The Oval Office,* 480–84; 483.

[121] Clinton, "Remarks at a Breakfast With Religious Leaders, September 8, 1995."

harder," Clinton said.[122] Hillary contributed to the discourse in her 1996 book, *It Takes a Village*, in which she wrote, "every society requires a critical mass of families that fit the traditional ideal....We are at risk of losing that critical mass in America today."[123] But sentiments about the need to protect traditional families were now undermined by the President's own conduct and his inability to control his sexual appetite. His performance as a husband and father had diminished the office and enfeebled any quasi-religious aura that still existed around the First Family. Clinton was easy prey for his critics. "Chronic indiscipline, compulsion, exploitation, the easy betrayal of vows, all suggest something wrong at a deep level—something habitual and beyond control," wrote William Bennett.[124] The mental weakness and the moral corruption exhibited by the head of the First Family had jeopardised his wife, his daughter, and the entire country.

Clinton's struggle for self-control was seized on by journalists who compared it unfavourably with McGwire's management of his mental health challenges. "Everybody needs therapy," McGwire had told reporters. "It brought so many things to my life. I can face the music now. I can face the truth."[125] The *New York Times* compared McGwire's openness to Clinton's reluctance to use personal therapy or marriage counselling, criticising his reliance on spiritual advisers for guidance and confession.[126] Admitting to any psychological flaw was not an option that the White House was prepared to countenance. "The President is not under medical treatment for any psychiatric or mental condition," his spokesperson told reporters. "He is seeking pastoral support and that of other caring people so that they can hold him accountable to the commitment he's made for repentance."[127] McGwire's experience told a different story: by publicly acknowledging his weaknesses through his use of therapy and cherishing his paternal duties, he was a servant of his family, his teammates, and, by

---

[122] William J. Clinton, "Remarks at the University of Texas at Austin, October 16, 1995," *American Presidency Project*.

[123] Hillary Rodham Clinton, *It Takes a Village*, 40.

[124] Bennett, *The Death of Outrage*, 29–30.

[125] Frank Rich, "Capital Shrink Rap," *New York Times*, October 7, 1998.

[126] Francis X. Clines, "The Therapy Question: Should Clinton Turn to Psychologists as Well as Religious Healers?," *New York Times*, September 17, 1998.

[127] William J. Clinton, "Press Briefing by Mike McCurry, September 11, 1998," *American Presidency Project*.

extension, the country. Clinton, on the other hand, had put the welfare of his family and his country at risk by succumbing to uncontrolled sexual impulses, which he seemed unwilling to confront. It was McGwire who filled the moral space in American public life vacated by the scandal-ridden First Family. And it begged the question—who was really America's national father?

If there was any uncertainty around the answer, one thing was clear; the holder of that title would inevitably be White. What had not changed was the dominant whiteness of the narrative of the McGwire-Sosa home run race. Despite the images of racial harmony and assertions of the symbolic triumph of multiculturalism associated with the McGwire-Sosa story, throughout the summer the mediation of the home run race had privileged the White player in assigning heroic status. McGwire's emphatic masculinity, which had been so meticulously constructed, overwhelmed Sosa's identity, pushing it into the background. The attributes of monumental physical stature which were assigned to McGwire were largely absent from the profiles of Sosa. The only reference to physique in a profile of Sosa that *Sports Illustrated* featured on its cover in June, was that he had been so slight as a teenager that MLB scouts thought he was malnourished. Admittedly, Sosa's story was usually presented positively in terms of the American Dream—the immigrant's journey from poverty to riches through baseball. But media reports of his wealth were laced with stereotypes of the flashy, Black professional athlete: gaudy jewelry, multiple sportscars (it was said Sosa did not know how many he owned) with personalized number plates, and a sixty-foot yacht.[128] McGwire, on the other hand, was apparently "missing the stud-jock-ego chromosome." He did not bother to put his baseball trophies on show and was "so hopelessly square he had one measly car."[129]

Unlike McGwire, portrayals of Sosa 'the father' were rare, despite his being married with four young children. Instead, Sosa's familial relationships were framed in terms of his humble childhood in the Dominican Republic and devotion to his mother.[130] "Sosa has been Sammy the Sequel all the way," wrote Rick Reilly in a column that tried to explain why

---

[128] Tom Verducci, "The Education of Sammy Sosa," *Sports Illustrated*, June 29, 1998.

[129] Reilly, "The Good Father."

[130] Mark Hermann, "Sosa Makes Journey From Rags to Glory," *Los Angeles Times*, July 19, 1998.

McGwire was so much the fans' favorite.[131] A *San Francisco Chronicle* columnist appeared to sum up the national mood. "Everybody is rooting for McGwire," he wrote, pointing to a poll confirming a landslide of public opinion supporting the White Cardinal over the Black Cub.[132]

To many, Sosa's race-rooted outsider status was discomforting—another sign that the self-congratulatory purity of the national pastime was illusory; that a successful challenge from a Black Latino to McGwire's celebrity status was not part of the summer's assumed plot. Even some baseball insiders, like the New York Mets manager Bobby Valentine, felt compelled to speak out about the racist undertones of media coverage: "There is some American pie in this whole thing. The interesting hypothetical would be the postseason story of Sammy winning the race. It might even be written as a disappointment."[133] Valentine's concerns were borne out by the lack of fanfare when Sosa drew level with McGwire on sixty-two home runs on September 13. There were no ceremonies for Sosa, there was no speech from Bud Selig, no member of the Maris family on hand to be hugged and no interruption to regular television programming.

But Sosa did get a congratulatory call from the President.[134] If there was an ambivalence in the media and the wider country about cheering on a Dominican immigrant against a White all-American icon, it was not shared by Clinton. For Clinton, Sosa's success was the embodiment of One America: a fusion of tradition (manifested by his excellence at baseball) and "the best of new America (the successful immigrant)."[135] Assimilation of talent like his was to the moral and economic benefit of the whole country. Finally drawing Sosa's fatherliness into the spotlight, Clinton invited him and his family to lead the ceremonial lighting of the National Christmas Tree in Washington. And a month later, at one of the most

---

[131] Rick Reilly, "Pride of the Yankees," *Sports Illustrated*, September 28, 1998.

[132] Tim Keown, "Sosa Adds More Bang to HR Race," *San Francisco Chronicle*, September 2, 1998.

[133] CBSNews.com Staff, "Sosa Hits No. 55 in Cubs Win," cbsnews.com, August 31, 1998.

[134] William J. Clinton, "Press Briefing by Mike McCurry, September 15, 1998," *American Presidency Project*.

[135] Draft SOTU speech with notes, OA/ID 14419, Folder: "SOTU [State of the Union] 1999 Speech Drafts 1/18/99 [Binder][1]," *Clinton Presidential Records*.

dramatic set piece speeches of his presidency—the 1999 State of the Union Address delivered by Clinton in the middle of his impeachment trial for high crimes and misdemeanours—Sosa was the honoured guest, sitting alongside the First Lady in the gallery of the House. As the first baseball player given that accolade, Sosa was the recipient of a bipartisan ovation: a hero in two countries, the President said, who taught our children the meaning of brotherhood.[136] In Sosa's presence, the synthesis of the national pastime's civil religious significance and its potential redemptive power was on display. Sosa represented brotherhood in an era of ultra-polarisation. In a climate of moral anxiety, he expressed the moral ascendancy of baseball through his demonstration of heroic qualities. And in the sanctification of record-breaking, Sosa's presence at one of the great rituals of state pointed to the promise of a virtuous future. Despite his failings as the 'national father,' Clinton, via his interactions with the home run race, was still endeavouring to fashion a unifying moment of national optimism.

The two dramas of the summer of 1998 had catapulted debates on the nature of virtue, morality, hope, and fatherhood into the public arena. They overlapped and enmeshed through performances by the principal actors—McGwire, Sosa, Clinton, Starr—in multiple forms of cultural output on multiple platforms. Their stories shared the same media space, competing for prominence in the national news agenda; their interplay was communicated in a common language—often the language of baseball mythology or the language of politics; sometimes the legal language of grand juries and constitutional crisis; occasionally the emboldened language of sex talk. At times, the actors placed themselves in the counter-narrative: Clinton with his telephone calls to the players, his White House invitations, and his self-identification as a home run hitter; the players in recognizing that they were competing with the President for page one and fulfilling a redemptive moral role assigned to them by the press. In fact, so entangled were the narratives that they effectively combined to become one complex story—in which expressions of baseball mythology provided a faith in American values through which a disgraced president and a failing political system could both be redeemed. In this context, Clinton tried to deploy baseball myth to his advantage by associating himself with the heroes of the national pastime, as he had done in previous years, he

---

[136] Clinton, "Address Before a Joint Session of the Congress on the State of the Union, January 19, 1999."

appeared to think he could again influence his own political fortunes. This time, however, the alternative moral framework offered by McGwire and Sosa presented such a stark contrast to Clinton's own behavior that he was unable to make his appropriation of baseball's virtues truly credible, a point emphasized by the *Washington Post* columnist Richard Cohen: "It is Clinton's bad luck to be compared to McGwire—a heroic standard no sitting president could match....McGwire reminds us how it could have been for Clinton....We want our presidents to be better than us, custodians of our childhood and our childhood dreams."[137]

While venerating the baseball myth, the events of the summer of 1998 had exposed the complexities of America's attitudes toward other cherished symbols, values, and beliefs. Challenges had emerged to the status of the presidency and the First Family and to the sanctity of traditional family models. The home run race had projected new constructions of masculinities, new behaviors, and new notions of fatherhood, all disseminated ever more widely via new forms of mass media. And in helping to redefine the idealized national father at a time of crisis for the presidency, it suggested a fluidity in some of the things which Americans held sacred. The home run race had signaled that baseball was capable of reflecting the changes in America's culture—especially in sexual and social liberalization—even as it projected itself as the guardian of many of the civil religious virtues more traditionally associated with America's national pastime—fatherhood, fortitude, humility, and grace.

In the moment, it seemed the McGwire-Sosa rivalry had restored baseball to its cultural pinnacle, finally rescuing it from the greed and petulance of the strike and vindicating the faith of the returning fans. America had indeed become a Baseball Nation again. Thus it was of little surprise that when news broke in late August of McGwire's long-term use of a performance-enhancing steroidal substance as part of his training regime, the moral qualms expressed in some quarters did little to disrupt the home run frenzy and the associated media narrative of baseball's intrinsic virtue. Eventually however, the reputations of McGwire and Sosa, along with dubious notions of the game's purity, would unravel, exposing a culture of deceit at the heart of baseball and adding ambiguity to the remembering of a nationally unifying event. In doing so, it would also change the terms of the comparisons between the ballplayers and the President, giving

---

[137] Cohen, "Two For The Record Books."

scandal and confession a lingering presence in the extended story of Sosa and McGwire, just as it had in the shaping of the public memory of the Clinton presidency.

Clinton throws his first Opening Day pitch as president,
Camden Yards, Baltimore, April 1993.

Courtesy William J. Clinton Presidential Library

Clinton in the broadcast booth, Opening Day,
Camden Yards, Baltimore, April 1993.
Courtesy William J. Clinton Presidential Library

Hillary Clinton takes a swing at the White House picnic on September 10, 1994, to mark the premiere of Ken Burns' *Baseball*.
Courtesy William J. Clinton Presidential Library

Don Baer's jottings on his invitation to the premiere of *Baseball*, September 10, 1994.
Courtesy William J. Clinton Presidential Library

10/10/94
3 pm
Rm. 472

Ken Burns
- serve something lgr than daily paper → posterity
- POTUS is m. effective when he is the "holy ghost"
- with end of Cold War - we have opportunity to define what we are for
- FDR: in restraint (of reporting on his polio) he had a better relationship w/ press
- seize high ground - don't be afraid of using relig themes.
- Take up tools of enemy.
- "E Pluribus Unum"
- mastery of rhetorical message - then step back + try to look at it in a new way
- "journalism is 1st draft of history"
- reverse inertia + apathy of conventional wisdom
- Alan: people are missing conversation (hence, attraction to "Baseball" + "Oprah")
- list of accomplishments: essentially reacting to someone's negatives
- Shakers: plant extra crops for thieves + crows → they have to eat too.
- Try to fashion rhetoric as if it was being read 10 yrs from now

Note made by Gabrielle Bushman of the White House speechwriters meeting with Ken Burns, October 10, 1994.

Courtesy William J. Clinton Presidential Library

Clinton exerts pressure on MLB acting commissioner Bud Selig at the White House baseball summit, February 7, 1995. Labor Secretary, Robert Reich, is sitting by the fireplace, with George Stephanopoulos looking over his shoulder.

Courtesy William J. Clinton Presidential Library

White House speechwriter's note of Clinton speaking about Cal Ripken Jr. breaking Lou Gehrig's consecutive game record, September 1995.

Courtesy William J. Clinton Presidential Library

Clinton with Cal Ripken Jr. in the Baltimore Orioles locker room before the record-breaking game, Camden Yards, September 6, 1995.
Courtesy William J. Clinton Presidential Library

Clinton and Al Gore, with their children at their side, celebrate Cal Ripken Jr. passing Lou Gehrig's consecutive game record at Camden Yards, September 6, 1995.

Courtesy William J. Clinton Presidential Library

Clinton with Kweisi Mfume, the chairman of the Congressional Black Caucus (left), and Kurt Schmoke, the mayor of Baltimore, at Camden Yards on Opening Day, April 1993.

Courtesy William J. Clinton Presidential Library

Chapter Six

Concealment and Confession in the Church of Baseball

"The News is Out: Popeye is Spiking His Spinach"

Like Mark McGwire, Raik Hannemann appeared to have the perfect physique for his chosen sport: tall, with strapping shoulders which could power his body through the water. It was the swimmer's classic triangular build, and Hannemann was a good swimmer, good enough to make the East German national team and to reach an Olympic final in 1988. His seventh place in the two hundred meters individual medley in Seoul was disappointing for the medal-obsessed East German state, but Hannemann was still part of a privileged elite. Spotted at an early age, he had attended the best schools and had access to world-class training facilities. Success had brought money and cars—undreamed of riches in a communist state. But when the Eastern Bloc collapsed and the two Germanys reunited, Hannemann turned from internationally competitive sportsman to eager-to-tell-all whistleblower, exposing the dark secrets of the East's sports machine, and becoming a minor celebrity in the process.[1] In 1998, Mark McGwire had never heard of Raik Hannemann, but they had more in common than a brawny upper body and the relative wealth of a successful athlete. They had both used the steroid precursor, androstenedione.

The steroid controversy that briefly embroiled McGwire in August 1998, and cast a fleeting shadow over the final weeks of his home run chase, had its chemical roots in the state-run doping program which had fueled East Germany's sporting success in the nineteen-seventies and eighties. Over those two decades, East German scientists developed an arsenal of performance enhancing drugs (PEDs) to help their athletes challenge the Olympic supremacy of the United States and the Soviet

---

[1] Mark Fritz, "Raik Hannemann: The Story of Steroids in Search of Privileges," *Associated Press*, December 8, 1990.

Union. Among the substances deployed in Seoul, and later exposed by Hannemnan, was a nasal spray which the East German coaches instructed their athletes to inhale before each race. The spray contained androstenedione, a naturally occurring androgenic steroid produced by the adrenal glands, ovaries, and testicles. Once released into the bloodstream it converted into testosterone, boosting levels of the male sex hormone for up to three hours, allowing athletes to work out harder and recover more quickly. After three days in the body, the substance was virtually undetectable. But ten years later, if Mark McGwire wanted to take androstenedione, he did not have to snort it illicitly up his nose. By the mid-nineties it had been patented in the United States in a more consumer-friendly form: it came in white pills and was marketed as the dietary supplement "Andro," available from any bodybuilding outlet in the country.

By the time the world became aware that McGwire was using Andro he had been taking the pills for more than a year. And he was not particularly secretive about doing so. Anyone wandering into the St. Louis clubhouse could have spotted them on the top shelf of McGwire's locker, in a clearly labelled brown bottle. But it was not until an *Associated Press* journalist, Steve Wilstein, found himself pressed against the locker in a postgame huddle in early August that anyone took any notice. Looking for detail to enliven a feature on McGwire, Wilstein made a note of what he could see scattered among the ballplayers belongings: a photograph of Matt in Cardinals uniform, a can of Popeye spinach, a golfing cap, packs of sugarless gum, a bottle of creatine, and the bottle of androstenedione pills. At the time, Wilstein did not recognize the name, but he wrote it down and later telephoned an acquaintance who was a cardiologist. Androstenedione, he was told, could be converted by the body into testosterone. Elevated levels of testosterone could improve athletic performance and also had the potential to damage the heart.[2] AP'S initial approach to the Cardinals for comment was rebuffed, but after being told what had been seen in McGwire's locker, the player confirmed his use. To McGwire it was not a controversial admission: androstenedione did not violate any of the rules of baseball and its use in the game, he said, was widespread.[3] But other sports saw things differently: the NFL had outlawed it years

---

[2] "Who Knew?" *ESPN Magazine Special Report, espn.com*, November 9, 2005.

[3] Steve Wilstein, "Drug OK in Baseball, Not Olympics," *Associated Press*, August 21, 1998.

earlier; it was on the NCAA list of proscribed drugs and banned in Olympic competition. Some experts believed it was also used as a masking agent for other anabolic steroids. As Charles Yesalis, a sports scientist at Penn State University, observed: "Androstenedione is one honest-to-God sex steroid: this is not Vitamin C."[4] Wilstein's story about McGwire and Andro, headlined "Drug OK in Baseball, Not Olympics," dropped on the AP wire on August 21, with McGwire on fifty-one home runs, three ahead of Sosa in the race for the record.

Although Wilstein was at pains to point out that McGwire had done nothing which breached either the law of the land or the rules of the game, his story ignited a brief debate about the use of PEDs in professional baseball. The *New York Times* led the way in raising questions about McGwire, headlining the story: "The News is Out: Popeye is Spiking His Spinach."[5] The *Times* suggested the home run race was now tainted; an editorial called on McGwire to stop taking androstenedione immediately.[6] As one newspaper acerbically pointed out, the ballplayer and Clinton had something in common—they both had a testosterone problem.[7] For a few days, arguments raged in multiple directions. Is it fair to make so much of McGwire's entirely legal use of androstenedione? Does androstenedione really give McGwire any advantage? What proof is there of harmful side effects? What are the ethics of a journalist poking around in a player's locker? So what if players use performance enhancers if it makes for more exciting baseball?

It was on this territory that the short-lived public skirmish over androstenedione was fought. And the arguments deployed by McGwire in his defense came straight out of the Bill Clinton playbook, reminiscent of the presidential fudging during the "inappropriate relationship" television address of August 17. To begin with there was the evasion. "Androstenedione?" said a Cardinals spokesman. "Mark doesn't even know how to

---

[4] Quoted in William C. Rhoden, "Baseball's Pandora's Box Cracks Open," *New York Times*, August 25, 1998.

[5] Harvey Araton, "The News is Out: Popeye is Spiking His Spinach," *New York Times*, August 23, 1998.

[6] New York Times Editorial Board, "Mark McGwire's Pep Pills," *New York Times*, August 27, 1998.

[7] Angus Hamilton, "McGwire, Clinton Share Problem," *The Oklahoman*, August 30, 1998.

spell it."[8] Within a few days McGwire's knowledge of androstenedione appeared to have improved. "Everything I've done is natural," he insisted. "Everybody that I know in the game of baseball uses the same stuff I use."[9] McGwire and the Cardinals management issued a statement, saying it was a natural substance with no proven anabolic-steroid effects and no significant side effects. At best, it made workouts a little more efficient. The rebuttal strategy was clear: the ethical concerns over the use of Andro were irrelevant—McGwire was acting entirely within the laws of baseball and there the argument should end. McGwire made the point forcefully: "This stuff is completely natural and legal! If they ban this, why not ban ginseng and coffee and, hell, red meat?"[10] It had echoes of the public defense Clinton was concurrently mounting in response to his admission of a relationship with Lewinsky: four days earlier, he too had insisted, that whatever the ethical boundaries of his case, he was legally clean. At no time had he asked anyone "to lie, to hide or destroy evidence or to take any other unlawful action."[11] When Clinton resorted to legal parsing, the political columnist David Broder had been scathing: "Clinton acted—and still, even in his supposed *mea culpa* acts—as if he does not recognize what it means to be the President of the United States."[12] It now appeared that McGwire was being similarly short-sighted about his moral, as opposed to legal, obligations. Did he not appreciate the responsibility that accompanied being America's most popular sportsman? Did this "pharmaceutically enhanced marvel" not understand his position as an exemplar of healthy living to other athletes?, asked a columnist in the *Toronto Star*.[13] As the most famous ballplayer of his era, McGwire had "the power to educate," lamented Wallace Matthews in the *New York Post*, adding that he owed children "the truth."[14] Instead, McGwire had allowed himself to

---

[8] Quoted in "Who Knew?"

[9] Quoted in Wilstein, "Drug OK in Baseball, Not Olympics."

[10] Quoted in Reilly, "The Good Father."

[11] Clinton, "Address to the Nation on Testimony Before the Independent Counsel's Grand Jury."

[12] David Broder, "A Deceitful, Disgraced Presidency," *Orlando Sentinel*, August 19, 1998.

[13] Randy Starkman, "McGwire, Baseball Crossing the Line," *Toronto Star*, August 26, 1998.

[14] Quoted in Bernie Miklasz, "Everyone Seems Pumped Up About McGwire and Andro," *St. Louis Post-Dispatch*, August 29, 1998.

unwittingly become the unofficial salesman for Andro, his image used in magazine advertisements to energize demand for a product which reported soaring sales in the weeks after the story broke, despite doctors warning of a looming health disaster from the possible side effects of uncontrolled usage—tumors, sterility, impotence, and hypertension.[15]

Major league players claimed not to see the problem. Jason Giambi, McGwire's former teammate at the Oakland Athletics, said, "The disappointing thing is that people are trying to take away from what Mark is doing....For someone to write that he's cheating the system is a joke."[16] Joe Girardi of the Yankees protested: "He's just doing things to help his body. We all do things to help our bodies, take protein. It's a health-conscious sport."[17] The players had another target too—the journalist who had opened this whole can of worms. Just as Clinton, in his August 17 confession, had condemned Starr's investigation for "hurting too many innocent people," so the Cardinals organization attacked Wilstein's investigative journalism. In declaring that "even presidents have private lives," Clinton had put violations of privacy at the center of national debate: now McGwire, and his team manager, Tony La Russa, did the same.[18] McGwire accused Wilstein of "snooping," while La Russa said it was "a clear invasion of privacy" that was "causing some real garbage here."[19] Mirroring Clinton's "it's nobody's business but ours" declaration, La Russa threatened to ban AP from the Cardinals' clubhouse.[20]

Indifferent to the press freedom issues wrapped up in threats to punish one of the world's largest newsgathering organizations, many journalists backed the Cardinals' display of indignation. Dan Le Batard described

---

[15] Associated Press, "McGwire Powers Andro Sales to 100,000 Users, Say Doctors," *Calgary Herald*, December 9, 1998.

[16] Quoted in Susan Slusser, "Giambi Defends McGwire's Use of Supplement," *SFGate.com*, August 24, 1998.

[17] Quoted in Buster Olney, "Opponents Don't Fault McGwire for Pills," *New York Times*, August 25, 1998.

[18] Clinton, "Address to the Nation on Testimony Before the Independent Counsel's Grand Jury."

[19] Quoted in, "Who Knew?"

[20] Mark Heilser, "La Russa Sounds Just a Little Slap-Happy," *Los Angeles Times*, August 31, 1998.

it as "the silliest sports story of the year," in the *Miami Herald*.[21] "I'm sorry, but when did Mark McGwire become Monica Lewinsky?" asked the columnist Bernie Miklasz of the *St. Louis Post-Dispatch*, who supported the Cardinals' line that Wilstein had been snooping for a scandal about the hometown hero.[22] "This Persecution of McGwire is a Crime," declared a headline in the *Boston Globe*, above a column which suggested the controversy had been stirred up by tabloid newspapers.[23] In truth the tabloid press had largely lined up behind McGwire. "McGwire is no cheater, and any attempt to paint him as such is just another example of the build-them-up-so-we-can-tear-them-down mentality poisoning today's society," wrote Tom Keegan in the *New York Post*.[24] The *Wall Street Journal* lent more heavyweight backing to McGwire in the form of the Harvard paleontologist, and baseball fan, Stephen Jay Gould. "What cruel nonsense to hold McGwire in any way accountable," Gould wrote, "simply because we fear that kids may ape him as a role model for an issue entirely outside his call, and within the province of baseball's rule makers."[25]

For Bud Selig, this story had the potential to undermine a memorable season. Baseball had spent much of the summer surfing a renewed wave of popularity thanks to the home run race. It had gradually reestablished its presence in the national psyche after the trauma of the 1994–95 strike, and the climax to the season promised even more drama as Sosa and McGwire battled it out for the home run crown, while the New York Yankees kept up a record-breaking winning pace in the American League. Selig had good reason, therefore, to treat McGwire's admission of androstenedione use with care, reluctant to upset the good news applecart. His first public comment reflected his caution: "The Cardinals are a disciplined

---

[21] Quoted in Miklasz, "Everyone Seems Pumped Up About McGwire and Andro."

[22] Bernie Miklasz, "Andro Isn't What Powers McGwire," *Pittsburgh Post-Gazette*, August 26, 1998.

[23] Dan Shaughnessy, "This Persecution of McGwire is a Crime," *Boston Globe*, August 26, 1998.

[24] Tom Keegan, "Slugger's Little Helper Falls Fair," *New York Post*, August 24, 1998.

[25] Stephen Jay Gould, "How the New Sultan of Swat Measures Up," *Wall Street Journal*, September 10, 1998.

organization and I don't think anything goes on there that shouldn't."[26] Selig then spent a couple of days making his own inquiries about the availability and properties of androstenedione before issuing another statement which avoided any mention of the ethical issues at stake: "I think what Mark McGwire has accomplished is so remarkable, and he has handled it all so beautifully, we want to do everything we can to enjoy a great moment in baseball history."[27] Like Clinton, who had closed his August 17 statement with the words, "It is time to…get on with our national life," Selig simply wanted to move matters on.[28]

The controversy had nevertheless raised issues for the baseball establishment. McGwire had not broken any rules because baseball had no rules which governed anabolic steroids or food supplements. If something was legal in law, it was legal in baseball, no matter what performance-enhancing capability it delivered. And along with no rules came no tests, a state of affairs the MLBPA was keen to preserve. Five days into the controversy, MLB and the MLBPA announced that they had agreed to fund scientific research into androstenedione, its muscle-building properties, and its potential health dangers. But their overarching ambition was to preserve the integrity of the home run race. Their joint statement of August 26 referenced the press coverage of androstenedione and reiterated that it was available, unregulated, over the counter: "In view of these facts, it seems inappropriate that such reports should overshadow the accomplishments of players such as Mark McGwire."[29]

Americans, fatigued by the seven-month long saga of presidential shame, appeared to have little appetite to engage with a second scandal in public life. Indeed, their enthusiasm for the home run race only escalated. In the days immediately after the AP story, McGwire attracted standing ovations and capacity crowds in Pittsburgh, the first time there had been three successive sellouts for regular season baseball in the twenty-seven-year history of the Three Rivers Stadium. Press coverage reflected the public mood and routinely gave greater prominence to the astonishing rate

---

[26] Quoted in Joe Drape "McGwire Admits Taking Controversial Substance," *New York Times*, August 22, 1998.

[27] Quoted in Pessah, *The Game*, 236–37.

[28] Clinton, "Address to the Nation on Testimony Before the Independent Counsel's Grand Jury."

[29] Murray Chass, "Baseball Tries to Calm Down Debate on Pills," *New York Times*, August 27, 1998.

of home run hitting by McGwire and Sosa over the allegations of artificial performance enhancement. It had echoes of another mass psycho-sociological phenomenon eighty years earlier, when the American public had displayed a similarly complex attitude to its flawed heroes—when the mythologised history of the game's righteousness and integrity had jarred with the reality of corruption and deceit. On that occasion, three Chicago White Sox ballplayers had confessed to a grand jury that they, along with five teammates, had agreed to throw the 1919 World Series at the behest of a gambling syndicate. Responding to what became known as the "Black Sox Scandal," the baseball owners and the press demanded stiff sanctions, including criminal charges and a ban from the game. But the public saw it differently. Crowds cheered when the accused players were acquitted in court, and though they were banned from the organized game, they became a popular attraction on barnstorming tours. Many Americans seemed to be determined to deny the entire affair and pretend nothing was wrong: at a time of national anxiety—with newspapers full of talk of "Red Scares" and waves of labor unrest breaking across the country—baseball was the one institution that was supposed to represent traditional American values. The historian Steven Riess summed up the prevailing mindset: "If baseball was no good what hope was there for the rest of our culture and society?"[30] It was psychological impulse which would be mirrored eight decades later, when, against the evidence, Americans again chose to believe in baseball at a time of national moral crisis. As the investigative journalist Howard Bryant commented: "McGwire had become untouchable, a national hero who had restored the national game even though it was clear that he had helped usher the game into a murky, unchartered space."[31]

This public's desire to put the androstenedione scandal behind them was matched by most in the media, who saw more merit in celebrating the drama of the home run chase than offering further investigations into the chemical properties of a legal dietary supplement. For the time being, the possibility that it was evidence of a bigger PED problem—demonstrated by the expanding body sizes of players and the unprecedented power-hitting numbers—gained little traction. There were other potential angles that reporters could have followed: McGwire's training partner was his

---

[30] Riess, *Touching Base*, 96.
[31] Bryant, *Juicing the Game*, 139.

brother Jay, a bodybuilder and self-identified steroid user.[32] But for the time being, the stories went unwritten. Instead, criticism of McGwire's dubious use of a bodybuilding supplement was limited to the occasional rebuke for bad judgement or foolishness—just as Clinton was criticized for attempting, on August 17, to explain away his encounter with Lewinsky as a "lapse of judgment."[33] So it was that *People* magazine lamented those who "carped" about McGwire, rather than celebrated his home runs, "his mile-wide smile and affectless candor," that had "shifted the gaze of a scandal-weary country from Monica's soiled blue dress to the clean green diamonds of the national game."[34]

The Soiling of Baseball's Clean Green Diamonds

For a few years the supposedly "clean green diamonds" of professional baseball, and the heroes who performed on them, would simultaneously be the subject of admiration as symbols of a revived American culture and the subject of a growing unease over the use of PEDs. The unease would be voiced by campaigning doctors and scientists, a handful of dogged investigative journalists, and a few retired players anxious about the vulnerability of their own records. All were concerned that doping was chipping away at the game's integrity and threatening the health of players. In contrast, the admiration for the national pastime's "clean green diamonds" came from the majority of professional baseball's stakeholders—the fans, the players union, the sports media, and the owners—whose blinkered desire to view baseball as an emblem of the purity of American values only increased in the aftermath of the terror attacks of 9/11, when ballparks became the rallying point for public displays of militarized patriotism. With millions of Americans convinced that the country faced an existential threat, the power exemplified by big-hitting ballplayers bound baseball and the military together in a metaphorical joint response to an enemy assault on home territory—American might was good in whatever form it came. And it was professional baseball that provided some of the most iconic post-9/11 images: the moment Sammy Sosa sprinted onto Wrigley Field for the first game in Chicago after the terror attacks, the stars-and-

---

[32] Jay McGwire, *Mark and Me,* 179–80.
[33] Clinton, "Address to the Nation on Testimony Before the Independent Counsel's Grand Jury."
[34] People Staff, "Mark McGwire," *People*, December 28, 1998.

stripes held aloft in his right hand, and the crowd roaring its approval, his immigrant background underlining the game's status as an unifying cultural emblem. Or President Bush, a bulletproof vest concealed beneath his baseball jacket, throwing the ceremonial opening pitch of Game Three of the 2001 World Series in New York, just a few weeks after the Twin Towers fell: "We were shaking with fear, we needed his hand to be steady," recalled one observer. "A thrown ball should not create a lump in our throats, but it did because baseball…remains the quintessential American sport."[35]

This fiction of baseball's ideological and physical purity, however, would not endure. It was clear that the game's green diamonds were as soiled as Lewinsky's blue dress—a culture of concealment as pervasive in professional baseball as it had been in the Clinton presidency. The lust for record-breaking from the press, the public, the players, and those running the game remained as strong as ever, but the suspicions about athletes who now appeared to have near-superhuman levels of strength and stamina made it increasingly difficult to continue turning a blind eye. Bodies were growing bigger, and balls were flying further, with greater frequency. In the year Clinton was first elected, MLB players hit 3,038 home runs; in 2000 they hit a record 5,693. Even allowing for the four extra franchises that were added to the MLB schedule in 1993 and 1998, the increase of eighty-seven percent in eight years was out of kilter. Before 1998, Roger Maris's single-season home run record had stood for thirty-seven years: McGwire's new mark of seventy stood for just three. It fell a few weeks after 9/11, to Barry Bonds of the San Francisco Giants, a prodigious slugger whose body size and shape had transformed late in his career. Rumors of steroid-taking stalked Bonds' record-breaking season and would, in time, envelop more players as investigative journalists and the federal authorities finally started asking questions about baseball's bulked-up physiques and eye-popping numbers.

Key to the unravelling of baseball's wholesome image was the whistleblowing of former ballplayers. First up was Jose Canseco, a former American League Most Valuable Player (MVP) who retired from the game, unhappily out of form, in 2002. In a farewell interview with AP, Canseco, who had been the subject of occasional press speculation about

---

[35] John Flynn, "Why George W. Bush's Post 9/11 Baseball Pitch Was Perfect," *elitedaily.com*.

PED use since the late-eighties, said up to eighty-five percent of major league ballplayers were taking steroids, adding: "There would be no baseball left if they drug-tested everyone today."[36] In a best-selling book published three years later, Canseco would go further, naming names and directly implicating his former teammate McGwire. "Right after batting practice, or right before the game, Mark and I would duck into a stall in the men's room, load up our syringes and inject ourselves."[37] Canseco's initial claims in 2002 had been met with familiar denials in ballpark clubhouses, but within a few weeks another former star confirmed the thrust of his story. In an interview with *Sports Illustrated*, Ken Caminiti, a National League MVP who had retired in 2001, admitted he had used steroids since the mid-1990s. And although he shaved several percentage points off the Canseco numbers, Caminiti still claimed that up to half of all major league ballplayers were doing the same.[38]

No longer could the baseball press ignore the story; players in locker rooms across the country were asked for their response to Caminiti's account of baseball's steroid culture. Most tried to deflect the issue or insist it had nothing to do with them. Sosa said he would be "first-in-line" if testing started, but ill-temperedly cut short a *Sports Illustrated* interview when pressed about why he did not just go ahead and get tested anyway. He explained to the reporter that his extra body bulk was down to having a tooth repaired which allowed him to eat more healthily.[39] For the time being, McGwire was able to avoid such contorted explanations—he had retired after the 2001 season, claiming to be "worn out."[40]

With negotiations over a new collective bargaining agreement underway, Selig saw an opportunity to insist on the inclusion of a deal with the union on testing: "We were the only major sport that couldn't test our players and the integrity of our competition—and our records—was an open question."[41] Meanwhile, federal authorities were beginning an investigation in San Francisco into the supply of illegal PEDs to professional athletes by the Bay Area Laboratory Co-operative (BALCO)—a probe

---

[36] Quoted in Bryant, *Juicing the Game*, 191.

[37] Canseco, *Juiced*, 7–8.

[38] Tom Verducci, "Totally Juiced," *Sports Illustrated*, June 3, 2002.

[39] Rick Reilley, "Excuse Me For Asking," *Sports Illustrated*, July 8, 2002.

[40] ESPN News Services, "'Worn out' McGwire retires from baseball," November 11, 2001, *espn.com*.

[41] Selig, *For the Good of the Game*, 228.

that would eventually ensnare the baseball stars Barry Bonds, Jason Giambi, and Gary Sheffield, all of whom would be summoned to give evidence to a federal grand jury.[42] And where federal investigators went, politicians usually followed. Under pressure from Congress to gauge the scale of the problem, MLB agreed to the anonymous drug testing of all players towards the end of the 2003 season. 104 produced positive results, although their names were not released at the time.[43] In April 2004, on the same day that the US Food and Drug Administration (FDA) announced a ban on the sale of androstenedione, MLB finally banned its use. Players would now be suspended if twice testing positive, although there was no public announcement of the ban or the potential sanctions.[44]

It was now open season for politicians to attack the integrity of the national pastime and its flawed heroes. A New York congressman, John Sweeney, called for an asterisk to be placed against Bonds' 2001 home run record.[45] Senator John McCain of Arizona said the game was in danger of "becoming a fraud in the eyes of the American people."[46] President Bush, who as part-owner of the Texas Rangers in the late-eighties and early-nineties was one of a generation of baseball executives who had collectively ignored the early warning signs of steroid use, used the platform of his State of the Union Address to urge the professional game "to send the right signal, to get tough, and to get rid of steroids now."[47] The House of Representatives followed up with a series of hearings, entitled "Restoring Faith in America's Pastime" at which McGwire and Sosa, were called to give evidence under oath. Sosa, who was still playing for the Chicago Cubs, denied taking illegal PEDs. Speaking through his lawyer he said: "I have not broken the laws of the United States or the Dominican Republic." Again, there were echoes of Clinton—careful wording, shrouded in legal technicality. McGwire pursued a different strategy, offering neither confirmation nor denial. He expressed support for stronger policies against

---

[42] Fainaru-Wada and Williams, *Game of Shadows*.

[43] Selig, *For the Good of the Game*, 254.

[44] AP, "Baseball Bans Andro," *Dubuque Telegraph Herald*, June 26, 2004.

[45] AP, "Bonds Refuses Comment; Others Issue Denials," *espn.com*, March 3, 2004,.

[46] Richard Sandomir, "Baseball Receives Steroid Warning," *New York Times*, March 11, 2004.

[47] George W. Bush, "Address Before a Joint Session of the Congress on the State of the Union, January 20, 2004," *American Presidency Project*.

performance enhancing drugs but offered no opinion on the scale of cheating in the sport during his playing career. When Representative Lacy Clay turned the questioning to the subject of paternal role models, McGwire became tearful.

> Clay: Mr. McGwire we are both fathers of young children. Both my son and daughter love sports and look up to stars like you. Can we look at those children with a straight face and tell them that great players like you played the game with honesty and integrity?
>
> McGwire: Like I said earlier, I am not going to go into the past and talk about my past. I am here to play a positive influence on this.[48]

It was a line McGwire repeated time after time during the testimony and one that was met with skepticism. Journalists who had celebrated his record-breaking feats in 1998 with such unquestioning glee were unimpressed with McGwire's evasiveness. The *New York Times* labelled McGwire a "role model in history" who was "avoiding the past."[49] His tears were no longer indicative of sensitive masculinity and emotional depth but a sign of weakness. He appeared to be physically and emotionally diminished, according to George Solomon in the *Washington Post* who described McGwire as "timid" in comparison to the "sheer power and dominance" of 1998.[50] Rick Reilly, whose "Good Father" article in September 1998 had done so much to carve out McGwire's heroic profile, was venomous: "You looked small and weak....They say getting off steroids will do that to your body. Can it do that to your morals too?" Americans forgive everything but lies, he wrote: "Even President Clinton said, 'I'm sorry' for cheating."[51]

---

[48] Committee on Government Reform, House of Representatives, March 17, 2005, "Restoring Faith in America's Pastime: Evaluating Major League Baseball's Efforts to Eradicate Steroid Use," *US Government Publishing Office*, 215–16.

[49] George Vecsey, "Avoiding the Past, a Role Model is History," *New York Times*, March 18, 2005.

[50] George Solomon, "Up on the Hill Baseball Finds a Mountain of Trouble," *Washington Post*, March 20, 2005.

[51] Rick Reilly, "Choking Up at The Plate," *Sports Illustrated*, March 28, 2005.

McGwire's Clinton-Style Confession

The five years between Mark McGwire's tearful stonewalling on Capitol Hill and his similarly tearful confession to steroid use in 2010 would see baseball riven by revelations of current and historic steroid use and struggling to respond. Just three weeks after the congressional committee hearing, Alex Sanchez became the first MLB player suspended under a new testing regime—other players would follow. Convictions of some of those involved in the supply of drugs to athletes by BALCO began in October 2005, and the shockwaves from that case would be felt in baseball for the rest of the decade and beyond. Senator George Mitchell's MLB-commissioned, twenty-month investigation into steroids in baseball was published in December 2007 and identified what one newspaper headlined, "An All-Star List" of eighty-nine steroid users.[52] In 2009 the names of those who had tested positively in the supposedly anonymous 2003 testing program began to leak into the media—they included Sosa, whose lawyer refused to comment.[53]

Given the awkwardness of his appearance at the 2005 congressional hearing, and the allegations that Canseco had made in his book, when McGwire finally admitted in 2010 that he had used steroids during his record-breaking season, few were surprised. McGwire's confession, however, did dredge up memories of 1998, drawing comparison in its mediation with the confessions of Bill Clinton, whose own flaws were still so strongly associated with that period. McGwire's written statement to AP on January 10 was initially fulsome: "It was a mistake, I truly apologise." But what began as contrition, swiftly turned to self-justification, projecting his victimhood rather than his culpability: he had only taken substances to recover from injury; it was the steroid era, and just happened to be playing at the time. Looking back, he said, he wished he had "never played in the steroid era."[54] His denial of agency was reminiscent of Clinton emphasizing his own victimhood at the hands of Starr's investigation. Just as

---

[52] "An All-Star List," *Baltimore Sun*, December 14, 2007.

[53] Michael S. Schmidt, "Another Blow to an Epic Chase," *New York Times*, June 17, 2009.

[54] "Text of Mark McGwire's Statement on Steroids," *USA Today*, January 11, 2010.

Clinton had admitted being less than fully truthful about his relationship with Lewinsky during legal proceedings in the Paula Jones case, so McGwire spoke of not being in a position "to come clean" during his congressional testimony. While Clinton called on the expertise of his White House communications department to handle the fallout from his scandal, so McGwire drew his media advice from a similar source: Ari Fleischer, the White House Press Secretary under George W. Bush, coordinated McGwire's media appearances, offering telephone interviews with his client to select journalists, and a single, sit-down TV interview, which was made available via AP. Often in tears, McGwire described his athletic ability as a "gift from the man upstairs"; there was not a pill or an injection, he insisted, that would give him the hand-eye coordination to hit a baseball. Even without steroids, he would have hit home runs at a record-breaking pace, he claimed. He admitted wrongdoing but, again like Clinton, argued that its consequences could be narrowly defined.[55] And in the same way that Clinton had sought to "turn away from the spectacle of the past seven months," to "move on" and get back to work for America, so McGwire asked for the freedom to "pour himself" into his new job as a hitting coach for the Cardinals "to help my team."[56]

The media recognized the structural similarities of the confessions of McGwire and Clinton, weaving together the narrative of the home run race and presidential scandal just as they had a dozen years earlier. Kevin Huffman in the *Washington Post* called it a "caveat" confession: "The prototype here is Bill Clinton's Monica Lewinsky apology—i.e. I apologize for my behavior. Now let me remind you that I was unfairly persecuted."[57] *Sports Illustrated* highlighted the timing of McGwire's apology, describing it as "a career move" to clear the way for his return to the game as a coach, just as newspapers in 1998 had portrayed Clinton's confession as a cynical act to salvage his presidency. The magazine also revived images of

---

[55] MLB Bash Brothers Videos, "Mark McGwire Steroids Admission #3," *YouTube*.

[56] "Text of Mark McGwire's Statement on Steroids"; Clinton, "Address to the Nation on Testimony Before the Independent Counsel's Grand Jury."

[57] Kevin Huffman, "Reid, Arenas and McGwire and the Art of Apology," *Washington Post*, January 13, 2010.

fatherhood, though it was no longer "The Good Father." Like Clinton, McGwire had surrendered that epithet, condemned for using his son as "a prop throughout the phony joyride."[58] FOX Sports accused him of "warping the record books."[59] McGwire had contaminated "a culturally transcendent moment," failing as a father and sinning against baseball's sacred records.[60]

Unlike Mark McGwire, Sammy Sosa has never confessed to steroid use, although over the years he has refined how he answers questions about it. From his legalistic denial on Capitol Hill in 2005, Sosa now offers the more ambiguous response: "I never failed a PED test in my career."[61] It is a formulation that has carried little weight with the Baseball Writers Association of America (BBWAA), the guardians of entry into the holy of holies, the Baseball Hall of Fame in Cooperstown. Despite posting career numbers that would otherwise justify election, Sosa, in his final year of automatic eligibility in 2022, failed to garner the votes required. It is the same for McGwire whose retirement was so long ago his name has long been absent from the annual BBWAA ballot. Confession or denial—it made no difference. Instead, both are remembered for the historic season when their achievements were inextricably bound up with the public's yearning for normality, for their big-hitting exploits which briefly eclipsed the trauma of a moral failure at the heart of political and national life, and for their fall from grace in the years that followed. Ballplayers in the 1990s, it turned out, were not heroic constructions of American masculinity, the inheritors of baseball's sacred ideology, but the bulked-up products of performance enhancing drugs. Although the myth of the game's purity powered a civil religious narrative of the saintly Sosa and McGwire, in truth, it obscured a culture of concealment and moral corruption—a culture which the national pastime shared with a presidency shamed by scandal.

---

[58] Selina Roberts, "Coming Clean: It's Complicated," *Sports Illustrated*, January 25, 2010.

[59] Ken Rosenthal, "McGwire's Confession Falls Short," *foxsports.com*, January 11, 2010.

[60] Josh Levin, "I'm Here To Talk About the Past," *Slate.com*, January 12, 2010.

[61] Paul Myerberg, "Sammy Sosa Says He Never Failed a Test for PED," *USA Today*, June 15, 2020.

In the summer of 1998, William Bennett, so often the scourge of the President, suggested that that the Clinton years offered "a window onto our times, our moral order, our understanding of citizenship," when a diffident public, with all the evidence of wrongdoing, had simply shrugged its shoulders.[62] Despite all its claims to civil religious virtue, baseball in the 1990s, it seemed, was playing in the same moral ballpark as the President.

---

[62] Bennett, *The Death of Outrage*, 10, 133.

Conclusion

Baseball, Civil Religion, and the Exercise of Presidential Power.

More than twenty years after he ceased spinning for the President, Mike McCurry offered this reflection on Bill Clinton's efforts to end the 1994–95 players strike: "I remember thinking to myself, this doesn't require spin, it's baseball. Presidents are supposed to do baseball. That's what they do. It's part of what the deal is if you're President of the United States." People searching for some other motive in Clinton's actions, McCurry added, were "overthinking."[1] At the risk of falling into the overthinking trap set by the former White House Press Secretary, I suggest that this view that presidents just "do baseball," while both banally reductive and culturally complex, is nevertheless a useful benchmark for this book. Underpinning McCurry's statement is an implicit understanding that the national pastime and the presidency have an unbreakable bond, a relationship grounded in a revealed faith enacted through the civil religious symbolism, rituals, and ideology of the game: and furthermore that the relationship, which some felt had diminished to the point of irrelevance by the time Clinton took office, made important contributions to shaping discourses around some of the most contested issues of the 1990s. These included debates on race, gender, and family; morality in private and public life; the work ethic and business culture; and affirmative action and the role of the state in welfare provision. These discussions inevitably informed a wider discourse on what it meant to be American in a society whose ethnic and racial composition was constantly changing, where economic forces were disrupting the fabric of the lives of millions, and in which rising political polarization was narrowing the grounds on which Americans had previously found a measure of consensus. Against this backdrop, the President and many political and media actors accepted that baseball exemplified a set of mythical national characteristics and values, which, when expressed

---

[1] McCurry, interview by author.

through a civil religious framework, could be utilized to appeal to citizens of what many believed was a fractured American community. Amidst the societal restlessness brought about by economic anxiety and cultural unease, Clinton deployed baseball-as-metaphor and mobilized baseball-as-civil-religion in his attempts, admittedly not always with success, to communicate controversial policies and sustain his sometimes-precarious presidential leadership.

It is in the output of the filmmaker Ken Burns where we observe vividly this dual cultural role for baseball—as a metaphor for a mythical American history and as an emblem of an American civil religion. And it was Burns' "gospel of Americanism" which connected the White House's embrace of baseball with Clinton's efforts to reenergize his presidency following the Republican landslide of 1994. Alongside Morris and his strategic triangulations, Clinton's aide, Don Baer, played a crucial part in enacting the pivot in 1995 which aimed to reconnect the presidency with the electorate. Enthused by Burns' "rhetorical artistry" and his promotion of the "enduring, eternal values" which he felt would resonate with middle-class Americans, Baer emboldened the President's communications with appeals to notions of compromise and community which would be the foundation for Clinton's later interactions with baseball.

This values-laden turn by Clinton from 1995 displayed itself in a raft of social initiatives and in a revised communications strategy which aimed to reboot his political message. Notably, it saw the civil religious rhetoric and symbolism of baseball brought to the fore through the connections made by Clinton between Cal Ripken Jr.'s embodiment of the work ethic and the reform of the welfare system. With Ripken as his workhorse avatar, Clinton could frame a controversial policy proposal within a quasi-religious framework of toil, responsibility, and endurance. Clinton's multifaceted civil religious performances on the night in Baltimore when Ripken broke Lou Gehrig's fifty-six-year-old consecutive game record, were part of a vibrant celebration of American values, which placed the veneration of work at the core of a national creed at the very moment contested welfare legislation lay before Congress. The Ripken parable boosted a key component of the president's domestic agenda and helped to revive the cultural relevance of baseball because it addressed the concerns of millions of White, middle-class Americans who supported the overhaul of the benefits system. It was this capacity of baseball to act as a cultural balm to some parts of society which felt aggrieved by economic uncertainty and alienated by cultural change which was so effectively instrumentalized by the President.

The enlistment of the heroic image of Ripken, with all its quasi-religious packaging, may have struck a chord with the White, middle-class supporters of welfare reform, but for much of Black America such associations were hollow, scarred as baseball was by a historic record of racial exclusion and a 1990s reality of persistent racial discrimination. Upholding his instinctive commitment to multiculturalism and One America, Clinton found himself caught between his symbolic obligations as president towards the national pastime and the reality of the professional game's institutionalized racism. These tensions surfaced in the public arena on two notable occasions: in a clash between Clinton and Jesse Jackson focused on the Opening Day Pitch in 1993; and during the celebrations in 1997 of the fiftieth anniversary of the integration of baseball. Looming over both were the issue of affirmative action and the mythologised memory of Jackie Robinson, baseball's original saint. Affirmative action had ignited some of the most racially charged debates of the Clinton years: fought out in the courts, in the voting booths, and in the media; on campuses, in workplaces, and in sports arenas. For some African American public intellectuals, such as Gerald Early, Robinson's breakthrough in 1947 was the "most magnificent case of affirmative action."[2] For Clinton, it was an embodiment of his own multicultural philosophy—Robinson's baseball career a powerful example of the positive effect, morally and economically, of drawing talent from all parts of society. To Jackson, however, Robinson's entry into professional baseball was an experiment in integration that had long-since stalled at the hands of racist baseball owners who routinely excluded non-Whites from the top jobs. Appropriating the Robinson myth, as Clinton did, was a convenient way for those in power to pay lip service to an iconic moment of African American progress while simultaneously backgrounding the pervasive presence of race-based inequality in the national pastime and in broader society. Despite his being a story that moved both Black and White Americans with its connections to the civil rights movement, Robinson was a problematical figure for a multicultural American civil religion, the ferocity of his condemnation of racism in his own country casting doubt on the existence of any national creed that embraced both Blacks and Whites.

---

[2] Early, "Performance and Reality."

Race in the national pastime also surfaced when two contrasting narratives grappled for attention over the summer of 1998. Competing discourses on morality, masculinity, fatherhood, family, and race flooded the public arena when the heroic baseball exploits of a White Californian, Mark McGwire, and a Black immigrant from the Dominican Republic, Sammy Sosa, were seized upon as a potential source of national redemption for the sins of a disgraced president. Those seeking to bring Clinton down saw opportunity in drawing contrasts between the baseball players' supposed moral excellence and the President's moral failings; equally, Clinton appeared to believe he could achieve a measure of personal redemption by associating himself with the excellence, dedication, and work ethic of the ballplayers. In reality, rather than presenting either side with an opening for some sort of victory in the culture wars, issues which already divided Americans according to their moral worldviews were brought into sharp focus: questions about private versus public morality; the status of the First Family and the structure of families in general; the role of fathers; the sexualization of heroes and the sexualization of popular culture in general. Declarations of a color-blind indifference to the outcome of the home run race appeared alongside coded assumptions about the inevitable whiteness of the victor, undermining notions of a multicultural civil religion expressed through baseball, however much Clinton would have wished otherwise.

The opening words of this book recalled the 1999 State of the Union Address in which, under the cloud of his impeachment trial, Clinton saluted Sammy Sosa to the bipartisan acclaim of Congress. It closes with an event a little more than two weeks later, with senators yet to deliver their verdict, when Clinton spoke at a dinner in Atlanta honoring the legendary hitter Hank Aaron. Like Jackie Robinson's breakthrough in 1947, Aaron's baseball story fused sporting excellence with symbolic meaning: he was a hero whose achievement in 1974 in eclipsing Babe Ruth's career home run record was marred by racist abuse and death threats directed at him for daring, as an African American, to remove Babe Ruth from the record books. In his comments that evening, Clinton reworked Jacques Barzun's famous observation: Aaron's life, Clinton said, was "the story of a changing America being manifest in baseball. Knowing it is necessary to know the mind and heart of modern America." Clinton then summoned the familiar tropes and symbols of the baseball mythos: heroism, the sanctity of records, Robinson, generational transmission, and the American Dream.

Aaron, he said, was being honored "not only for the power of his swing but for the power of his spirit; not only for breaking records but for breaking barriers; not only for chasing his dream but, even more, for giving children…the chance to chase theirs."[3] This brief speech, delivered with his own political future in the balance, contained the essence of Clintonian baseball rhetoric presented in a civil religious setting—an optimistic synthesis of imagined ideals and images drawn from a national collective memory, linking America's destiny, and by implication his own, to the fortunes of the national pastime.

The President was not alone in wanting to believe that baseball supplied a set of metaphors and myths which had a common meaning to millions of Americans as the twentieth century drew to a close. And while Clinton attempted to capitalize on that emotional link for his own political purposes, he also expressed the hope that, at a time of social and economic disruption, the cultural power exerted by baseball could serve his vision for a community of One America. In the context of the culture wars, where values were the main battleground, and where a polarizing president was condemned by his opponents as the incarnation of a corrupt moral code inherited from the sixties, Clinton recognized that his challenge was to find ways to talk about values that unified rather than divided, to find symbols of a common inheritance which could draw people together. There were precious few opportunities to do this, but the mythology of baseball offered him one plausible route. By invoking the game's ideals and heroes in this speech in Atlanta, the President was once again embracing one of America's most cherished institutions, and, through the communication of its civil religious meaning, using it in the exercise of political power.

---

[3] William J. Clinton, "Remarks at a Gala Honoring Hank Aaron in Atlanta, Georgia, February 5, 1999," *American Presidency Project*.

Selected Bibliography and Sources

Books and Scholarly Articles

Abbott, Philip. "A 'Long and Winding Road': Bill Clinton and the 1960s." *Rhetoric & Public Affairs* 9, no. 1 (2006): 1–20.

Adut, Ari. *On Scandal: Moral Disturbances in Society, Politics and Art*. New York: Cambridge University Press, 2008.

Alexander, Lisa Doris. *When Baseball Isn't White, Straight and Male: The Media and Difference in the National Pastime*. Jefferson, NC: McFarland & Company, 2013.

Anderson, Benedict. *Imagined Communities: Reflections on the Origin and Spread of Nationalism*. Revised edition. London: Verso, 2016.

Anderson, Terry H. *The Pursuit of Fairness: A History of Affirmative Action*. Oxford: Oxford University Press, 2004.

Angell, Roger. *A Pitcher's Story: Innings With David Cone*. New York: Warner, 2001.

Annas, George J. *American Bioethics: Crossing Human Rights and Health Law Boundaries*. Oxford: Oxford University Press, 2005.

Armour, Mark, and Daniel R. Levitt. "Baseball Demographics, 1947–2016." *Society For American Baseball Research*. https://sabr.org/research/article/baseball-demographics-1947-2012/. Accessed March 2023.

Associated Press, ed. *Home Run! The Year the Records Fell*. Champaign, IL: Sports Publishing, 1998.

Baker, William. *Of Gods and Games: Religious Faith and Modern Sports*. Athens: University of Georgia Press, 2016.

Barber, Benjamin R. *The Truth of Power: Intellectual Affairs in the Clinton White House*. New York: W. W. Norton & Co., 2001

Barzun, Jacques. *God's Country and Mine: A Declaration of Love Spiced With a Few Harsh Words*. Boston: Little Brown, 1954.

Bellah, Robert N. "Civil Religion in America." *Daedalus: Journal of the American Academy of Arts and Sciences* 96, no. 1 (1967): 1–21.

———. *The Broken Covenant: American Civil Religion in a Time of Trial*. 2nd ed. Chicago: University of Chicago Press, 1992.

Bennett, William J. *The Death of Outrage: Bill Clinton and the Assault On American Ideals*. New York: Touchstone, 1999.

Bercovitch, Sacvan. *The American Jeremiad*. Madison: University of Wisconsin Press, 1978.

Berlant, Lauren, and Lisa Duggan, eds. *Our Monica Ourselves: The Clinton Affair and the National Interest*. New York: New York University Press, 2000.

Berrett, Jesse. *Pigskin Nation: How the NFL Remade American Politics*. Urbana: University of Illinois Press, 2018.

Blumenthal, Sidney. *The Clinton Wars*. London: Viking, 2003.

Bodley, Hal. *How Baseball Explains America*. Chicago: Triumph, 2014.

Branch, Taylor. *The Clinton Tapes: A President's Secret Diary*. London: Simon & Schuster, 2009.

Briley, Ron. "Baseball and America in 1969: A Traditional Institution Responds to Changing Times." In *Class at Bat, Gender on Deck and Race in the Hole: A Line-up of Essays on Twentieth Century Culture and America's Game*, 196–211. Jefferson, NC: McFarland & Company, 2003.

Bryant, Howard. *Juicing the Game: Drugs, Power and the Fight for the Soul of Major League Baseball*. New York: Plume, 2006.

Burk, Robert F. *Much More Than a Game: Players, Owners and American Baseball Since 1921*. Chapel Hill: University of North Carolina Press, 2001.

Burns, Adam and Rivers Gambrell, eds. *Sports and the American Presidency: From Theodore Roosevelt to Donald Trump*. Edinburgh: Edinburgh University Press, 2022.

Burns, Ken, and Geoffrey C. Ward. *Baseball: An Illustrated History*. New York: Alfred A. Knopf, 2000.

Busby, Robert. *Defending the American Presidency: Clinton and the Lewinsky Scandal*. New York: Palgrave, 2001.

Butterworth, Michael L. *Baseball and the Rhetorics of Purity: The National Pastime and American Identity During the War on Terror*. Tuscaloosa: University of Alabama Press, 2010.

———. "George W. Bush as the 'Man in the Arena': Baseball, Public Memory and the Rhetorical Redemption of a President." *Rhetoric & Public Affairs* 22, no. 1 (2019): 1–31.

———. "Race in 'the Race': Mark McGwire, Sammy Sosa, and Heroic Constructions of Whiteness." *Critical Studies in Media Communication* 24, no. 3 (2007): 228–44.

———. "Ritual in the 'Church of Baseball': Supressing the Discourse of Democracy After 9/11." *Communication and Critical/Cultural Studies* 2, no. 2 (2005): 107–29.

Canseco, Jose. *Juiced: Wild Times, Rampant 'Roids, Smash Hits and How Baseball Got Big*. New York: Regan, 2005.

Caro, Robert A. *Master of the Senate: The Years of Lyndon Johnson*. New York: Alfred A. Knopf, 2002.

Carter, Daryl A. *Brother Bill: President Clinton and the Politics of Race and Class*. Fayetteville: University of Arkansas Press, 2016.

Chidhester, David. "The Church of Baseball, the Fetish of Coca-Cola and the Potlatch of Rock 'N' Roll: Theoretical Models for the Study of Religion in American Popular Culture," *Journal of the American Academy of Religion* 64, no. 4 (2011): 743–65.

Clinton, Bill. *Between Hope and History: Meeting America's Challenges for the 21st Century*. New York: Hutchinson, 1996.

———. *My Life*. London: Hutchinson, 2004.

Clinton, Bill and Al Gore, *Putting People First: How We Can All Change America*. New York: Time Books, 1992.

Clinton, Hillary Rodham. *It Takes a Village*. London: Pocket, 1996.

Cohen, Morris R. "Baseball: A Moral Equivalent for War." *Dial*, July 26, 1919.

Connell, R.W. *Masculinities*. Cambridge: Polity, 2005.

Denton Jr, Robert E. and Rachel L. Holloway. *Images, Scandal, and Communication Strategies of the Clinton Presidency*. Westport, CT: Praeger, 2003.

DeParle, Jason. *American Dream: Three Women, Ten Kids and a Nation's Drive to End Welfare*. New York: Penguin, 2005.

Dershowitz, Alan M. *Sexual McCarthyism: Clinton, Starr and the Emerging Constitutional Crisis*. New York: Basic Books, 1998.

Dinces, Sean, and Christopher Lamberti. "Sports and Blue-Collar Mythology in Neoliberal Chicago." In *Neoliberal Chicago*, edited by Larry Bennett, Roberta Garner, and Euan Hague, 119–38. Urbana: University of Illinois Press, 2017.

Dowd Hall, Jacquelyn. "The Long Civil Rights Movement and the Political Uses of the Past." *Journal of American History* 91, no. 4 (2005): 1233–63.

Dreier, Peter. "Jackie Robinson's Legacy: Baseball, Race and Politics." In *Baseball and the American Dream: Race, Class, Gender and the National Pastime*, edited by Robert Elias, 43–63. Armonk, NY: M. E. Sharpe, 2001.

Du Bois, W. E. B. *The Souls of Black Folk*. Seattle: AmazonClassics, 2017.

Durant, Robert F. "A 'New Covenant' Kept: Core Values, Presidential Communications and the Paradox of the Clinton Presidency." *Presidential Studies Quarterly* 36, no. 3 (2006): 345–72.

Edgerton, Gary R. *Ken Burns's America*. New York: Palgrave, 2001.

———. "'Mystic Chords of Memory': The Cultural Voice of Ken Burns." In *In the Eye of the Beholder: Critical Perspectives in Popular Film and Television*, edited by Gary R. Edgerton, Michael T. Marsden, and Jack Nachbar, 11–26. Bowling Green, OH: Bowling Green State University Popular Press, 1997.

Eig, Jonathan. *Luckiest Man: The Life and Death of Lou Gehrig*. New York: Simon & Schuster, 2005.

———. *Opening Day: The Story of Jackie Robinson's First Season*. New York: Simon & Schuster, 2007.

Eisenbath, Mark. "For Mark McGwire, It Was the Culmination of a Season-Long Quest." In *The St. Louis Baseball Reader*, edited by Richard F. Peterson, 426. St. Louis: University of Missouri Press, 2006.

Eisenberg, John. *The Streak: Lou Gehrig, Cal Ripken Jr., and Baseball's Most Historic Record.* New York: Houghton Mifflin, 2017.

Elias, Robert, ed. *Baseball and the American Dream: Race, Class, Gender and the National Pastime,* Armonk, NY: M. E. Sharpe, 2001.

Evans, Christopher H. "Baseball as Civil Religion: The Genesis of a Creation Story." In *The Faith of Fifty Million: Baseball, Religion and American Culture*, edited by Christopher H. Evans and William R. Herzogg II, 13–34. Louisville: Westminster John Knox Press, 2002.

Fackre, Gabriel, ed. *Judgment Day at the White House: A Critical Declaration Exploring Moral Issues and Political Use and Abuse of Religion.* Grand Rapids, MI: Eerdman's, 1998.

Fainaru-Wadu, Mark, and Lance Williams. *Game of Shadows: Barry Bonds, Balco and the Steroids Scandal That Rocked Professional Sports.* New York: Avery, 2007.

Florio, John, and Ouisie Shapiro. *One Nation Under Baseball: How the 1960s Collided with the National Pastime.* Lincoln: University of Nebraska Press, 2017.

Fornay, Craig A. *The Holy Trinity of American Sports: Civil Religion in Football, Baseball and Basketball.* Macon, GA: Mercer University Press, 2007.

Gardella, Peter. *American Civil Religion: What Americans Hold Sacred.* New York: Oxford University Press, 2014.

Gartman, David. *Auto Slavery: The Labor Process in the American Automobile Industry, 1897–1950.* New Brunswick, NJ: Rutgers University Press, 1986.

Gerstle, Gary. *American Crucible: Race and Nation in the Twentieth Century.* New Paperback Edition. Princeton: Princeton University Press, 2017.

Giamatti, Bartlett. "Baseball and the American Character." In *A Great and Glorious Game: Baseball Writings of A. Bartlett Giamatti*, edited by Kenneth S. Robson, 41–65. Chapel Hill, NC: Algonquin Books of Chapel Hill, 1998.

———. *Take Time for Paradise: Americans and Their Games.* New York: Summit, 1991.

Gillon, Steven M. *The Pact: Bill Clinton, Newt Gingrich and the Rivalry That Defined a Generation.* New York: Oxford University Press, 2008.

Gormley, Ken. *The Death of American Virtue: Clinton vs. Starr.* New York: Crown, 2010.

Gorski, Philip. *American Covenant: A History of Civil Religion from the Puritans to the Present.* Princeton: Princeton University Press, 2017.

Gould IV, William B. "The 1994–'95 Baseball Strike and the National Labor Relations Board: To the Precipice and Back Again." *West Virginia Law Review*, no. 110 (2008): 983–97.
Guttman, Bill. *Sammy Sosa: A Biography*. New York: Pocket, 1998.
Guttmann, Allen. *From Ritual to Record: The Nature of Modern Sports*. New York: Columbia University Press, 2004.
Greenberg, Stanley G. *Dispatches From the War Room: In the Trenches with Five Extraordinary Leaders*. New York: Thomas Dunne, 2009.
Hall, Jonathan. *Mark McGwire: A Biography*. New York: Pocket, 1998.
Harris, John F. *The Survivor: Bill Clinton in the White House*. New York: Random House, 2005.
Haskins, Ron. *Work Over Welfare: The Inside Story of the 1996 Welfare Reform Law*. Washington, DC: Brookings, 2007.
Haupert, Michael J. "The Economic History of Major League Baseball." *EH.Net Encyclopedia*, edited by Robert Whaples. December 3, 2007. https://eh.net/encyclopedia/the-economic-history-of-major-league-baseball/.
Hester, Michael. "America's #1 Fan: A Rhetorical Analaysis of Presidential Sports Encomia and the Symbolic Power of Sports in the Articulation of Civil Religion in the United States." PhD diss., Georgia State University, 2005.
Higgs, Robert J. and Michael C. Braswell, *An Unholy Alliance: The Sacred and Modern Sport* Macon, GA: Mercer University Press, 2004.
Hollinger, David A. *Postethnic America: Beyond Multiculturalism*. Revised 10th Anniversary Edition. New York: Basic Books, 2005.
Hunt, Darnell M. *O. J. Simpson Facts and Fictions: News Rituals in the Construction of Reality*. Cambridge: Cambrdge University Press, 1999.
Hunter, James Davison. *Culture Wars: The Struggle to Define America*. New York: Basic, 1992.
Jeffords, Susan. *Hardbodies: Hollywood Masculinity in the Reagan Era*. New Brunswick, NJ: Rutgers University Press, 1994.
Jennings, Kenneth M. *Swings and Misses: Moribund Labour Relations in Professional Baseball*. Westport, CT: Praeger, 1997.
Jhally, Sut, and Justin Lewis. *Enlightened Racism: The Cosby Show, Audiences and the Myth of the American Dream*. Boulder, CO: Westview, 1992.
Johnson, Haynes. *The Best of Times: America in the Clinton Years*. New York: Harcourt, 2001.
Johnson, Paul Christopher. "The Fetish and McGwire's Balls." *Journal of the American Academy of Religion* 68, no. 2 (2000): 243–64.
Kim, Claire Jean. "Clinton's Race Initiative: Recasting the American Dilemma." *Polity* 33, no. 2 (2000): 175–97.

Klein, Joe. *The Natural: The Misunderstood Presidency of Bill Clinton*. New York: Broadway, 2002.

Kurtz, Howard. *Spin Cycle: Inside the Clinton Propaganda Machine*. London: Pan, 2015.

Linder, Robert D. "Universal Pastor: President Bill Clinton's Civil Religion." *Journal of Church and State* 38, no. 4 (1996): 733–49.

Logan, Bob. *More Tales from the Cubs Dugout*. Champaign, IL: Sports Publishing, 2006.

Lowenfish, Lee. *The Imperfect Diamond: A History of Baseball's Labor Wars*. Lincoln: University of Nebraska Press, 2010.

Lowenthal, David. *Possessed by the Past: The Heritage Crusade and the Spoils of History*. New York: The Free Press, 1996.

Lucas, Shelley. "Lost in Translation: Voice, Masculinity, Race and the 1998 Home Run Chase." In *Fame to Infamy: Race, Sport and the Fall from Grace*, edited by David C. Ogden and Joel Nathan Rosen, 61–75. Jackson: University Press of Mississippi, 2010.

Lupica, Mike. *Summer of '98: When Homers Flew, Records Fell and Baseball Reclaimed America*. Chicago: Contemporary, 1999.

MacCambridge, Michael. *America's Game: The Epic Story of How Pro Football Captured a Nation*. New York: Anchor, 2005.

Malin, Brenton J. *American Masculinity under Clinton: Popular Media and the Nineties "Crisis of Masculinity."* New York: Peter Lang, 2005.

Maney, Patrick J. *Bill Clinton: New Gilded Age Presidency*. Lawrence: University Press of Kansas, 2016.

Maraniss, David. *First In His Class: The Biography of Bill Clinton*. New York: Touchstone, 1996.

———. *The Clinton Enigma: A Four-and-a-Half Minute Speech Reveals the President's Entire Life*. New York: Simon & Schuster, 1998.

McGwire, Jay. *Mark and Me: Mark McGwire and the Truth About Baseball's Worst-Kept Secret*. Chicago, Triumph Books, 2010.

Mead, William B., and Paul Dickson. *Baseball: The Presidents' Game*. Washington, DC: Farragut, 1993.

Meyer, Birgit. "'Praise the Lord': Popular Cinema and Pentecostalite Style in Ghana's New Public Sphere." *American Ethnologist* 31, no. 1 (2004): 92–110.

Morgan, Iwan. *Reagan: American Icon*. London: I. B. Tauris, 2016.

Morris, Dick. *Behind The Oval Office: Getting Reelected Against the Odds*. Los Angeles: Renaissance, 1999.

Nathan, Daniel A. "Baseball as The National Pastime: A Fiction Whose Time Is Past." *The International Journal of the History of Sport* 31, no. 1–2 (2014): 91–108.

―――. *Saying It's So: A Cultural History of the Black Sox Scandal*. Urbana: University of Illinois Press, 2003.

Nathan, Daniel A., and Mary G. Mcdonald. "Yearning for Yesteryear: Cal Ripken Jr., The Streak, And the Politics of Nostalgia." *American Studies* 42, no. 1 (2001): 99–123.

Nathanson, Mitchell. *A People's History of Baseball*. Urbana: University of Illinois Press, 2012.

Neustadt, Richard E. *Presidential Power and the Modern Presidents: The Politics of Leadership from Roosevelt to Reagan*. New York: The Free Press, 1990.

Newman, Roberta. "The American Church of Baseball and The National Baseball Hall of Fame." *Nine: A Journal of Baseball History and Culture* 10, no. 1 (2001): 46–63.

Novak, Michael. *The Joy of Sports: Endzones, Bases, Baskets, Balls and the Consecration of the American Spirit*. Lanham, MD: Madison, 1976.

Nylund, David. *Beer, Babes and Balls: Masculinity and Sports Talk Radio*. Albany: State University of New York Press, 2007.

Office of the Independent Counsel. *The Starr Report: Referral to the United States House of Representatives Pursuant to Title 28, United States Code, 595 I*. London: Orion, 1998.

Ogden, David C., and Joel Nathan Rosen. *Fame to Infamy: Race, Sport and the Fall from Grace*. Jackson: University Press of Mississippi, 2010.

Packer, George. *Our Man: Richard Holbrooke and the End of the American Century*. London: Vintage, 2020.

Patterson, James T. *Restless Giant: The United States from Watergate to Bush v. Gore*. Oxford: Oxford University Press, 2005.

Pessah, Jon. *The Game: Inside the Secret World of Major League Baseball's Power Brokers*. New York: Back Bay, 2015.

Petrash, Jack. *Covering Home: Lessons in the Art of Fathering From the Game of Baseball*. Beltsville, MD: Robin Lane, 2000.

Pierman, Carol J. "Cal Ripken and the Condition of Freedom: Theme and Variations on the American Work Ethic." *Nine: A Journal of Baseball History and Culture* 7, Fall (1998): 59–74.

Polumbaum, Judy. "News For the Culture: Why Editors Put Strong Men Hitting Baseballs on Page One." *Newspaper Research Journal* 21, no. 2 (2000): 23–39.

Pratkanis, Anthony R., and Marlene E. Turner. "Nine Principles of Successful Affirmative Action: Mr Branch Rickey, Mr Jackie Robinson and the Integration of Baseball." In *Out of the Shadows: African American Baseball from the Cuban Giants to Jackie Robinson*, edited by Bill Kirwen, 194–222. Lincoln: University of Nebraska Press, 2005.

Price, Joseph L. *Rounding the Bases: Baseball and Religion in America*. Macon, GA: Mercer University Press, 2006.

Putnam, Robert D. "Bowling Alone: America's Declining Social Capital." *Journal of Democracy* 6, no. 1 (1995): 65–78.

———. *Bowling Alone: The Collapse and Revival of American Community.* New York: Simon & Schuster, 2000.

Rable, George C. "Patriotism, Platitudes and Politics: Baseball and the American Presidency." *Presidential Studies Quarterly* 19, no. 2 (1989): 363–72.

Rawls, John. "The Best of All Games." *Boston Review*, March 1, 2008.

———. "Two Concepts of Rules." *The Philosophical Review* 64, no. 1 (1955): 3–32.

Reich, Robert B. *Locked in the Cabinet.* New York: Alfred A. Knopf, 1997.

Remillard, Arthur. "Sports and Religion in America." *Oxford Research Encyclopedias.* March 3, 2016. https://doi.org/10.1093/acrefore/9780199340378.013.145.

Renshon, Stanley. *High Hopes: Bill Clinton and the Politics of Ambition.* New York: New York University Press, 1996.

Richmond, Peter. *Ballpark: Camden Yards and the Building of an American Dream.* New York: Simon & Schuster, 1993.

Riess, Steven A. *Touching Base: Professional Baseball and American Culture in the Progressive Era.* Urbana: University of Illinois Press, 1999.

Riess, Steven A., Jules Tygiel, Larry Gerlach, and S. W. Pope. "Roundtable: Ken Burns's Baseball." *Journal of Sport History* 23, no. 1 (1996): 61–77.

Riley, Russell L. *Inside the Clinton White House: An Oral History.* New York: Oxford University Press, 2016.

Ripken Jr., Cal, and Mike Bryan. *The Only Way I Know.* New York: Penguin, 1997.

Ripken Sr., Cal. *The Ripken Way: A Manual For Baseball and Life.* New York: Diversion, 1999.

Robinson, Jackie. *I Never Had It Made: Jackie Robinson, An Autobiography.* New York: Ecco, 1995.

Rodgers, Daniel T., *Age of Fracture.* Cambridge, MA: Belknap, 2011.

———. *The Work Ethic in Industrial America 1850–1920.* Chicago: University of Chicago Press, 1978.

Rosenfeld, Harvey. *Iron Man: The Cal Ripken Jr. Story.* New York: St. Martin's, 1995.

Roth, Philip, *The Human Stain.* London: Vintage, 2001.

Said, Edward W. "The President and the Baseball Player." *Cultural Critique* 43 (1999): 133–38.

Sandomir, Richard. *The Pride of the Yankees: Lou Gehrig, Gary Cooper and the Making of a Classic.* New York: Hachette, 2018.

Sarantakes, Nicholas Evan. *Fan in Chief: Richard Nixon and American Sports, 1969–74.* Lawrence: University Press of Kansas, 2019.

Sayle Watterson, John. *The Games Presidents Play: Sport and The Presidency.* Baltimore: John Hopkins University Press, 2009.

Schlesinger Jr., Arthur M. *The Disuniting of America: Reflections on a Multicultural Society.* Knoxville: Whittle Direct, 1991.

Selig, Bud. *For The Good of The Game: The Inside Story of the Surprising and Dramatic Transformation of Major League Baseball.* New York: William Morrow, 2019.

Smith, Curt. *The Presidents and the Pastime: The History of Baseball and the White House.* Lincoln: University of Nebraska Press, 2018.

Smith, Stephen, ed. *Bill Clinton on Stump, State and Stage: The Rhetorical Road to the White House.* Fayetteville: University of Arkansas Press, 1994.

Stanton, Tom. *Hank Aaron and the Home Run That Changed America.* New York: Perenniel Currents, 2005.

Starr, Kenneth. *Contempt: A Memoir of The Clinton Investigation.* New York: Sentinel, 2019.

Staudohar, Paul D. "The Baseball Strike of 1994–1995." In *Diamond Mines: Baseball and Labor*, edited by Paul D. Staudohar, 48–61. Syracuse: Syracuse University Press, 2000.

Stephanopoulos, George. *All Too Human: A Political Education.* Boston: Little Brown, 1999.

Sullivan, Patricia A., and Steven R. Goldzwig. "Seven Lessons From President Clinton's Race Initiative: A Post-Mortem on the Politics of Desire." In *Images, Scandal, and Communication Strategies of the Clinton Presidency*, edited by Robert E. Denton Jr. and Rachel L. Holloway, 143–71. Westport, CT: Praeger, 2003.

Takiff, Michael. *A Complicated Man: The Life of Bill Clinton As Told by Those Who Know Him.* New Haven: Yale University Press, 2010.

Troy, Gil. *Affairs of State: The Rise and Rejection of the Presidential Couple Since World War II.* New York: Simon & Schuster, 1997.

———. *The Age of Clinton: America in the 1990s.* New York: St. Martin's, 2015.

Tygiel, Jules. *Baseball's Great Experiment: Jackie Robinson and His Legacy.* Oxford: Oxford University Press, 2008.

———. "Unreconciled Strivings: Baseball in Jim Crow America," in *Past Time: Baseball as History*, 116–43. Oxford: Oxford University Press, 2000.

Waldman, Michael. *POTUS Speaks: Finding the Words That Define the Clinton Presidency.* New York: Simon & Schuster, 2000.

Weiss, Jana. "Remember, Celebrate and Forget? Martin Luther King Day and the Pitfalls of Civil Religion." *Journal of American Studies* 53, no. 2 (2019): 428–48.

Wenger, Michael R. *My Black Family, My White Privilege: A White Man's Journey Through the Nation's Racial Minefield.* Bloomington, IN: iUniverse, 2012.

White, G. Edward. *Creating the National Pastime: Baseball Transforms Itself 1903–1953*. Princeton: Princeton University Press, 1996.
White, Mark, ed. *The Presidency of Bill Clinton: The Legacy of a New Domestic and Foreign Policy.* New York: I. B. Tauris, 2012.
Will, George. *Bunts*. New York: Touchstone, 1999.
———. *Men at Work: The Craft of Baseball*. New York: Harper, 2010.
Wood, Gordon S. "History and Heritage." In *The Purpose of the Past: Reflections on the Uses of History*, 180–95. New York: Penguin, 2009.
———. "Truth in History." In *The Purpose of the Past: Reflections on the Uses of History*, 133–45. New York: Penguin, 2009.
Woodward, Bob. *The Agenda: Inside the Clinton White House*. New York: Simon & Schuster, 1995.
Zimbalist, Andrew. *In the Best Interests of Baseball? The Revolutionary Reign of Bud Selig*. Hoboken: John Wiley & Sons, 2006.

Archival Collections

Arkansas State Archives, at One Capitol Mall, Little Rock, Arkansas.
Clinton Presidential Records at the William J. Clinton Presidential Library and Museum, Little Rock, Arkansas.
Garland County Historical Society Archives at 328 Quapaw Avenue, Hot Springs, Arkansas.

Web-based Sources

American Presidency Project. Presidency.ucsb.edu.
American Rhetoric. Americanrhetoric.com/speechbank.htm.
AP Archive. Aparchive.com.
Bill Clinton Presidential Oral History Project. Millercenter.org/the-presidency/presidential-oral-histories/bill-clinton.
Bill of Rights Institute. Billofrightsinstitute.org.
Clinton Digital Library. Clinton.presidentiallibraries.us.
Clinton Foundation YouTube Channel. Youtube.com/user/clintonfoundationorg/videos.
Congressional Record Online. Congress.gov/congressional-record.
C-SPAN Video Library. C-span.org/quickguide/.
FDR Library. Fdrlibrary.org/digital-collections.
Gallup. News.gallup.com.
Ibiblio. ibiblio.org.
Justia. Law.justia.com.
Media Burn Independent Video Archive. Mediaburn.org.
National Baseball Hall of Fame and Museum. Baseballhall.org.

Pew Information and Technology Research Center. pewinternet.org.
Scribd. Scribd.com.
Smithsonian Institution. Si.edu.
Society for American Baseball Research. Sabr.org.
Statista Business Database. Statista.com.
UPI Archives. Upi.com/archives.
US Government Publishing Office. Gpo.gov.
US National Archives. Archives.gov.
Vanderbilt Television News Archive. News.vanderbilt.edu.
YouTube. Youtube.com.
4President.Org. 4president.org.

Interviews by Author

Ashbrook, Gail, Clive Convington, Liz Robbins. *Garland County Historical Society*, Hot Springs, Arkansas. January 17, 2019.
Baer, Don. New York. April 26, 2018.
Curiel, Carolyn. Chicago via Skype. July 23, 2020.
Kusnet, David. Washington, DC via Zoom. August 4, 2020.
McCurry, Mike. Washington, DC. November 6, 2019.
Waldman, Michael. New York. June 18, 2019.
Wenger, Michael. Washington, DC September 13, 2019.

A Note on Sources

In June 2019, I interviewed Bill Clinton's former Director of Speechwriting, Michael Waldman, at his office at the Brennan Center for Law in New York City. Towards the end of our session, we discussed why Clinton made repeated attempts to broker an end to the baseball strike of 1994–95, the first time a president had personally and publicly intervened in a labor dispute in professional sports. Waldman recalled one occasion when he interrupted a meeting in the Oval Office involving the President, his assistant, Bruce Lindsey, and Robert Reich, the Labor Secretary. The three were discussing the ongoing negotiations between the players union and the owners. "They were all there talking about it, and I realized nobody was writing any of it down, and it wasn't being taped or anything like that," Waldman told me. "And I was thinking, what a loss that this is happening, and that history will never know what is being said in this meeting about the baseball strike." Waldman then looked at me and said: "And then here *you* are!"[1]

In a sense, Waldman, with this casual account of a meeting of which he admits he can recall nothing of substance, encapsulates both the challenges and opportunities facing me in researching this book. Compared to most modern presidencies, Clinton's White House was, at best, inconsistent with its record keeping. Some meetings were taped by those involved to provide a record of the discussions that would be transcribed and worked-off later; most were not. Sometimes personal taping machines were switched off mid-meeting if the subject strayed into sensitive areas around the various real and not-so-real scandals boiling around the President, especially if Clinton began venting against his political and institutional foes. The paper trail is equally incomplete. Waldman, who contributed to about two thousand presidential speeches, estimates that his own records, stored at the Clinton Presidential Library only include about twenty percent of the paperwork he generated while at the White House. Other staffers simply did not take notes so fearful were they of the legal minefields surrounding the President. Joe Lockhart, Clinton's Press Secretary from 1998 to 2000, has this warning for historians: "[If] they ever

---

[1] Waldman, interview by author.

want to find a piece of paper I generated, don't bother looking. They don't exist. I didn't keep them."[2] As the oral historian Russell Riley notes, at the time of the Clinton presidency, "the twin perils of leaks and subpoenas chilled virtually every form of serious internal writing."[3] Thus the recollections of the individuals working at the White House, mined from the published oral histories and the recordings of the University of Virginia's presidential oral history project have become an important source of information about many aspects of debate, policy formulation and execution. Similarly, the limitations in the presidential archive obliged me to supplement the existing oral record with my own interviews with former staff in the Clinton Administration.

However, even allowing for the aversion to written recordkeeping by many in Clinton's sphere, his presidency still generated a voluminous quantity of archival material which remains under-explored by scholars. By April 2020, only an estimated two percent of the collection of seventy-eight million text documents at the Clinton Presidential Library in Little Rock had been digitized. A further body of processed documents were available in hard copy at the library and the remainder (the vast majority) were unprocessed and therefore only accessible through requests under freedom of information (FOIA) legislation. Similarly, of the two-and-a-half- million photographic images held at the library, only one hundred thirteen thousand had been processed. As a result, it is a resource which is difficult to interrogate with efficiency. Many of the documents cited and photographs reproduced in this book have only emerged through my own FOIA requests. This challenge is compounded by the fact that one is not dealing with discrete policy areas such as welfare reform, the federal budget or health care, subjects which naturally throw up a wealth of draft speeches, position papers, draft legislation, documents, memos, and correspondence. Instead, the archive reveals references to baseball scattered throughout the presidential records: in speeches and interviews, mentioned in policy papers on welfare, education, race, and crime, and on invitation lists to official events; in letters from the public and from advocates of campaigns wishing to press their point on subjects ranging from affirmative action to raising academic standards in schools.

---

[2] Joseph Lockhart Interview, September 19–20, 2005, *Bill Clinton Presidential Oral History.*

[3] Riley, *Inside the Clinton White House,* ix.

Of course, the familiar popular vocabulary of baseball—*hitting a home run, touching base, stepping up to the plate, throwing a curveball, in the ballpark, grand slam, left field, getting to first base, three strikes and you're out*—crops up in many documents, the language of sports used figuratively, for descriptive purposes, or deployed as shorthand for expressions of success and failure and admissions of responsibility. Sometimes the most unlikely events received the baseball linguistic treatment. For example, when a new Chief of Naval Operations was named in June 1996, the communications team drew up a briefing note for Clinton which offered a tortured baseball analogy: "A baseball coach looks for a specific quality in a lead-off hitter: speed, a good batting average and the smarts necessary to get on base and score runs that win games. Today's navy is the lead-off hitter for our nation's defense."[4] Baseball metaphors like this surfaced in other forms and contexts. The historian and former JFK advisor Arthur Schlesinger Jr. wrote to Clinton in November 1993 criticizing a fellow scholar for providing an unreliable guide to the "hits, runs and errors of the Kennedy administration."[5] Benjamin Barber's account of an 'ideas dinner' at which Clinton sought the views of prominent academics was laced with the vocabulary of the ballpark.

> I was on deck—it would be after coffee that I would actually come to the plate....[Bill] Galston turned to me: 'You're batting clean-up Ben. Go.' I went but felt less compelling than I'd been the preceding year at Camp David. I made contact, but it felt like an infield single.[6]

The language in the briefing note, the language of Barber's recollections and the words and phrases deployed at the White House dinner—*get on base, leadoff, on deck, come to the plate, batting cleanup, made contact, infield single*—all illustrate the banal presence of baseball in everyday conversation and communication. Just like any workplace in America, such

---

[4] Draft comments for President, June 5, 1996, OA/ID 3381, Folder: Chief of Naval Operations Announcement, 6/5/96, Speechwriting – Anthony Blinken, National Security Council, *Clinton Presidential Records*.

[5] Letter, Arthur Schlesinger Jr. to Bill Clinton, November 23, 1993, OA/ID 4284, Folder G: President's Letters, David Kusnet, Speechwriting, *Clinton Presidential Records*.

[6] Barber, *The Truth of Power*, 147. Until May 1995, William Galston was a deputy assistant for domestic policy. He was subsequently retained by the White House to plan 'ideas' dinners.

language was part of the backdrop of daily life, as were conversations about the sport itself, discussed over the water-cooler for seven months a year, fueled by what Clinton's press secretary Mike McCurry describes as a press corps of "sports rabid guys" who spent long days lingering in the West Wing, often with little to do on a quiet news day except follow the latest scores.[7] Such emotions and informal social relationships can be difficult for the historian to capture, but taken together, all these threads allow baseball's influence in the White House to be pieced together as a constant cultural presence deployed by the President in several ways: sometimes contextualizing policy by placing it in a framework of national ideals; by contributing role models to exemplify national virtues; and by offering a language, understood by large parts of the population, with which to communicate ideas, policies, and some elements of a national vision.

Beyond the White House, baseball's capacity to be a nationally cohesive force was as dependent on the media propagating its mythical narrative as it had been for the previous hundred years. Thus, to assess this aspect of the presidential engagement with the national pastime, I carried out a qualitative analysis of mainstream media which, across many genres, carried detailed descriptions and comment about the occasions when baseball and the presidency came together in the Clinton years, both at moments of sacred and ceremonial celebration and during periods of political and personal drama. Indeed, commentators in the major opinion-forming newspapers, *The New York Times, Washington Post, Wall Street Journal,* and *Los Angeles Times,* and syndicated columnists who reached readerships away from the coasts, were often quicker to identify the common values at stake in concurrent political and sporting dramas than were the actors themselves. The major weekly news magazines, *Time, Newsweek,* and *US News & World Report,* sometimes juxtaposed baseball and politics in their reporting, while their sports counterpart, *Sports Illustrated,* commonly constructed articles around themes of American values, masculinity, and fatherhood, especially when such subjects surfaced in the news agenda. Equally, the content and style of television coverage was essential to reinforce baseball's elevated, quasi-religious status, both through the live broadcasts of 'sacred' moments (such as Ripken's $2,131^{st}$ consecutive game and McGwire's 62nd home run), through the endless recycling of those moments on network news programs and cable channels, and in the

---

[7] McCurry, interview by author.

documentary narratives of myth contained in more meditative television series, such as Burns' *Baseball*.

Of course, the stories, images, and words were filtered by a journalistic profession that, on both the baseball and political beats, was overwhelmingly male and White. Sportswriters invariably viewed professional baseball in the light of sentimentalized childhood memories and were fiercely protective of its masculine-oriented traditions and rituals. This lack of diversity in press box personnel contributed to a uniformity in perspective of much of the output, notably the foregrounding of White men in heroic and fatherly roles while their Black colleagues were marginalized as players in a supporting cast (for example, the 1998 home run race) or assigned racial stereotypes of laziness and overindulgence (for example, media comparisons between Ripken and successful African American athletes). Representations of women, meanwhile, were largely confined to roles of mother, daughter, wife, and occasionally victim of the powerful men who were the principal actors in the journalists' dramatic plots. A handful of women occupied lonely outposts in the male-dominated sports media of the 1990s: Claire Smith, an African American journalist, spent much of the decade as a trailblazing baseball columnist for the *New York Times*, offering sharp opinions on issues of racism and diversity in the game. But when Smith left the *Times* in 1998, the number of women on the national baseball beat, let alone African American women, dropped to zero.[8] Thus, the media's controlling images which are reflected here and which were so important in framing baseball as an expression of civil religion, portray mythological enactments of White masculinity produced by the overwhelmingly White-male power structures.

Throughout the Clinton years, a significant body of writing for the mass publishing market contributed to a vigorous discourse surrounding declining morality in national life—with values in both the political and sporting culture of America being at the center of public debate. Clinton's polarizing presence in the political landscape generated its own raft of mass-market literature, much of which articulated a jeremiad rhetoric of outrage with the intention of influencing public opinion, particularly as the impeachment crisis unfolded in late 1998. And the moral fury of the right was amplified in the rapidly expanding, Rush Limbaugh-dominated

---

[8] Claire Smith, "Women Sportswriters Confront New Issues," *niemanreports.org*, September 15, 1999.

world of conservative talk radio, where broadcasters were liberated from offering a balance of viewpoints thanks to Ronald Reagan's scrapping of the "fairness doctrine" in broadcasting in 1987. Meanwhile, in old-fashioned book publishing, hagiographic mini biographies of baseball stars such as Cal Ripken Jr., Mark McGwire, and Sammy Sosa were rushed to press and sold for a few dollars on newsstands, affirming idealized images of masculinity and virtue exemplified by sporting icons.

And the debate played out in a new, vibrant, arena too: in 1994, the year the White House's first website went online, eleven million American households had access, in the newly minted language of cyberspace, to the "information superhighway." By the end of the century, more than eighty million Americans were online and "surfing the internet." The World Wide Web was the public platform on which the President's sex scandal first surfaced in January 1998 via the *Drudge Report* and where Lewinsky was first publicly linked with him, forcing the more cautious traditional media to confront the story. And seven months later, the web was an important conduit for the rapid dissemination of Kenneth Starr's report into Clinton's alleged perjury and obstruction of justice following his confession of an "inappropriate relationship" with Lewinsky, ensuring that a great slab of the American population had acquired a detailed knowledge of their President's sexual tastes within hours of Congress authorizing its publication. Alongside all the dramatic disruptions to social and economic life brought about by de-industrialization, globalization, and technological change; alongside the revolution in attitudes towards sex, morality, and the lives of public figures; alongside shifting definitions of what constituted the American family, the way in which Americans were consuming their news was changing as well.

Acknowledgments

The seeds for this book were sown almost thirty years ago, on September 6, 1995, when I sat in a press seat at Camden Yards to witness Cal Ripken Jr. breaking Lou Gehrig's record for consecutive major league appearances. In a sky box to my right President Bill Clinton stood alongside his daughter, Chelsea, and Vice President Al Gore, arms aloft, celebrating with almost fifty thousand fans inside the ballpark and millions watching on TV, one of American sports greatest-ever individual achievements. I have my then-employers, the BBC, to thank for my ticket for that memorable night in Baltimore, and over subsequent years, as I immersed myself in US politics and presidential elections on behalf of a variety of news broadcasters, I would often find myself contemplating the intimate relationship between sports, the American people, and the nation's political culture. It was a subject I frequently debated with my baseball-watching companion, Simon Buglione, during the long driving hours of our annual road trips which, over many years, have taken in every franchise in Major League Baseball. From such experiences an idea of a book took hold, but it is the historian, Uta Balbier, then of King's College London, now of the University of Oxford, who has helped shape my thoughts into the framework I present here—the interplay of the presidency and baseball as American civil religion. Further, help, advice, and comments at various stages of this project came from Iwan Morgan, Andrew Fearnley, Clare Birchall, Dan Matlin, Lynda Marlowe, and Ben Pelling. King's was generous with financial support through the Professor Sir Richard Trainor Scholarship and travel grants which allowed me to spend time in Arkansas, New York, and Washington, DC. I also received great encouragement from Cara Rodway at the Eccles Centre for American Studies at the British Library, where I was provided with a welcoming intellectual home and the opportunity to share my research with the public. In the United States, I am grateful to the archivists at the William J. Clinton Presidential Library who handled my Freedom of Information requests with such efficiency, despite being locked out of their workplace for parts of my research period due to the federal government shutdown of 2018–2019 and, more recently, the Covid-19 pandemic. I am especially pleased to have had the opportunity to work with them in person in Little Rock in January 2020. While

ACKNOWLEDGMENTS

in Arkansas, I enjoyed the hospitality of the Garland County Historical Society in Hot Springs where I learned a great deal from those who knew Bill Clinton in his youth. At Mercer University Press, Joe Price, the editor of the Sports and Religion series, has been a constant source of wisdom and guidance: whatever its remaining faults, his interventions have undoubtedly made this a better book. Others at Mercer have been invaluable in supporting this project, notably Mark Jolley, Marsha Luttrell, and Mary Beth Kosowski. I am also grateful to Edinburgh University Press for allowing me to reuse, in chapter two, parts of my essay, "'He'd Like to be Savior of the National Pastime': Bill Clinton and the 1994–1995 Baseball Strike," which first appeared in *Sports and the American Presidency: From Theodore Roosevelt to Donald Trump*, ed. Adam Burns and Rivers Gambrell (Edinburgh University Press, 2022) at pages 78–99.

It is custom in writing acknowledgements, that the thanks to those closest to the author get the final mention. By all rights, they should, of course, come first; for they are the most important building block on which all writers depend—even more so in the case of this book, much of which was written during the United Kingdom's Covid-19 lockdowns, when family was often my sole company, sustenance, and source of hope. So, with apologies to my wife Lynda, and my children Pepa and Freddy, for not getting to you until this very last sentence, thank you for keeping life in perspective when everything Clinton and baseball was in danger of overwhelming me—you have my everlasting gratitude and love.

Chris Birkett, London, October 2022

Index

Aaron, Hank, 5, 19, 92, 119, 207-208
Acosta, Gloria, 80-81
Adut, Ari, 174
affirmative action, 2, 38, 77, 113-135, 138-139, 142, 146-148, 204, 206, 222.
African American Jeremiad, 110-111, 126
Aid to Families With Dependent Children (AFDC), 107.
Alexander, Lisa Doris, 166
Ali, Mohammed, 137-138
American League, 4, 81, 92, 192, 197
AmeriCorps, 35
Anaheim Angels, 149. *See also* California Angels
Anderson, Terry, 130
androstenedione (Andro), 187-195, 198. *See also* performance enhancing drugs
Angelos, Peter, 101
Arafat, Yasir, 70
Arkansas, 12, 20, 38-39, 40, 65, 76, 83-84, 116, 132, 159
Arthur, Chester, 5
Ashcroft, John, 168
Atlanta Braves, 21-22, 24, 73
Augusta Masters, 141

Baer, Don, 14, 33-39, 42n60, 43, 47-50, 78, 205
Bagwell, Jeff, 24-25
Baird, Zoe, 42n54
Ball Four – The Fans Are Walking, 58
Ball Park Tour, 58
Baltimore, 4, 20, 53, 68, 86, 104, 105, 107, 108, 124, 126-129, 139, 180, 205
Baltimore Orioles, 67, 81, 88, 91-109, 124, 127, 128. *See also* Camden Yards
Baltimore & Ohio Railroad warehouse, 96, 99

Bancells, Richie, 93
Barber, Benjamin, 90, 222-223
Barzun, Jacques, 8-9, 207
Baseball (TV series), 3-4, 27-35, 38-39, 40, 49, 59-60, 147, 175-176. *See also* Ken Burns Baseball Fans and Communities Protection Act (1995), 66
baseball strike: 27, 29, 50-79, 82, 95, 100, 185, 192, 204, 220; Clinton intervention in, 3-4, 49-50, 51-54, 56-75; end of, 75-76; impact of, 31-32, 79, 98; origins of, 54-56; White House summit, 69-74, 76
Baseball Writers Association of America (BBWAA), 202
Bay Area Laboratory Co-operative (BALCO), 198, 200
Baylor, Don, 130
Bellah, Robert, 7-8. *See also* civil religion
Belle, Albert, 24
Bennett, William, 164, 181, 203
Berman, Chris, 100, 139-140
Black Sox Scandal, 68, 194
Blackmun, Harry, 55
Blumenthal, Sydney, 135
Bonds, Barry, 196, 198
Bosnia, 65
Boxer, Barbara, 161
Branch, Taylor, 19, 41, 67, 75, 90
Brigham Young University, 157
Brokaw, Tom, 62
Brooklyn, 110, 111, 141
Brooklyn Dodgers, 138. *See also* Ebbets Field
Bryant, Howard, 194
Buchanan, Pat, 15
Burns, Ken, 4, 23, 24, 27-28, 29-39, 40, 42-44, 47, 49, 50, 52-53, 59-61, 147, 156, 175-177, 205. *See also* *Baseball*; civil religion; *Lewis &*

Clark; The Civil War; Thomas Jefferson
Busch Stadium, 151-152, 158, 169. *See also* St. Louis Cardinals
Bush, George H.W., 15, 21, 63, 115, 120, 135
Bush, George W., 122, 196, 198, 201
Boston, 171
Boston Red Sox, 113

California, 131, 142, 155, 169
California Angels, 95, 99. *See also* Anaheim Angels
Camden Yards, 95-102, 105, 125-128, 139. *See also* Baltimore Orioles
Caminiti, Ken, 197
Camp David, 16, 48, 222
Campbell, Tevin, 140
Canseco, Jose, 196-197, 200
Caray, Harry, 20
Carter, Jimmy, 120
Carter, Stephen, 45, 47
Carville, James, 18
Chechnya, 65
Chevrolet Trucks, 93-94
Chicago, 81, 165
Chicago Cubs, 1, 6, 155, 198. *See also* Sammy Sosa; Wrigley Field
Chicago White Sox, 71, 122, 194
Chiles, Lawton, 63
Chowning, Martha, 28
Cincinnati Reds, 118-119, 128, 146. *See also* Marge Schott; Riverfront Stadium
Civil Rights Commission (CRC), 122, 123, 125
Civil Rights Act (1991), 117
Cisneros, Henry, 49
civil religion: African American, 110-111, 126-127, 128, 130, 133; American, 7, 39, 59, 89, 96, 110, 120, 132, 147; baseball as, 8-12, 17, 19, 23, 35, 39, 53, 58-59, 82, 89, 96, 119, 127, 128, 130, 133, 139, 140, 147, 148-149, 151, 175, 176, 184-185, 202-203,205-207, 208;

224; Burns and 35-38; meaning of, 7-8, 39, 101, 110-111, 125, 131, 208; multicultural 128, 132, 140, 207; Robinson and 110-114, 148-149, 150
Clay, Lacy, 199
Clemens, Roger, 24-25
Cleveland, 4, 12, 58, 105
Cleveland Indians, 19, 56. *See also* Jacobs Filed
Clinton, Chelsea: 18; at Ripken record-breaking game, 97-99, 180; relationship with father, 98, 179-180
Clinton, Hillary Rodham: 1, 18, 184, 179-180, 181; at baseball picnic, at 26-27; defends husband,163, 180
Clinton, William J. (Bill): Aaron speech (1999), 207-208; affirmative action and, 114-115, 117, 122, 129-130, 131-134, 204, 206; approval ratings of, 41, 53, 129; August 17 confession, 160-161, 179, 189-190, 193, 195, 200-202; baseball fan as 18-19, 62; basketball fan as 19-20; baseball mythology and 2-4, 7, 12, 17, 23- 24, 29, 34, 62, 74, 78-79, 185, 204-205, 208; baseball strike intervention, 3, 50-53, 56-79; Burns and, 27-29, 32, 35, 37-39, 43-44, 49; Chelsea, relationship with, 98, 179-180; communications strategy of, 42-47; community and, 12-14, 16-17, 28-29, 44-45, 48-50, 205; *Conversation With the President* (TV program), 146-147; culture wars and, 14-15, 208; D-Day anniversary speeches, 43-44; Democratic Leadership Council speech (1991), 12; Democratic National Convention (1992), 38, 117, 180; domestic agenda, of, 40-41; economy (*See also* financial crisis), 40, 44-45; father, as, 176-177, 179-182; golf and, 18, 72; health-care reform and, 13, 28, 40, 42, 76; home run

Index

race and, 3, 152, 154, 161, 169-172, 183-185, 207; impeachment, of, 1, 40, 152, 159, 161, 163, 172, 173, 184, 207, 225; Inaugural Address (1993), 59, 78; Inaugural Address (1997), 134-135; Jackson, relationship with, 116, 124-125, 127, 130, 148, 206; jogging and, 18, 64; Lewinsky and, 108-109, 152-153, 156-157, 159-160, 163-164, 172-175, 179, 190, 192, 201, 225; Los Angeles riots and, 116; Maraniss biography, 65-66; Moscow visit, 158; National Archives speech (1995), 131-132; New Democratic philosophy of 38, 44; Oklahoma City bombing and 46; Opening Day pitch (1993), 20-21, 53, 120-122, 124-130, 148, 206; Opening Day pitch (1994), 19, 20, 53; Opening Day pitch, (1996), 20; politically formative years of, 14-15; prayer breakfast speech (1995), 80-82; President's Initiative on Race, 142-145; Putnam, relationship with, 16-17, 28-29, 45, 48; race and, 116-118, 134-137, 142-145; Republican criticism of, 41-42, 49; rhetoric of, 34, 40-41, 48, 67, 77-79, 83, 135, 205, 208; Ripken and, 3, 81- 82, 86-87, 90, 96-99, 102-103, 107-108, 112, 149, 175, 180, 205-206; Robinson fiftieth anniversary and, 3, 110, 111, 112, 113-115, 138, 139-141, 144, 145, 148, 206; Ruth and, 68-69, 74; scandals, 40n54 (*See also* Lewinsky; Whitewater); Sister Souljah, criticism of, 116, 124; sports broadcaster, as, 21-23, 98-99, 128, 139-140; sports fan, as, 18-25; Starr and, 65, 152, 157, 159-160, 163, 167-168, 171-172, 191, 201, 205, 225; State of the Union Address (1995), 47-49, 66; State of the Union Address (1999), 1-2, 183-184, 207-208; State of the Union Address (2000), 5; stepfather, relationship with, 20; welfare reform and, 12-13, 40, 67, 79, 82-87, 95, 105-107, 134, 204, 205; youth of, 20, 39, 44, 83-84. *See also* civil religion; elections, Mark McGwire, Sammy Sosa

Clinton, William J. Presidential Library, 221
Coca-Cola, 8, 111
Cohen, Morris, 9
Cold War, 14-15, 44, 55, 115
Colorado Rockies, 130
Cone, David, 71, 108
Congressional Black Caucus (CBC), 84, 116, 127
Contract with America, 41-42, 47
Cooper, Gary, 89
Cooperstown, 11. *See also* National Baseball Hall of Fame
Cosby, Bill, 137
Cox, Bobby, 21
Curiel, Carolyn, 47, 132
Davis, Ossie, 61
Dershowitz, Alan, 163
DiMaggio, Joe, 92, 100-101
Dobson, James, 164
Dole, Robert, 54, 70, 95, 131
Dominican Republic, 1, 183, 199, 207
Doubleday, Abner, 11
Dowd Hall, Jacqueline, 149
Du Bois, W.E.B., 113
e pluribus unum, 36-37
Early, Gerald, 30-31, 112
East Germany, 187-188
Ebbets Field, 110. *See also* Brooklyn Dodgers
Eckhart, William, 6
Edgerton, Gary, 37
Edmonds, Terry, 138
Eig, Jonathan, 110
Eisenhower, Dwight D., 6
elections: 1992 (presidential), 38, 63, 115, 117-118; 1994 (midterms) 23, 41-42, 47-48, 57 78, 85, 129-

130, 132, 161; 1996 (presidential), 54, 63-64, 134; 1998 (midterms), 169-170
Empire State Building, 151
Equal Employment Opportunities Commission (EEOC), 122, 125
Espada Jr., Pedro, 583
ESPY Awards (TV program), 137-138
Evans, Christopher, 11
Family Support Act (1988), 84
Fans First, 58
Fayetteville, 19
Fehr, Donald 57, 64
Feinstein, Diane, 112
Field of Dreams (film), 74, 78
financial crisis, 158-159
Finkelman, Paul, 138-139
Fleischer, Ari, 201
Fletcher, Arthur, 123
Florida Marlins, 21, 133, 149
Food and Drug Administration (FDA), 198
Ford, Gerald, 64
Forneris, Tim: meets Clinton, 169-170; retrieves McGwire ball, 152, 158
Foster, Vince, 40
Gabler, Neil, 119
Garth, David, 116
Gehrig, Lou: consecutive game record, 11, 67, 73, 81-82, 86, 87, 95, 99-101, 107, 130, 205; disease, 88-89; Gary Cooper, as, 89; Ripken, comparisons with, 11, 88- 89, 92, 97, 105, 107
General Motors, 33, 93-94
Georgetown University, 84
Gerlach, Larry, 32
Giamatti, A. Bartlett, 10, 112-113
Giambi, Jason, 191, 198
Giles, William, 129
Gingrich, Newt: 2, 54, 94-95; baseball strike and 70, 74; midterms (1994) and, 41-42
Girardi, Joe, 191
Glavine, Tom, 72-73

Goodman, Ron, 104
Goodman, Walter, 32-33
Gore Jr., Albert: 117, 129, 171; baseball strike and, 52, 71, 73; Ripken record and, 97
Gould, Stephen Jay, 192
Gould IV, William, 57
Graham, Bob, 63
Graham, Katherine, 35
Great Society, 84
Green Light Letter, 6
Greenspan, Alan, 158
Grella, George, 61
Griffey Jr., Ken, 24
Gulf War, 115
gun control, 40, 78
Guttman, Allen, 11
Gwynn, Tony, 56
Hackney, Sheldon, 136-137
Hannemann, Raik, 187
Harrison, Benjamin, 5
Henderson, Ricky, 103-104
Holbrooke, Richard, 77
Hollinger, David, 136
Hollings, Fritz, 161
home run race, 3, 9, 150, 151-186, 189, 192-193, 207, 224. *See also* Mark McGwire; Sammy Sosa
Hoover Dam, 151
Hoover, Herbert, 6
Hornsby, Bruce, 96
Hot Springs, 20
Houston, 146
Hunter, James Davison, 15, 164, 176
Illinois, 170
International Monetary Fund, 158
Irby, Ken, 156
Irby, Sherry, 156
Ireland, 159
Jackson, Jesse, 115, 138: affirmative action in baseball 120-131, 146-148; All-Star Game protest, 129; Clinton, letter to 124-125; Opening Day boycott, and, 124-127, 141, 206; Schott and, 118; Sister Souljah and, 116.

Index

Jacobs Field, 19. *See also* Cleveland Indians
Japan, 71
Jeter, Derek, 149
Johnson, Andrew, 5
Johnson, Connie, 26
Johnson, Haynes, 29
Johnson, Lyndon B., 6, 70-71
Johnson, Randy, 24-25
Jones, Paula, 40, 42n54, 159, 201
Jonniaux, Alfred, 71
Jordan, Michael, 55
Justice Department, 66, 105, 122
Kansas City, 95
Kantor, Mickey, 47
Keegan, Tom, 192
Kennedy, Edward, 171
Kennedy, John F., 37, 136, 143, 173, 222,
King, Rodney, 115-116
King, Jr., Dr. Martin Luther, 114, 122, 125, 126, 146, 149
Klein, Joe, 134
Krugman, Paul, 158
Kusnet, David, 13, 23
La Russa, Tony, 191
Lader, Phil, 42n60
Lagatutta, Bill, 17
Lake, Anthony, 65
Leahy, Patrick, 103
Leibovitz, Annie, 174-175
Leno, Jay, 172
Letterman, David, 172-173
Lewinsky, Monica: blue dress, 160, 196; Clinton, relationship with, 108-109, 152-153, 156- 157, 159-160, 163-164, 172-175, 179, 190, 201, 225; jokes about affair, 173-174, 192
Lewis & Clark (TV series), 39. *See also* Ken Burns
Ley, Jim, 146
Lieberman, Joe, 161
Limbaugh, Rush, 225
Lindsey, Bruce, 57, 63-64, 74-75, 220
Little League, 45, 60, 61, 78

Little Rock, 13, 115, 221
Lockhart, Joe, 220-221
Los Angeles, 58, 105, 116, 122
Los Angeles County Superior Courthouse, 104
Los Angeles Police Department, 105
Los Angeles riots, 105, 115-116
Maddux, Greg, 24-25
Maher, Bill, 172
Major League Baseball (MLB), 3-4, 25, 27, 91, 92, 95, 120, 138, 140, 146, 182, 196; performance enhancing drugs and, 193, 198, 200; racism in, 118-119, 121-123, 125, 129, 141, 142, 149. *See also* baseball strike
Major League Baseball Players Association (MLBPA), 54, 56, 64, 73, 193, 195, 220. *See also* baseball strike
Major League Baseball Restoration Act (1995), 66
Major League Play Ball Act (1995), 74
Mantle, Mickey, 92
Maraniss, David, 65-66
Maris, Roger, 11, 154, 157, 183, 196
Marsalis, Branford, 96
Martha's Vineyard, 179
Maryland, 91, 96, 102
masculinity, 1, 162, 175, 177-179, 182, 199, 202, 207, 223, 224, 225
Mayflower Hotel, 69
McCain, John, 198
McCurry, Mike, 46-47, 53, 69-71, 76, 77, 90, 97-99, 204, 223
McDonald's, 8, 111
McGovern, George, 39
McGwire, Jay, 195
McGwire, Mark: Clinton, congratulations from, 162, 169; confesses taking performance enhancing drugs, 200-202; congressional hearing, appearance at, 198-200, counselling and, 181-182; hits sixty-second home run, 151-152, 154-158; home run race and 1, 2, 3, 9, 11,

151-158, 162, 164-186; Jay
  McGwire, relationship with, 195;
  jokes about, 172-174; masculinity
  of, 174-175, 177-179, 182; Matt
  McGwire, as father of, 152, 154-
  155, 176-177, 180; media coverage
  of, 165-167, 171, 178; Nike com-
  mercial and, 174; performance en-
  hancing drugs and, 185-186, 187-
  195, 197, 198-203; Sosa, compari-
  sons with, 155-156, 165, 167-168,
  182-183; *Sports Illustrated* Sports-
  man of the Year (1998), 168; *Time*
  Hero of the Year (1998), 169
McGwire, Matt, 152, 154-155, 176-
  177
Medicaid, 85, 106
Meek, Carrie, 112
Memphis, 136
Mfume, Kweisi, 127
Middle Atlantic Milk Marketing Asso-
  ciation, 94
Mikulski, Barbara, 102-103
Miller, Jon, 22, 99
Mitchell, George, 200
Molloy, Joe, 123
Moores, John, 146
Moreno, Arte, 149, 132
Morgan, Joe, 146
Morris, Dick: 49, 205; baseball strike,
  advice on, 65-66; fatherhood, ad-
  vice on, 180; welfare reform, advice
  on, 84, 86, 105
Mount Rushmore, 151
multiculturalism, 1, 35-36, 93, 116-
  119, 120-121
Musial, Stan, 19, 78
National Amateur All-Star Baseball
  Tournament, 76
National Baseball Hall of Fame, 111,
  158, 169, 202
National Basketball Association (NBA)
  3, 55
National Collegiate Athletic Associa-
  tion (NCAA): 189; Clinton attends
  Championship game, 19

National Commission on Professional
  Baseball Act (1995), 66
National Endowment for the Humani-
  ties (NEH), 28, 137,
National Football League (NFL), 3,
  55-56, 103, 122, 188
National Governors Association
  (NGA), 84
National Labor Relations Board
  (NLRB), 57, 75
National League: 4, 21, 24, 60; Cham-
  pionship Series (1992), 19
National Museum of American His-
  tory, 111
National Pastime Preservation Act
  (1995), 76
National Theatre, Washington DC,
  27, 33
National Union of Fans and Families,
  58-59
Negro Leagues, 27, 113
Nestlé, 68
Neuhaus, Rev. Richard John, 165
Neustadt, Richard, 52
New Deal, 6, 38
New York, 38, 58, 67, 111, 123, 137,
  138, 159, 198, 220
New York Mets, 138-139, 183. *See also*
  Shea Stadium
New York Stock Exchange, 159
New York Yankees, 21, 24, 67, 71,
  123, 191, 192. *See also* Yankee Sta-
  dium
Newman, Roberta, 10-11
Nike: 111; TV commercial featuring
  McGwire, 174
Nixon, Richard M., 5-6, 20
Nobel Peace Prize (1905), 71
Noonan, Peggy, 171
North Korea, 65
Novak, Michael, 10
O'Neil Jr., John 'Buck', 26
Oakland Athletics, 191
Office of Independent Counsel (OIC),
  65, 159. *See also* Kenneth Starr
Oklahoma City bombing, 46

234

Index

Olympics, 189: Seoul (1988), 187
Opening Day pitch: Bush, H.W. and, 21, 120; Clinton and, 19, 20-21, 53, 75, 121, 124-130, 148, 206; Nixon and, 20; presidential ritual of, 5, 53, 120-121; Reagan and, 20, 120; Taft and, 5, 120
Owens, Pamela, 52
Oxford, 38-39
Parks, Rosa, 114, 140
Patterson, James, 105
Pearl Harbor, 6
performance enhancing drugs (PEDs), 185, 187-203. *See also* androstenedione.
Personal Responsibility Act (1995), 85
Personal Responsibility and Work Opportunity Reconciliation Act (1996), 107
Petrash, Jack, 175
Philadelphia Phillies, 129
Piazza, Mike, 24
Pittsburgh Pirates, 39. *See also* Three Rivers Stadium
Poitier, Sidney, 137-138
Pope John Paul II, 96
Povich, Shirley, 68, 97
Presidential National Fatherhood Initiative, 181
Price, Joseph, 8, 10
Professional Baseball Antitrust Reform Act (1995), 66
Professional Sports Fans Association, 58
Putnam, Robert, 16-17, 36, 45, 48
Queens, 170
Rable, George, 6-7
Rainbow Coalition, 116, 121, 122-123
Rainbow Commission for Fairness in Athletics, 121-122
Rather, Dan, 166-167
Ratvich, Richard, 57-58
Rawls, John, 9
Razorbacks, University of Arkansas, 19
Reagan, Ronald, 6, 16, 20, 115, 120, 164, 171, 225

Reagan-Democrats, 117
Rector, Rickey Rey, 116
Reed Amar, Akhil, 161
Reed, Bruce, 19, 84,
Reich, Robert, 29, 52, 57, 64, 70-73, 76, 220
Reich, Tom, 154
Reilly, Rick, 177, 183, 199
Reinsdorf, Jerry, 122
Renshon, Stanley, 160
Republican National Convention (1992), 15
Riess, Steven, 32, 110n2, 194
Riley, Russell, 221
Ripken Jr., Calvin: 3, 11 22, 78, 80-109, 112, 130, 174, 224; baseball strike and, 67; Clinton and, 3, 81-82, 86-87, 90, 96-99, 102-103, 107-108, 112, 149, 175, 180, 205-206; consecutive game 'streak' and, 81, 87-95, 107-109, 162, 165-166; early career, 91-93; Gehrig, comparisons with, 11, 88-89, 92, 97, 105, 107; race and, 104-105; record breaking game, 95-103, 139, 180, 224; *Sports Illustrated* Sportsman of the Year (1995), 93; 'streak' begins, 88; 'streak' ends, 108-109; upbringing, 90-91, 94; welfare reform and, 64, 67, 86-87, 95, 105-106, 107, 205; work ethic and, 81-82, 90, 91, 94, 106, 107, 205
Ripken Sr., Calvin, 92, 94
Ripken, Kelly, 101
Ripken, Rachel, 96, 101
Ripken, Ryan, 96, 101
Ripken, Violet, 91
Ripken, William (Billy), 92
Rittner, Kurt, 93-94
Riverfront Stadium, 118-119. *See also* Cincinnati Reds
Robinson, Jackie: 3, 38, 92, 101, 110-115, 121, 126, 129, 137-142, 147-150, 207; affirmative action, as example of, 113-115, 138-139, 147, 206; anniversary celebrations,

fiftieth, of breaking race barrier, 110-115, 134, 137-142, 143-144, 145, 148-150; Clinton and, 110, 111, 112, 113-115, 138, 139-141, 144, 145, 148, 206; *ESPY* tribute to, 137-138; Shea Stadium celebration, of, 139-142
Robinson, Rachel, 112, 138, 140-141
Robinson Simms, Jesse, 139
Rodgers, Daniel, 16, 28, 83
Roosevelt, Franklin D., 6, 71
Roosevelt, Theodore, 5, 71,
Roth, Phillip, 9-10, 164
Rousseau, Jean Jacques, 7
Russia, 71, 158
Ruth, Herman 'Babe': 88, 92, 95; anniversary of birth (100th), 68; Clinton compares himself with, 68-69, 74; home run record of, 11, 152, 154, 207
Said, Edward, 9, 162
San Diego Padres, 56, 146
San Francisco Giants, 4, 56, 196
Sanchez, Alex, 200
Sanders, Deion, 103-104
Sanderson, Scott, 71
Schlesinger Jr., Arthur, 36-37, 222
Schmoke, Kurt, 127
Schott, Marge: 118-120, 121, 122, 124, 126, 128, 130; media portrayal of, 118; punishment of, 118-120
Schwarzenegger, Arnold, 178
Selig, Bud: baseball strike and, 64, 72, 77; home run race and 157, 183, 192-193; performance enhancing drugs and, 192-193, 197; Robinson and, 112, 140-141, 142; World Series, cancels, 60
Shannon, Mike, 165
Shea Stadium, 123-126
Sheffield, Gary, 198
Shipley, David, 134-135
Shorin, Arthur, 67
Simpson, Nicole, 104
Simpson, O. J., 104-105, 134, 135
Sister Souljah, 116, 124, 130

Smith, Claire, 52, 120, 178, 224
Smithsonian Institution, 111
Sosa, Sammy: Clinton and, 1-2, 169-171, 183-184, 185, 207; congressional hearing, appearance at, 198-199; family and, 183; home run race and, 3, 11, 153, 155-157, 165-172, 173, 184, 189, 192, 194, 207; McGwire, comparisons with, 155-156, 165, 167-168, 182-183; performance enhancing drugs and, 186, 194, 197, 198-199, 200, 202-203; State of the Union Address (1999), 1-2, 5, 184, 207; *Sports Illustrated* Sportsman of the Year (1998), 168; 9/11 tribute, 196
Sotomayor, Sonia, 75
Soviet Union, 15, 187-188
Sports Broadcasting Act (1961), 55
Sports Fans United, 58
spring training, 63-64
St. Louis Cardinals: 1, 151-152, 154, 155, 156, 165, 169, 176, 201; Clinton listens to radio broadcasts of, 20, 98; Clinton, trip to as boy, 20; performance enhancing drugs and 188, 190-193. *See also* Busch Stadium; Mark McGwire
Stallone, Sylvester, 178
Starr, Kenneth: 65, 157, 163, 167; Clinton and, 65, 152, 157, 159-160, 163, 167-168, 171-172, 191, 201, 205, 225. *See also* Office of Independent Counsel; Starr Report
Starr Report, 152-153, 159-160, 172, 225. *See also* Office of Independent Counsel
Stephanopoulos, George, 124, 125-126, 129, 131
Stewart, Riley, 26
Strike Back, 58
Strike Three – The Fans Are Out, 58
Strikebusters '94, 58
Stubbart, Audrey, 81
Surratt, Alfred 'Slick', 26
Sweeney, John, 198

Index

Taft, William Howard, 5, 120
Texas Rangers, 122, 198
Texas Southern University, 19
The Civil War (TV series), 4, 27, 29, 35. *See also* Ken Burns
The Man from Hope (film), 98, 180.
Thomas Jefferson (TV series), 39. *See also* Ken Burns
Three Rivers Stadium, 193-194. *See also* Pittsburgh Pirates
Topps Trading Cards, 67
Toronto Blue Jays, 88
Tripp, Linda, 171-172
Troy, Gil, 179
Truman, Harry S., 110, 140
Tygiel, Jules, 110
University of California, San Diego, 142
University of Massachusetts, Amherst, 112
US Mint, 111
US Supreme Court, 54-55, 75, 131
US Treasury, 152, 154
Usery, William, 64-66, 68-73, 76
Valentine, Bobby, 183
Verducci, Tom, 108, 151, 154, 174, 178
Vietnam War, 6, 7, 15
Waldman, Michael, 20, 24, 38-39, 44, 48, 57, 134, 142-143, 220
Walt Disney World, 169-170
Ward, Geoffrey, 30, 39
Warner, Mark, 103
welfare reform, 2, 42, 80-109, 130, 205, 206, 221: bill passes, 107; Clinton and, 12-13, 40, 67, 79, 82-87, 95, 105-107, 134, 204, 205; Democratic Party and, 84-85, 134; ideology of, 82-83; Morris and, 84, 86, 105; Republicans and 85, 107; Ripken and, 64, 67, 86-87, 95, 105-106, 107, 205; Senate vote (September 1995), 106
Wenger, Michael, 143-144
West, Cornel, 114
West Point, 6

Wheaties, 111
Whetstone, Martha, 19
Whitewater, 40, 65
Will, George, 10, 17, 93, 156
Williams, Matt, 56
Williams, Ted, 92
Wilstein, Steve, 188-189
Winfrey, Oprah, 36
Winston, Judith, 145
Winter, William, 143-144
Wood, Gordon, 24, 136
Woods, Tiger, 141
Woodward, Bob, 40-41
Work First Bill (1995), 86
World Cup (1994), 3
World Series (1919), 68, 194
World Series (1983), 92
World Series (1994): cancellation of 31, 40, 50-51, 60, 62. *See also* baseball strike
World Series (1995), 78-79, 133
World Series (1997), 133
World Series (2001), 196
World War Two, 12, 42
Wright, Betsey, 65
Wrigley Field, 196. *See also* Chicago Cubs
Yale Law School, 39
Yankee Stadium, 58, 89. *See also* New York Yankees
Yeltsin, Boris, 158
Yesalis, Charles, 189
Zimbalist, Andrew, 89